Contents

About
Geography Centers
Grades 3-4

What's Great About This Book

Centers are a wonderful, fun way for students to practice important skills. The 13 centers in this book are self-contained and portable. Students may work at a desk, table, or even on the floor. Once you've made the centers, they're ready to use any time.

What's in This Book

The teacher direction page includes how to make the center and a description of the student task.

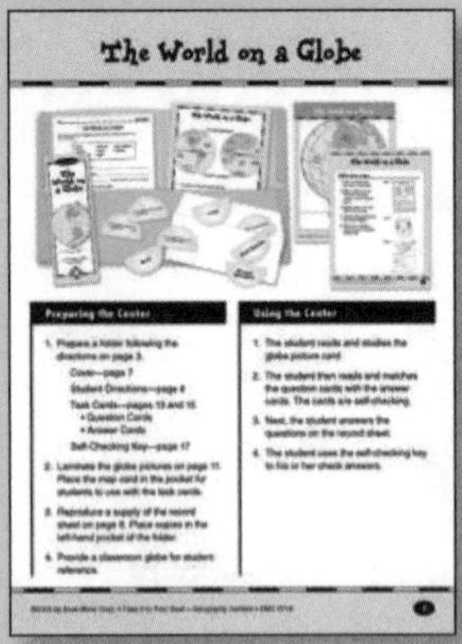

The World on a Globe

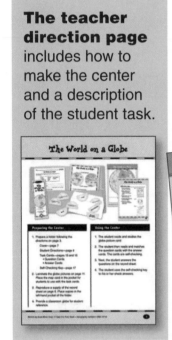

Full-color materials needed for the center

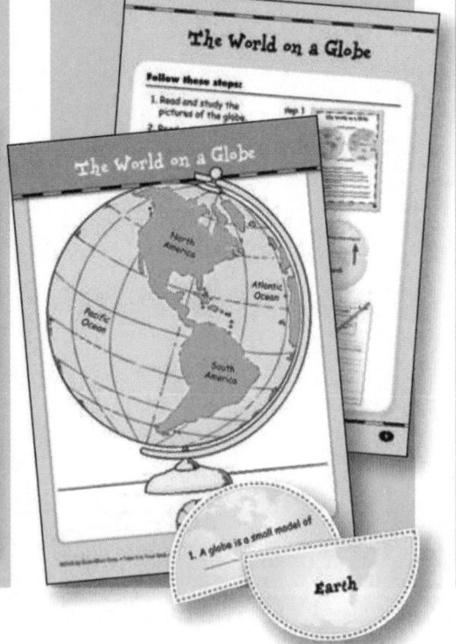

The World on a Globe
The World on a Globe
North America
Atlantic Ocean
Pacific Ocean
South America
1. A globe is a small model of
Earth

Reproducible record sheets

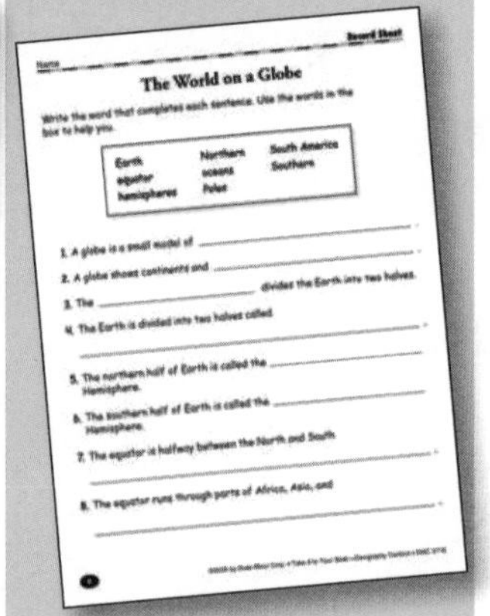

The World on a Globe
Earth
equator
hemispheres
Northern
oceans
Poles
South America
Southern

Self-checking answer keys

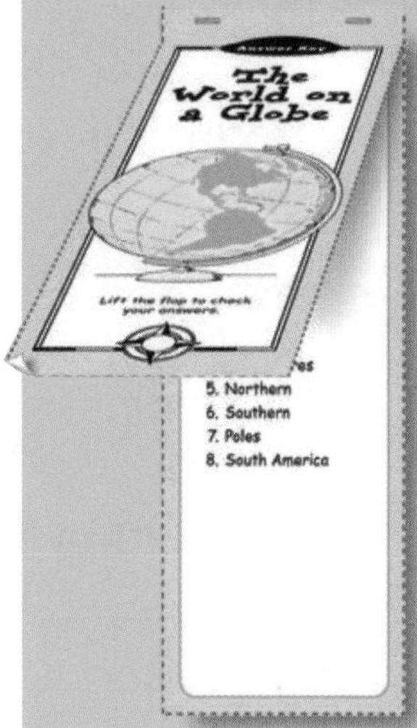

The World on a Globe
Lift the flap to check your answers.
5. Northern
6. Southern
7. Poles
8. South America

How to Use the Centers

The centers are intended for skill practice, not to introduce skills. It is important to model the use of each center before students do the task independently.

Questions to Consider:

- Will students select a center, or will you assign the centers?
- Will there be a specific block of time for centers, or will the centers be used throughout the day?
- Where will you place the centers for easy access by students?
- What procedure will students use when they need help with the center tasks?
- Where will students store completed work?
- How will you track the tasks and centers completed by each student?

Making a File Folder Center

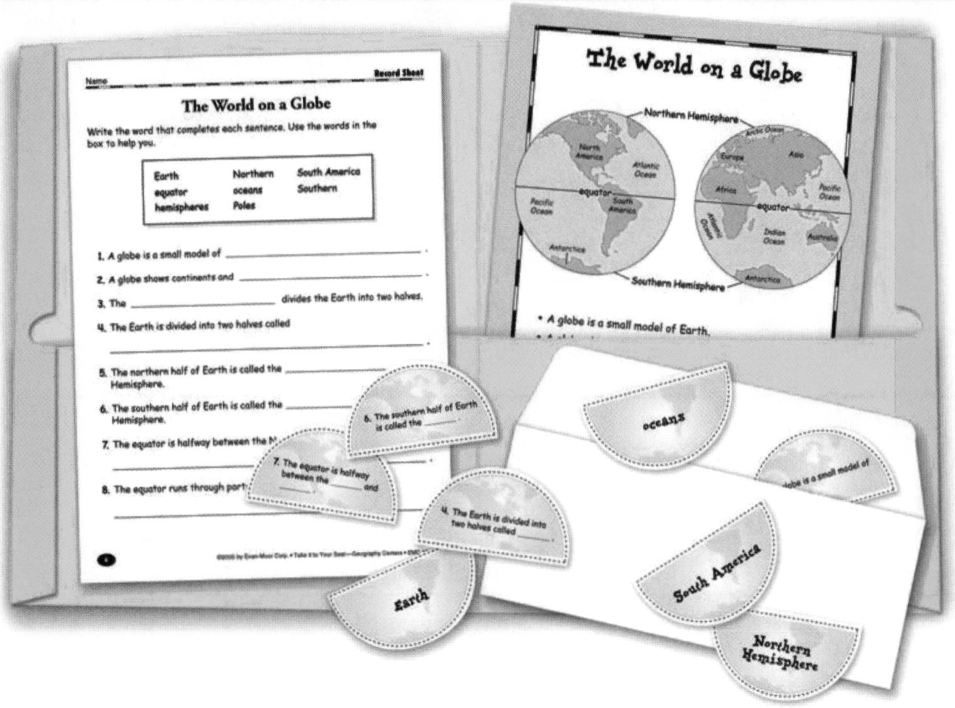

The World on a Globe
Record Sheet
The World on a Globe
Earth
Northern
South America
equator
oceans
Southern
hemispheres
Poles
oceans
South America
Earth
Northern Hemisphere

Folder centers are easily stored in a box or file crate. Students take a folder to their desks to complete the task.

Materials

- folder with pockets
- envelopes
- marking pens and pencils
- scissors
- stapler
- two-sided tape

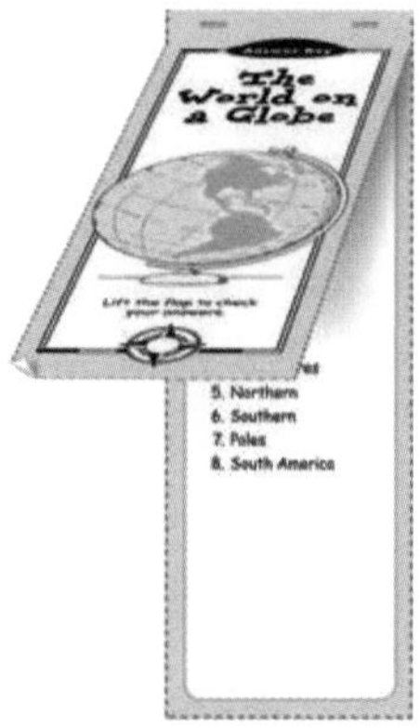

The World on a Globe
5. Northern
6. Southern
7. Poles
8. South America

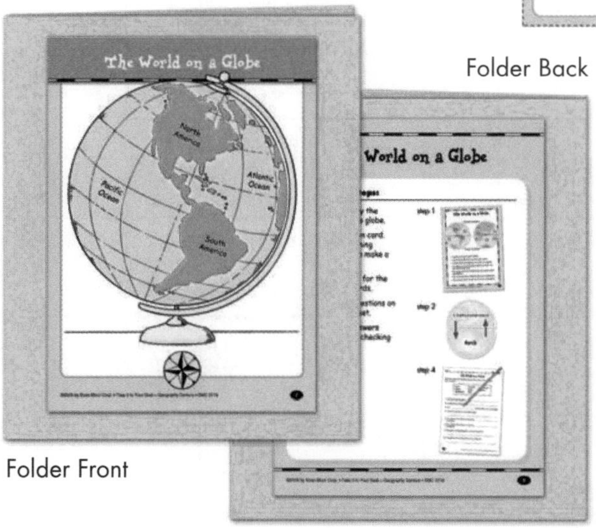

The World on a Globe
World on a Globe

Folder Back

Folder Front

Steps to Follow

1. Laminate the cover. Tape it to the front of the folder.
2. Laminate the student direction page. Tape it to the back of the folder.
3. Laminate the self-checking answer key(s) for each center. Cut the page in half. Staple the cover on top of the answer key. Place the answer key in the left-hand pocket.
4. Place record sheets, writing paper, and any other supplies in the left-hand pocket.
5. Laminate the task cards. Place each set of task cards in an envelope. Place the labeled envelopes in the right-hand pocket.
6. If needed for the center, tape the sorting mat together. Laminate it and fold in half before placing it in the right-hand pocket of the folder.

Center Checklist

Student Names

Centers

The World on a Globe												
The World on a Map												
Introducing North America												
Regions of the United States												
The Compass Rose												
Using a Map Key												
A Map Grid												
Parts of a Map												
Types of Maps												
Earth's Landforms												
Bodies of Water												
Name That Landmark!												
A Trip to Arizona												

The World on a Globe

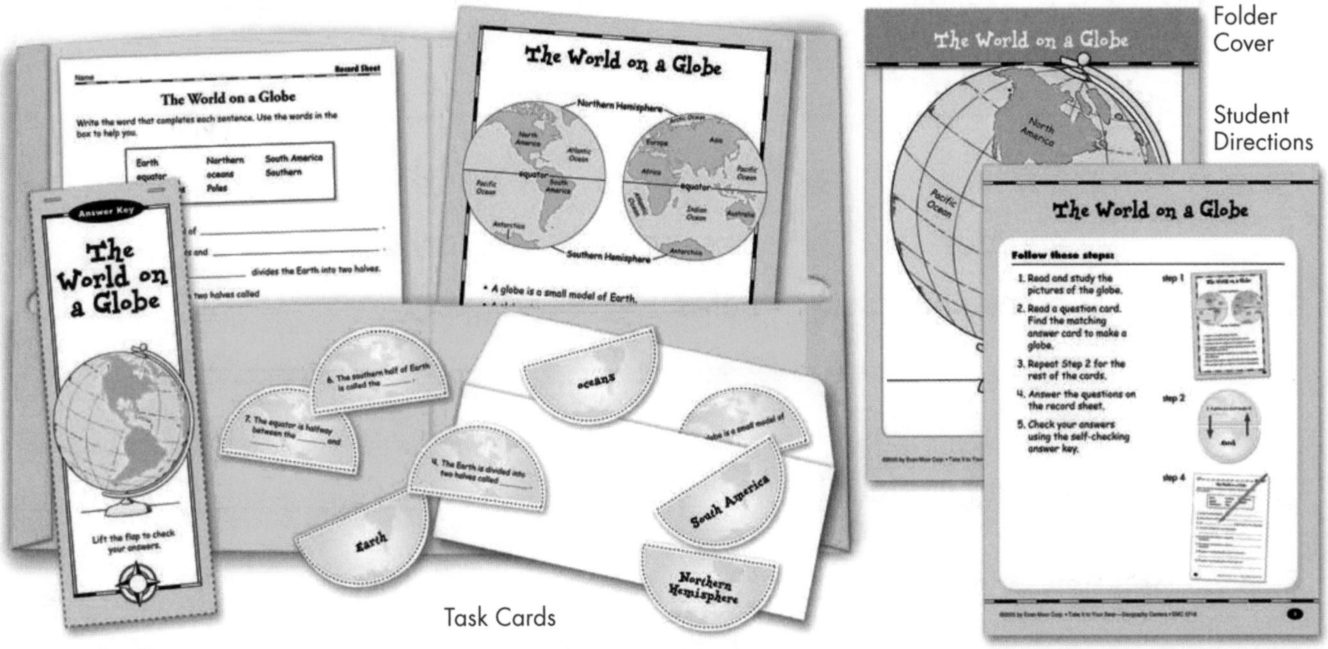
Folder Cover
Student Directions
Task Cards
The World on a Globe
Answer Key
Lift the flap to check your answers.
Follow these steps:
oceans
South America
Earth
Northern Hemisphere

Preparing the Center

1. Prepare a folder following the directions on page 3.

   Cover—page 7

   Student Directions—page 9

   Task Cards—pages 13 and 15
   - Question Cards
   - Answer Cards

   Self-Checking Key—page 17

2. Laminate the globe picture card on page 11. Place the map card in the pocket for students to use with the task cards.

3. Reproduce a supply of the record sheet on page 6. Place copies in the left-hand pocket of the folder.

4. Provide a classroom globe for student reference.

Using the Center

1. The student reads and studies the globe picture card.

2. The student then reads and matches the question cards with the answer cards. The cards are self-checking.

3. Next, the student answers the questions on the record sheet.

4. The student uses the self-checking key to check his or her answers.

The World on a Globe

Write the word or words that complete each sentence. Use the words in the box to help you.

Earth	Northern	South America
equator	oceans	Southern
hemispheres	Poles	

1. A globe is a small model of ______________________.
2. A globe shows continents and ______________________.
3. The ______________________ divides the Earth into two halves.
4. The Earth is divided into two halves called

   ______________________.
5. The northern half of Earth is called the ______________________ Hemisphere.
6. The southern half of Earth is called the ______________________ Hemisphere.
7. The equator is halfway between the North and South

   ______________________.
8. The equator runs through parts of Africa, Asia, and

   ______________________.

The World on a Globe

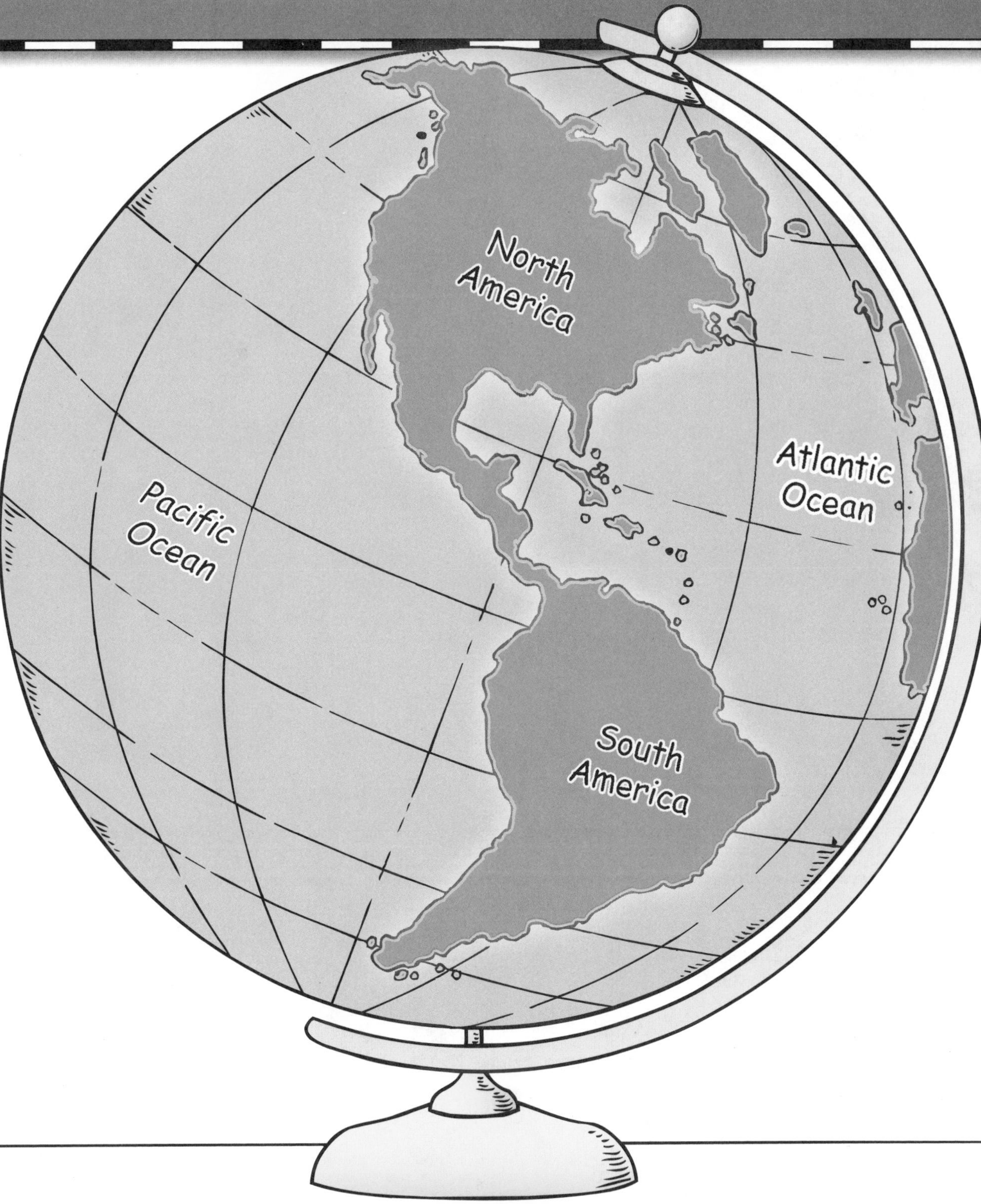
North America
Atlantic Ocean
Pacific Ocean
South America

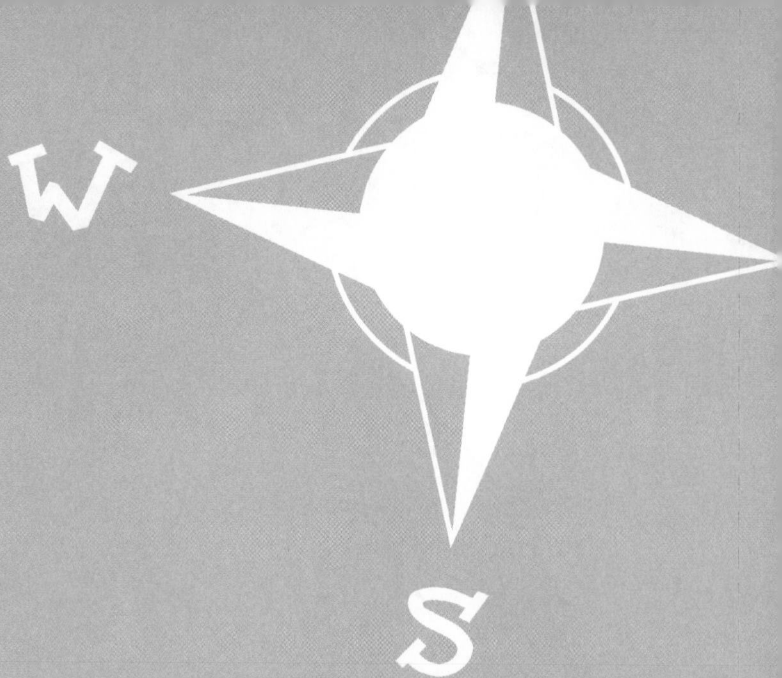
W
S

N
E
S

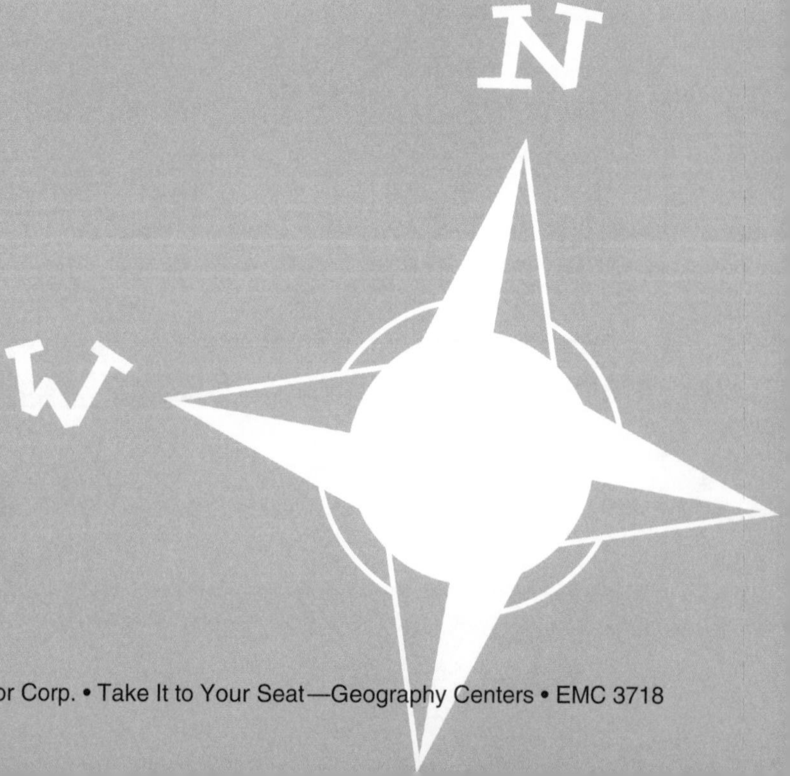
N
W

The World on a Globe

Follow these steps:

1. Read and study the pictures of the globe.
2. Read a question card. Find the matching answer card to make a globe.
3. Repeat Step 2 for the rest of the cards.
4. Answer the questions on the record sheet.
5. Check your answers using the self-checking answer key.

step 1

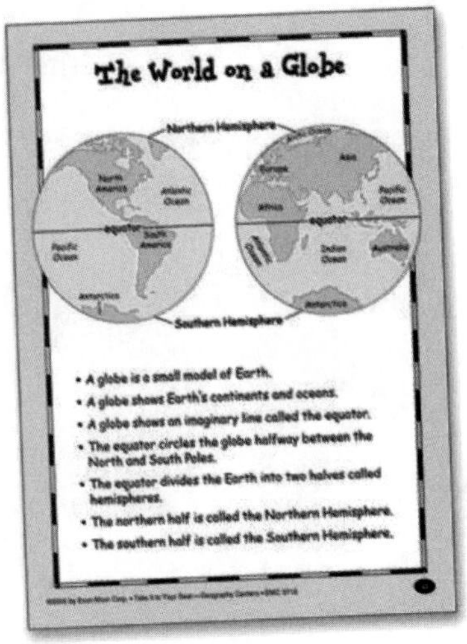
The World on a Globe

step 2

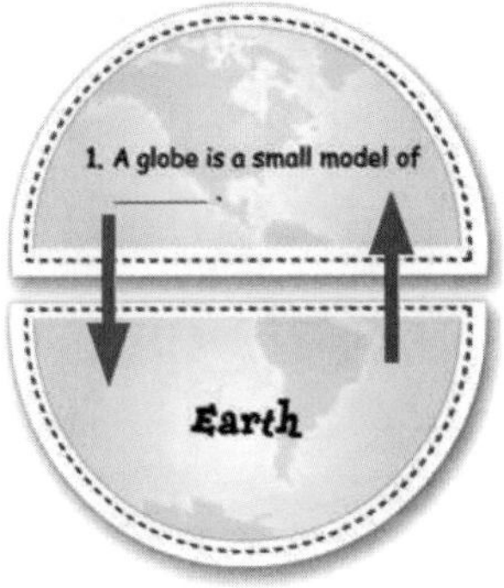
1. A globe is a small model of
Earth

step 4

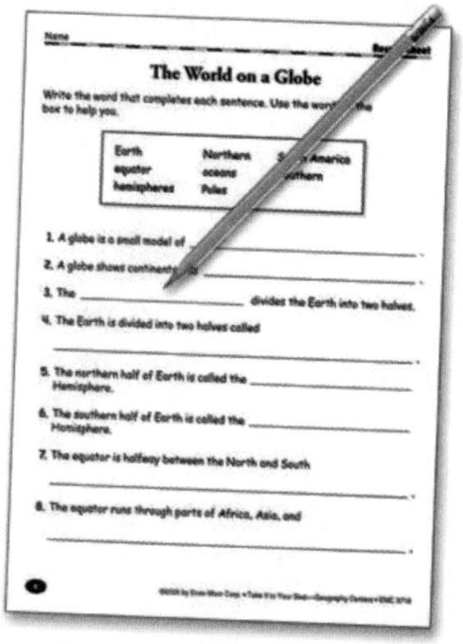
The World on a Globe

W
S

N
E
S

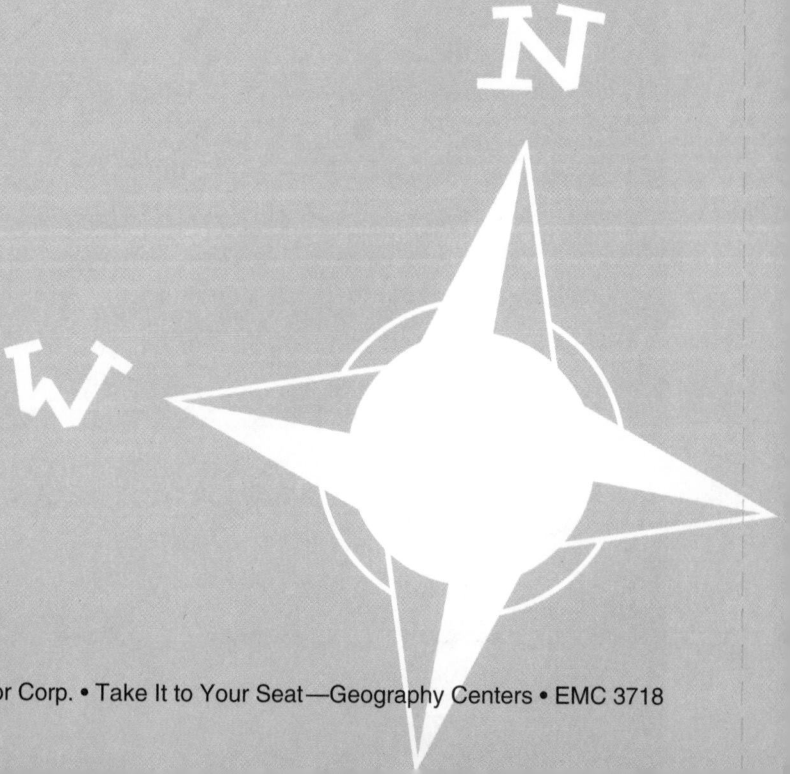
N
W

The World on a Globe

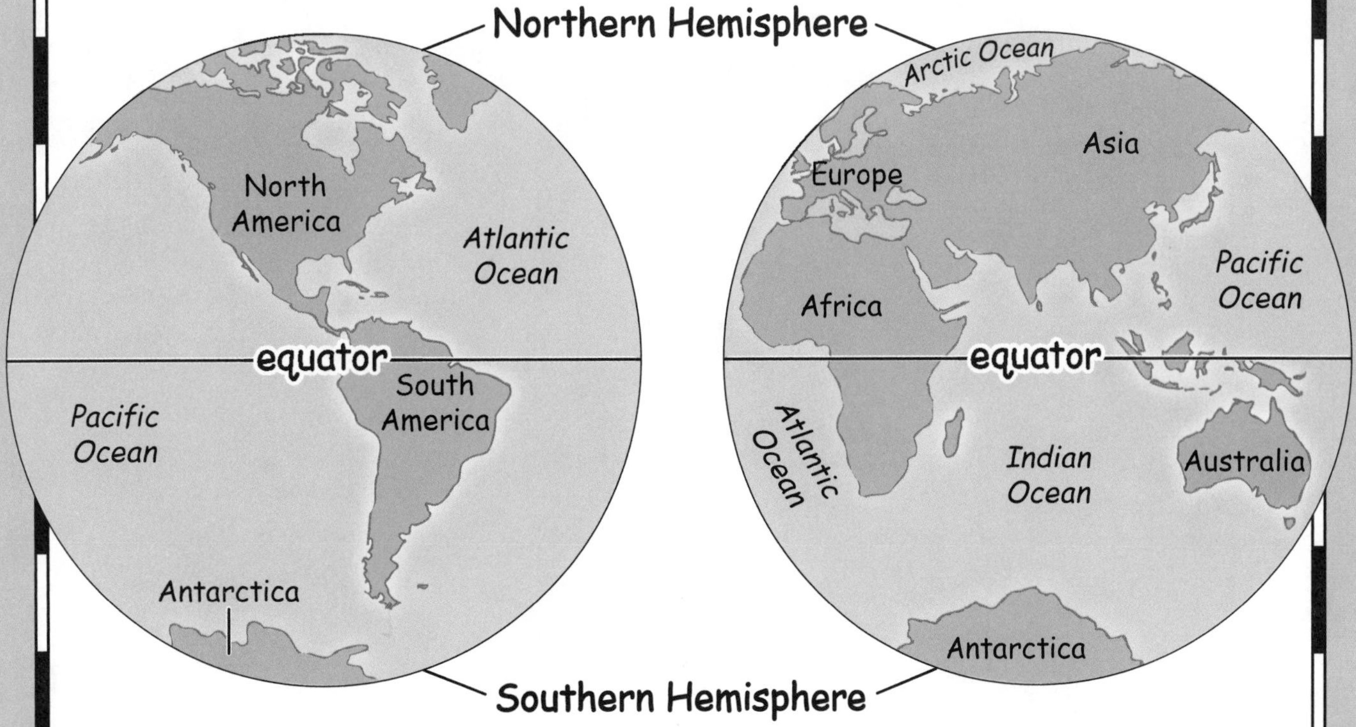
Northern Hemisphere
North America
Atlantic Ocean
equator
South America
Pacific Ocean
Antarctica
Arctic Ocean
Asia
Europe
Pacific Ocean
Africa
equator
Atlantic Ocean
Indian Ocean
Australia
Antarctica
Southern Hemisphere

- A globe is a small model of Earth.
- A globe shows Earth's continents and oceans.
- A globe shows an imaginary line called the equator.
- The equator circles the globe halfway between the North and South Poles.
- The equator divides the Earth into two halves called hemispheres.
- The northern half is called the Northern Hemisphere.
- The southern half is called the Southern Hemisphere.

W
S

N
E
S

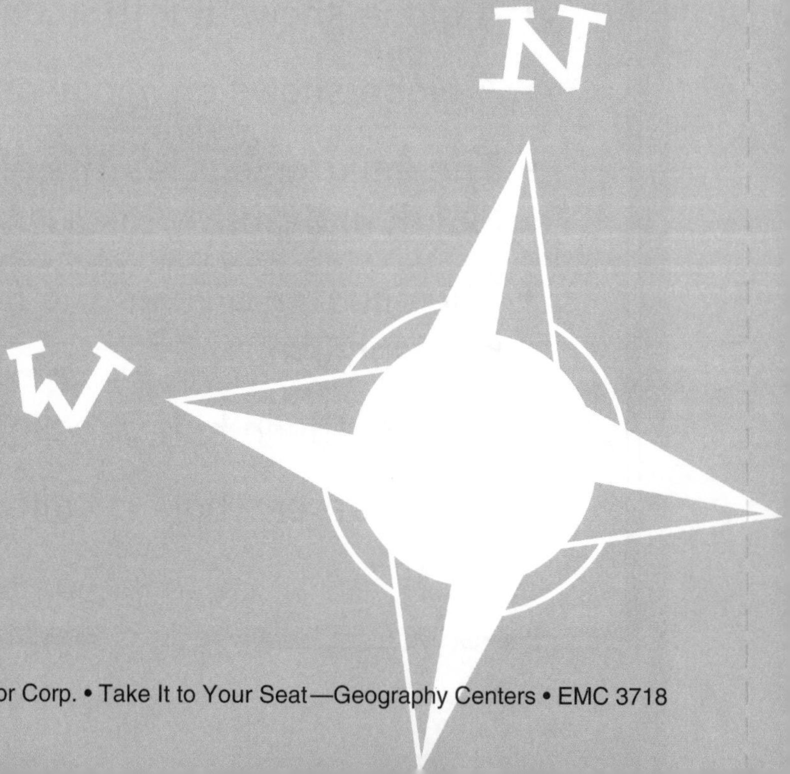
N
W

1. A globe is a small model of _______ .

2. A globe shows continents and _______ .

3. The _______ divides the Earth into two halves.

4. The Earth is divided into two halves called _______ .

5. The northern half of Earth is called the _______ .

6. The southern half of Earth is called the _______ .

7. The equator is halfway between the _______ and _______ .

8. The equator runs through parts of Africa, Asia, and _______ .

The World on a Globe

The World on a Globe

The World on a Globe

The World on a Globe

The World on a Globe

The World on a Globe

The World on a Globe

The World on a Globe

Earth

oceans

equator

hemispheres

Northern Hemisphere

Southern Hemisphere

North Pole and South Pole

South America

The World on a Globe

The World on a Globe
©2005 by Evan-Moor Corp. • EMC 3718
The World on a Globe
©2005 by Evan-Moor Corp. • EMC 3718
The World on a Globe
©2005 by Evan-Moor Corp. • EMC 3718
The World on a Globe
©2005 by Evan-Moor Corp. • EMC 3718
The World on a Globe
©2005 by Evan-Moor Corp. • EMC 3718
The World on a Globe
©2005 by Evan-Moor Corp. • EMC 3718
The World on a Globe
©2005 by Evan-Moor Corp. • EMC 3718

Answer Key

The World on a Globe

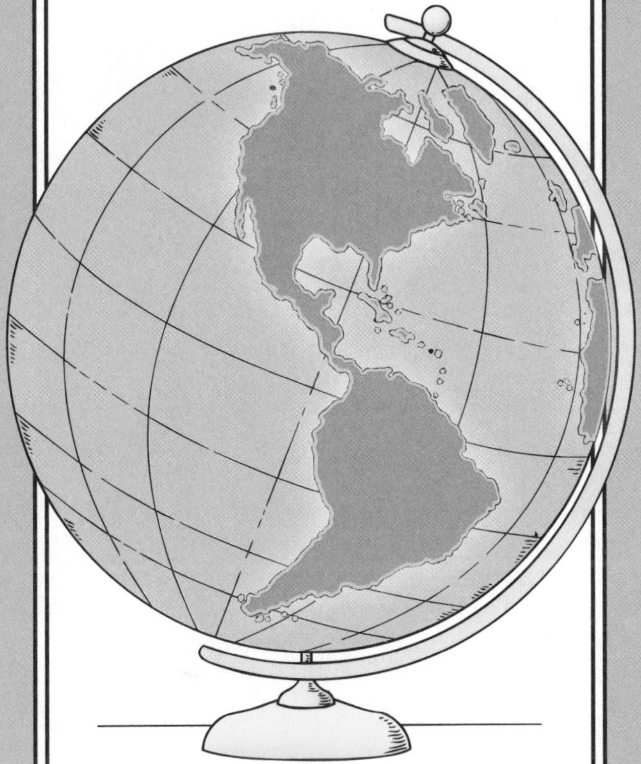

Lift the flap to check your answers.

The World on a Globe

1. Earth
2. oceans
3. equator
4. hemispheres
5. Northern
6. Southern
7. Poles
8. South America

The World on a Globe

The World on a Globe

©2005 by Evan-Moor Corp. • EMC 3718

The World on a Map

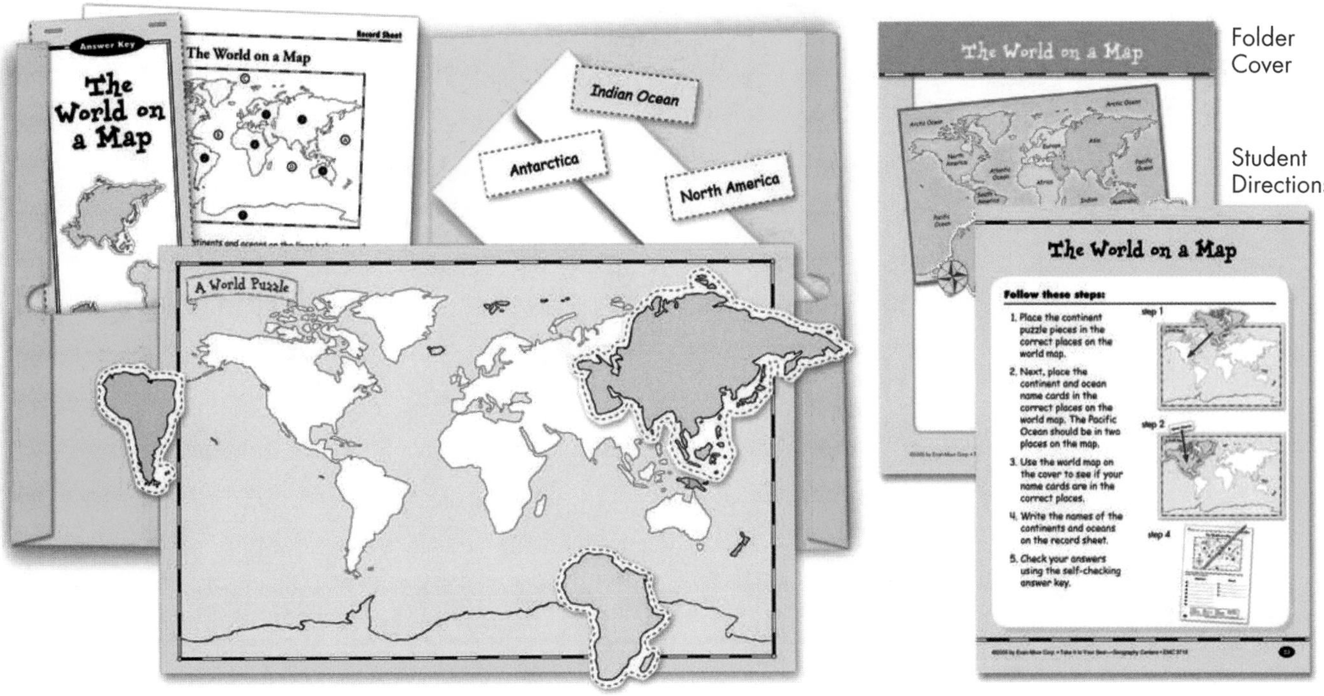
Answer Key
The World on a Map
Record Sheet
The World on a Map
Indian Ocean
Antarctica
North America
A World Puzzle
The World on a Map
The World on a Map
Follow these steps:

Folder Cover

Student Directions

Task Cards and Sorting Mat

Preparing the Center

1. Prepare a folder following the directions on page 3.

   Cover—page 21

   Student Directions—page 23

   Task Cards—pages 29–33
   - Continent Puzzle Pieces
   - Continent and Ocean Name Cards

   Sorting Mat—pages 25 and 27

   Self-Checking Key—page 35

2. Reproduce a supply of the record sheet on page 20. Place copies in the left-hand pocket of the folder.

Using the Center

1. The student places the continent puzzle pieces in the correct places on the sorting mat.

2. Next, the student places the continent and ocean name cards in the correct places on the sorting mat. The student uses the labeled world map on the cover as reference.

3. Then the student writes the names of the continents and oceans on the record sheet.

4. Finally, the student uses the self-checking key to check answers.

The World on a Map

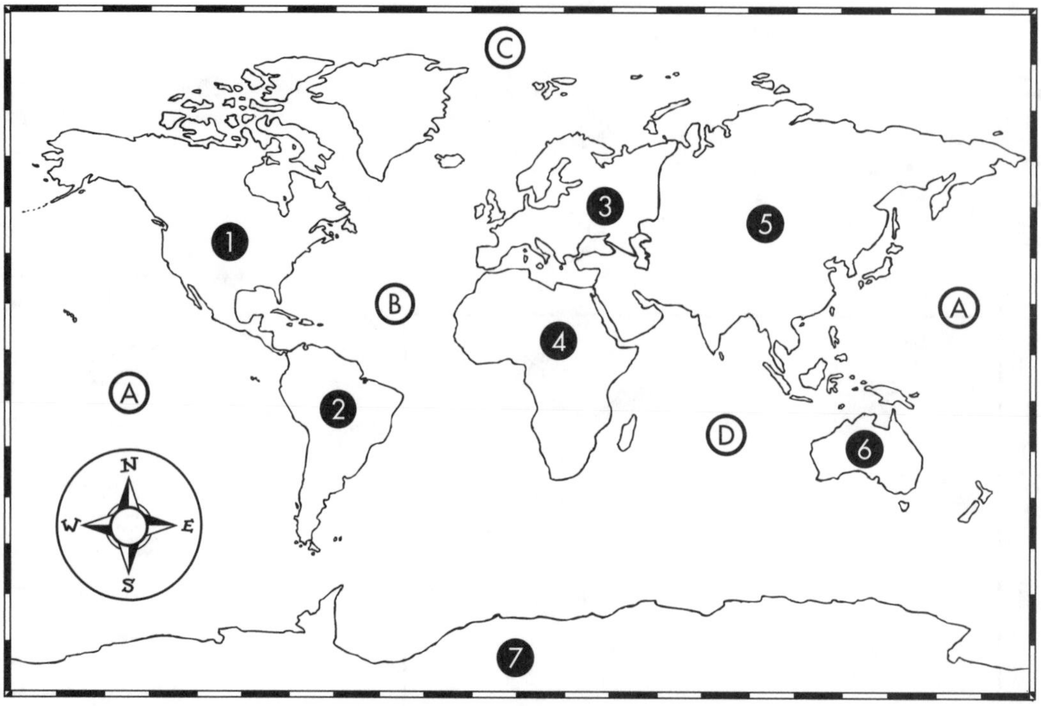
C
1
3
5
B
A
A
4
2
D
6
7
N
W
E
S

Write the names of the continents and oceans on the lines below. Use the words in the box to help you.

Continents

1. ______________________
2. ______________________
3. ______________________
4. ______________________
5. ______________________
6. ______________________
7. ______________________

Oceans

A. ______________________
B. ______________________
C. ______________________
D. ______________________

Africa	Asia	Europe	Pacific Ocean
Antarctica	Atlantic Ocean	Indian Ocean	South America
Arctic Ocean	Australia	North America	

The World on a Map

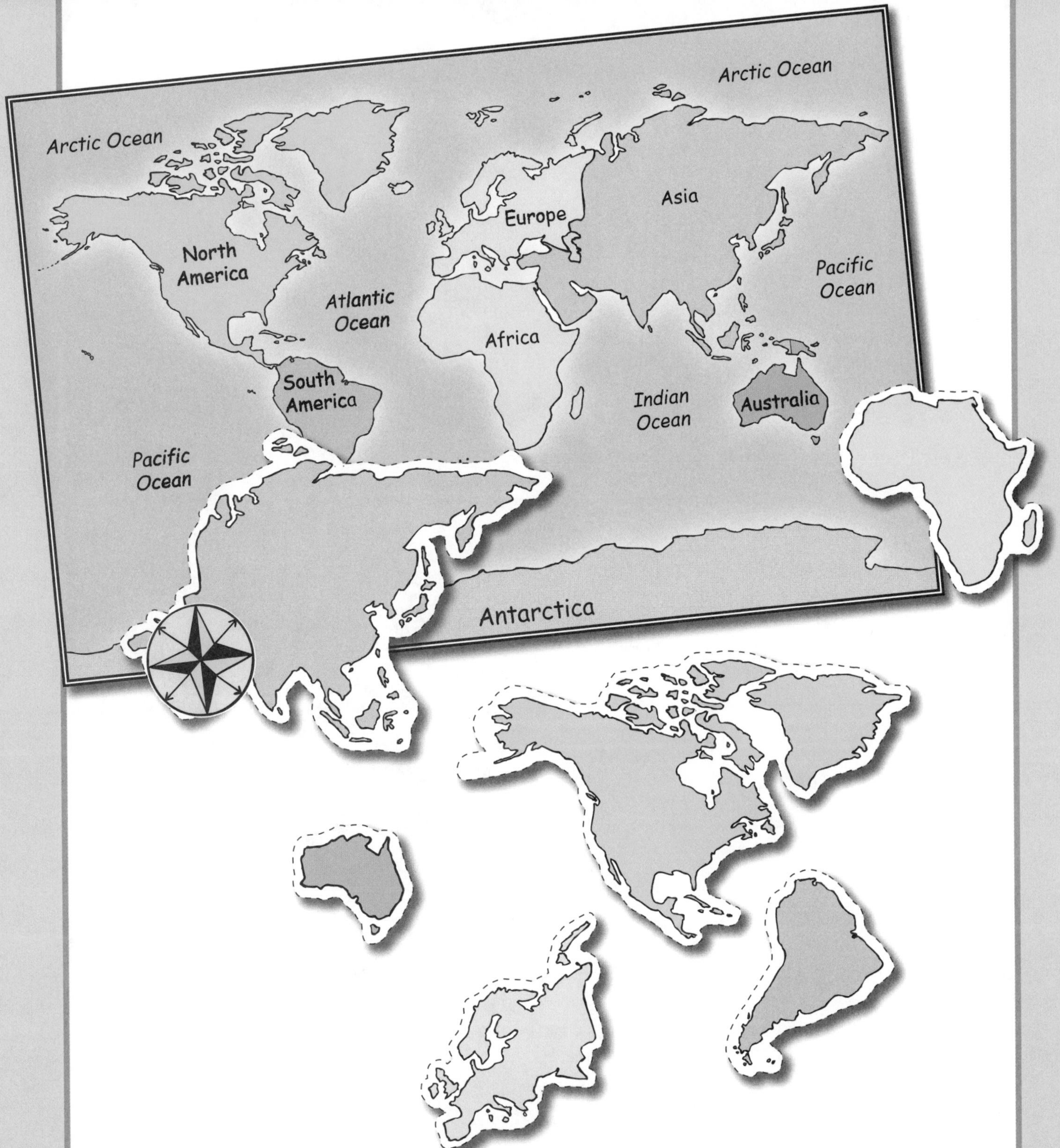
Arctic Ocean
Arctic Ocean
Asia
Europe
North America
Pacific Ocean
Atlantic Ocean
Africa
South America
Indian Ocean
Australia
Pacific Ocean
Antarctica

W
S

N
E
S

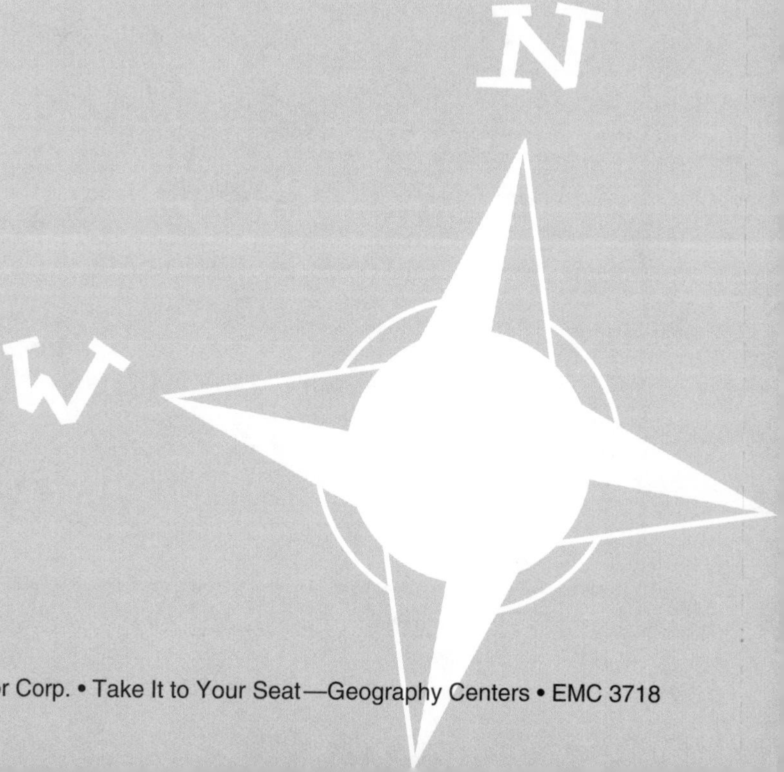
N
W

The World on a Map

Follow these steps:

1. Place the continent puzzle pieces in the correct places on the world map.
2. Next, place the continent and ocean name cards in the correct places on the world map. The Pacific Ocean should be in two places on the map.
3. Use the world map on the cover to see if your name cards are in the correct places.
4. Write the names of the continents and oceans on the record sheet.
5. Check your answers using the self-checking answer key.

step 1

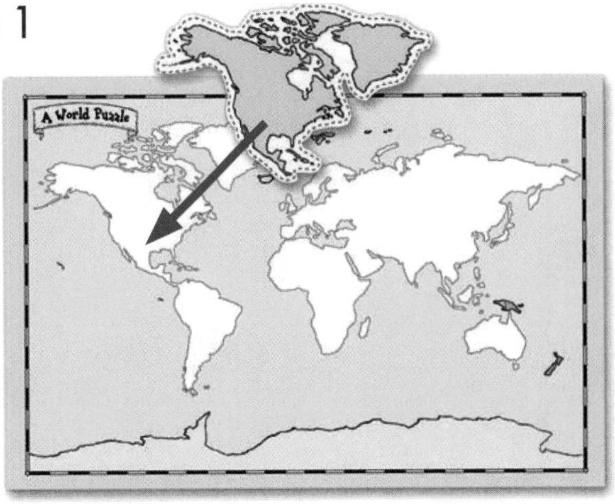
A World Puzzle

step 2

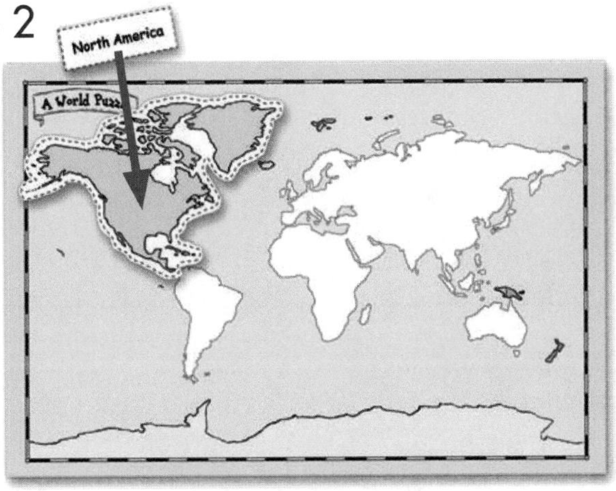
North America

step 4

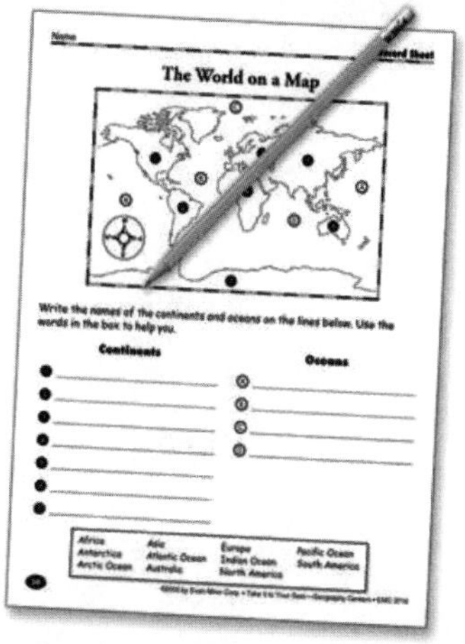
The World on a Map

W
S

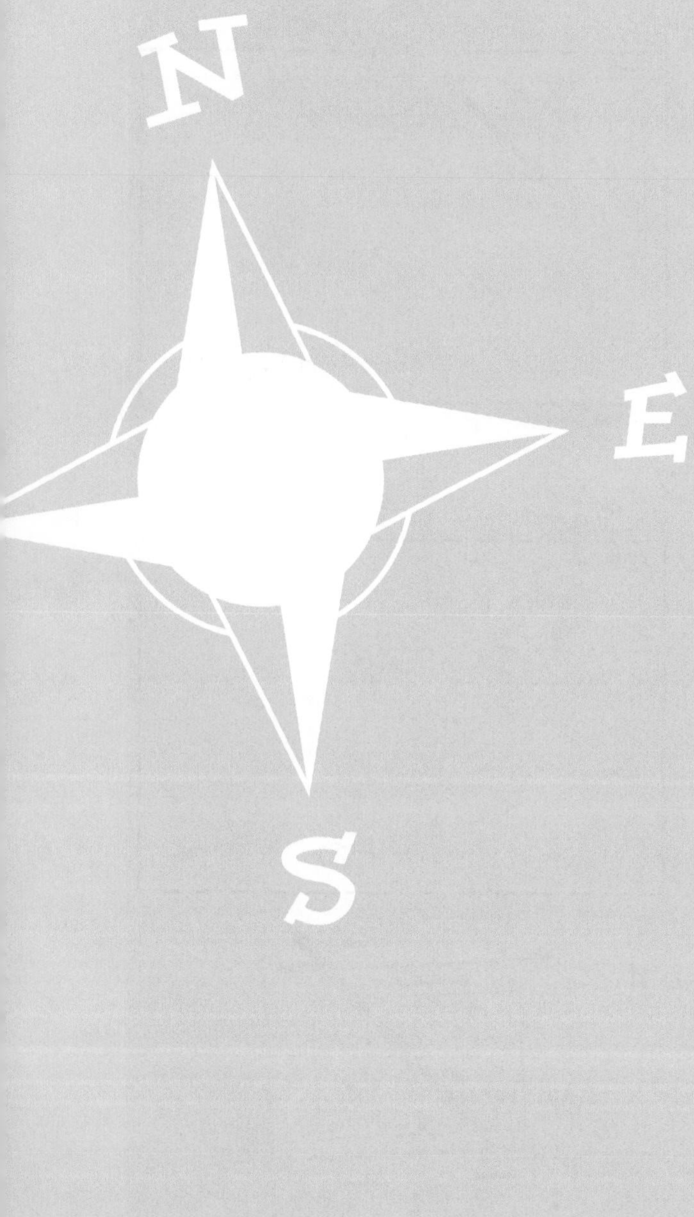
N
E
S

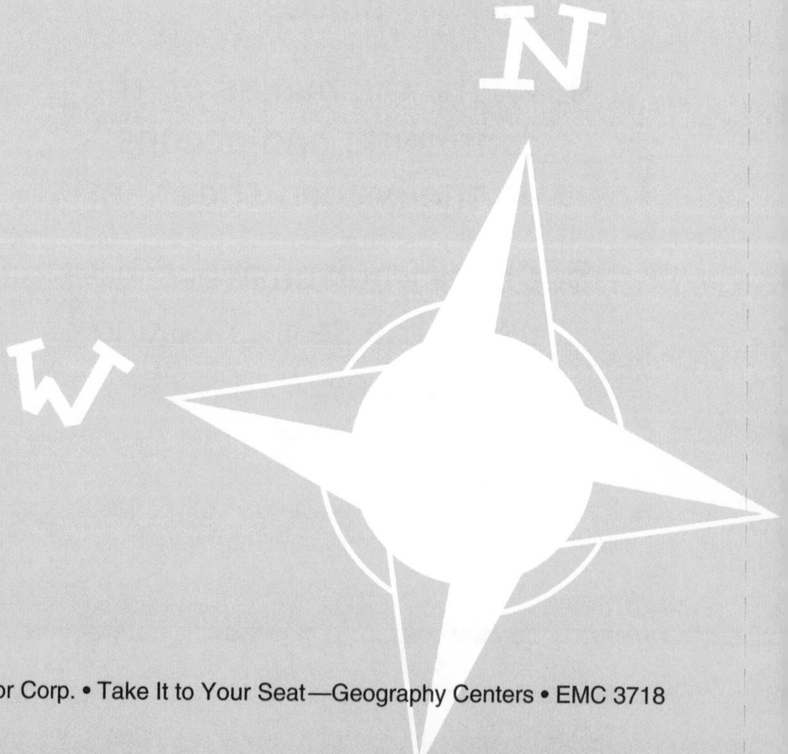
N
W

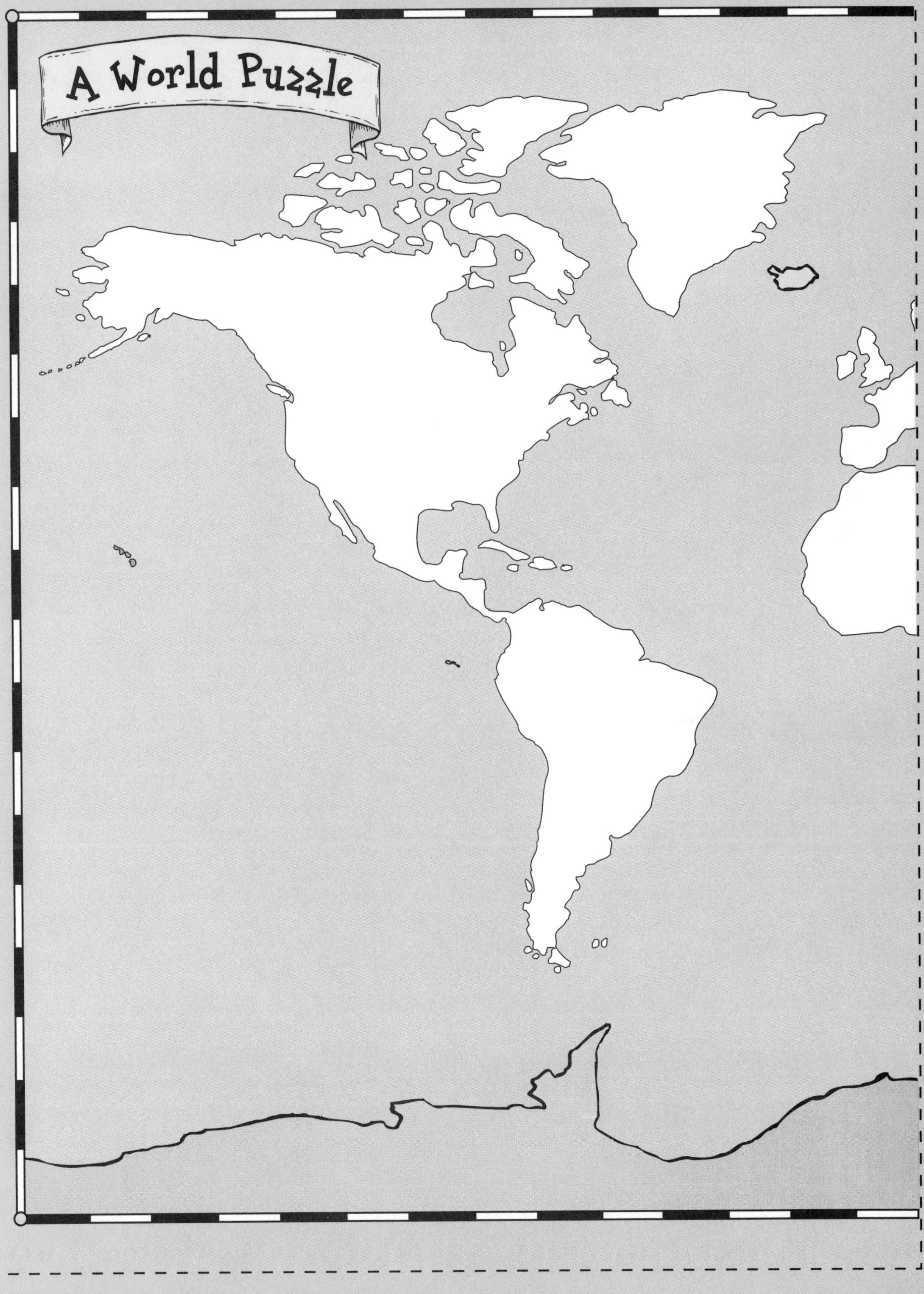
A World Puzzle

The World on a Map

glue

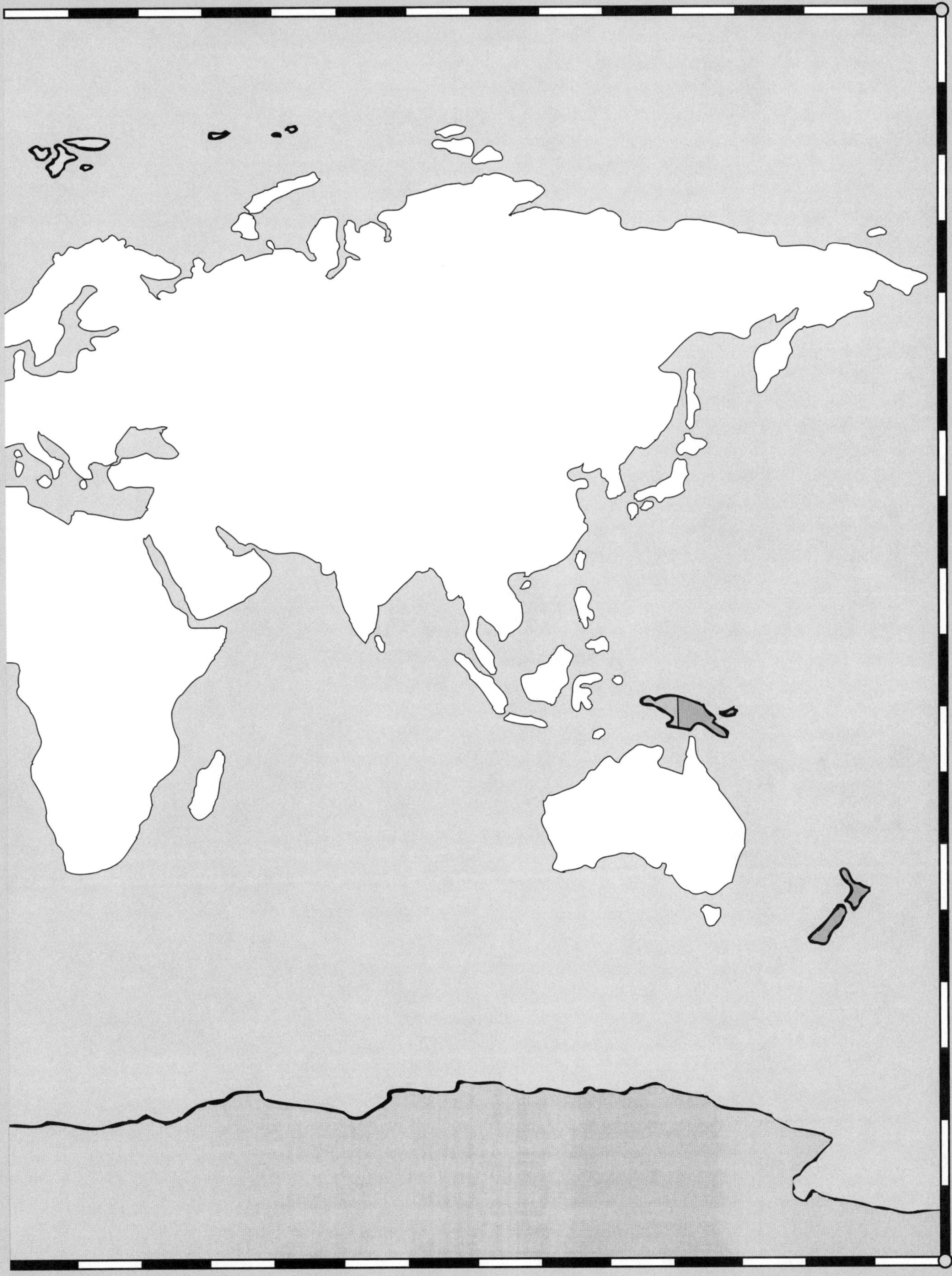

The World on a Map

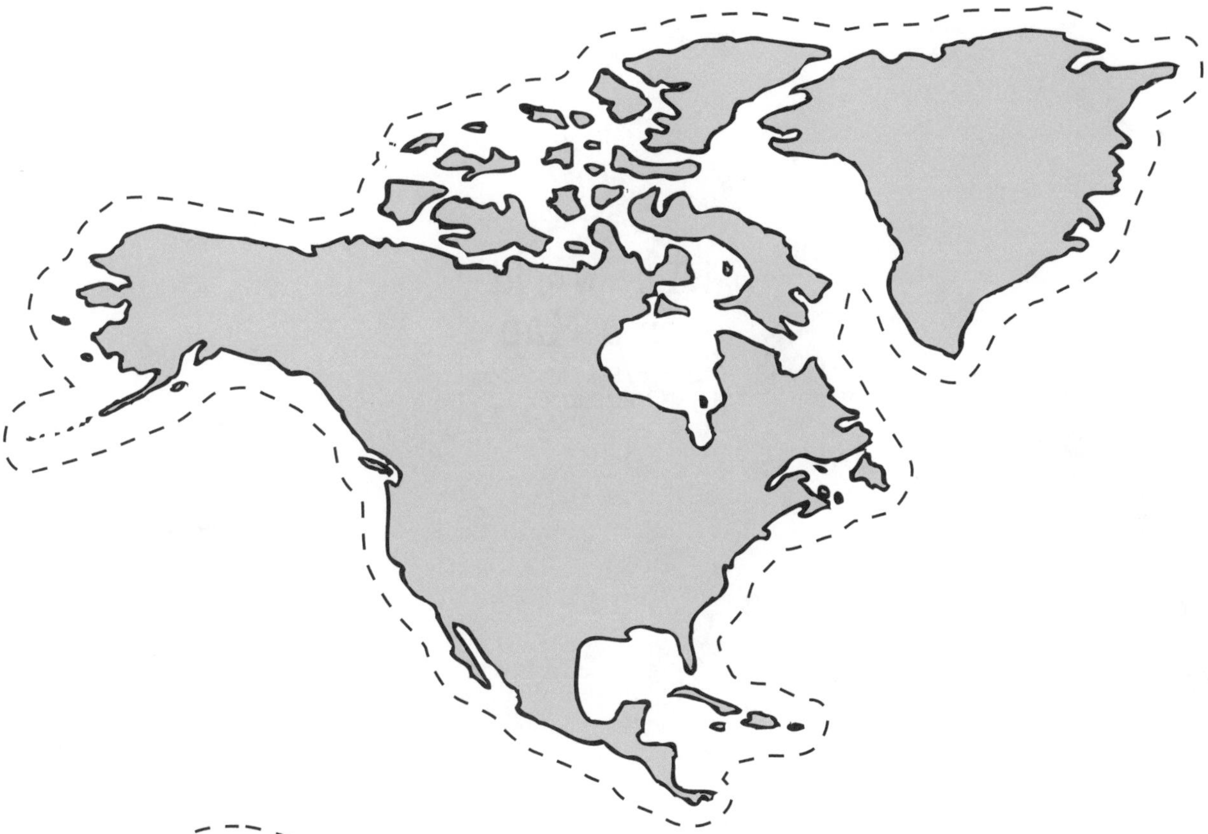

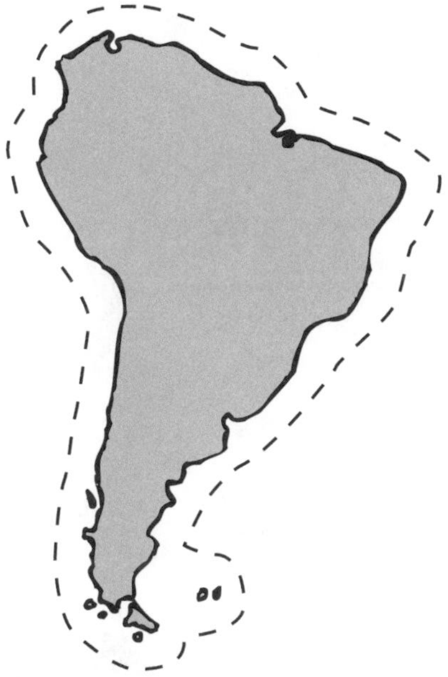

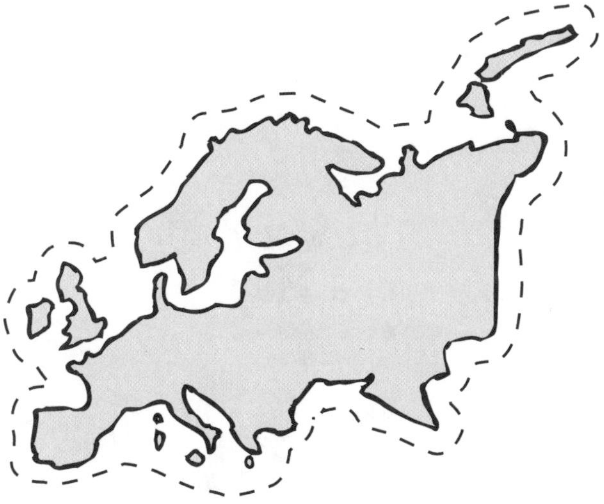

The World on a Map

The World on a Map

The World on a Map

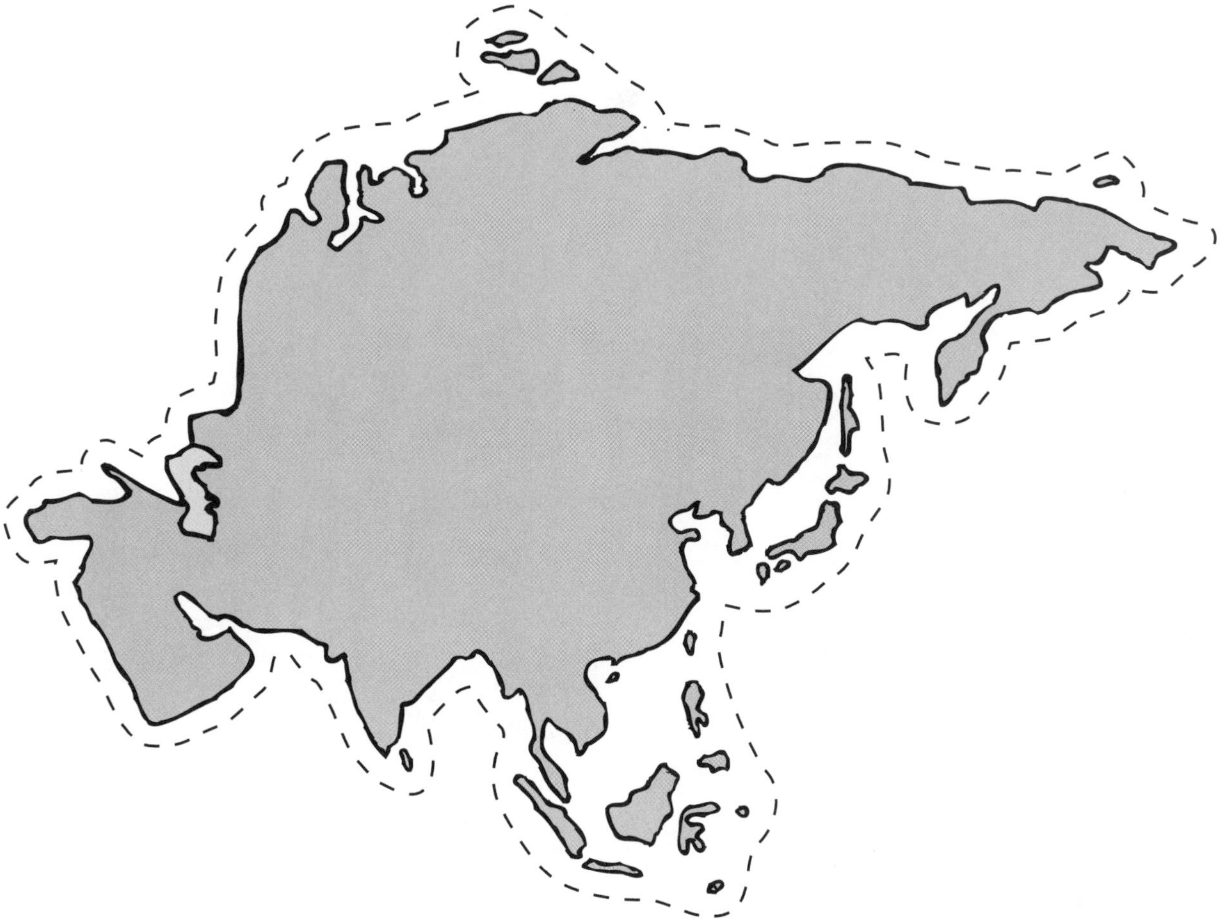

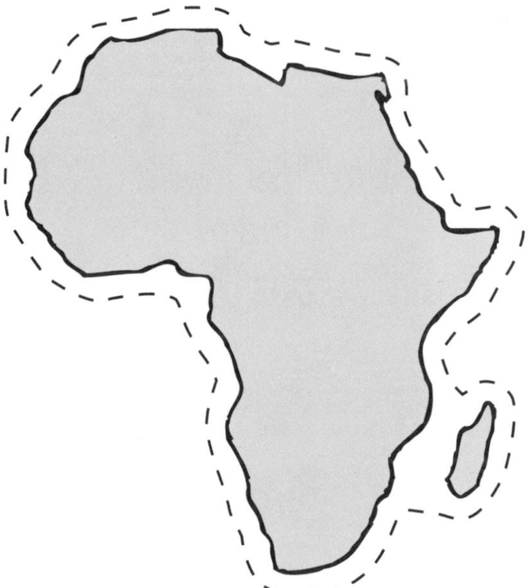

The World on a Map

The World on a Map

The World on a Map

Africa	South America
Antarctica	*Arctic Ocean*
Asia	*Atlantic Ocean*
Australia	*Indian Ocean*
Europe	*Pacific Ocean*
North America	*Pacific Ocean*

The World on a Map

©2005 by Evan-Moor Corp. • EMC 3718

The World on a Map

©2005 by Evan-Moor Corp. • EMC 3718

The World on a Map

©2005 by Evan-Moor Corp. • EMC 3718

The World on a Map

©2005 by Evan-Moor Corp. • EMC 3718

The World on a Map

©2005 by Evan-Moor Corp. • EMC 3718

The World on a Map

©2005 by Evan-Moor Corp. • EMC 3718

The World on a Map

©2005 by Evan-Moor Corp. • EMC 3718

The World on a Map

©2005 by Evan-Moor Corp. • EMC 3718

The World on a Map

©2005 by Evan-Moor Corp. • EMC 3718

The World on a Map

©2005 by Evan-Moor Corp. • EMC 3718

The World on a Map

©2005 by Evan-Moor Corp. • EMC 3718

The World on a Map

©2005 by Evan-Moor Corp. • EMC 3718

Answer Key

The World on a Map

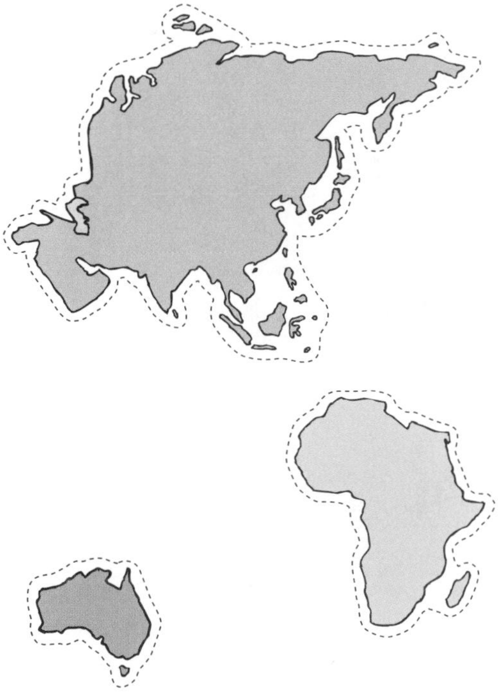

Lift the flap to check your answers.

The World on a Map

Continents

1. North America
2. South America
3. Europe
4. Africa
5. Asia
6. Australia
7. Antarctica

Oceans

Ⓐ Pacific Ocean
Ⓑ Atlantic Ocean
Ⓒ Arctic Ocean
Ⓓ Indian Ocean

The World on a Map

The World on a Map

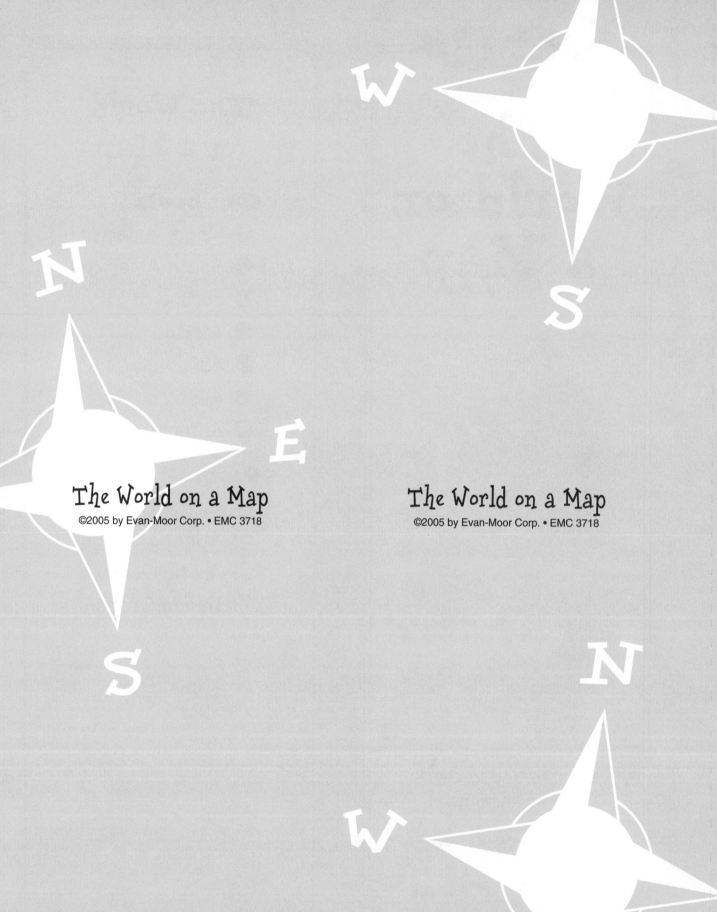

©2005 by Evan-Moor Corp. • EMC 3718

Introducing North America

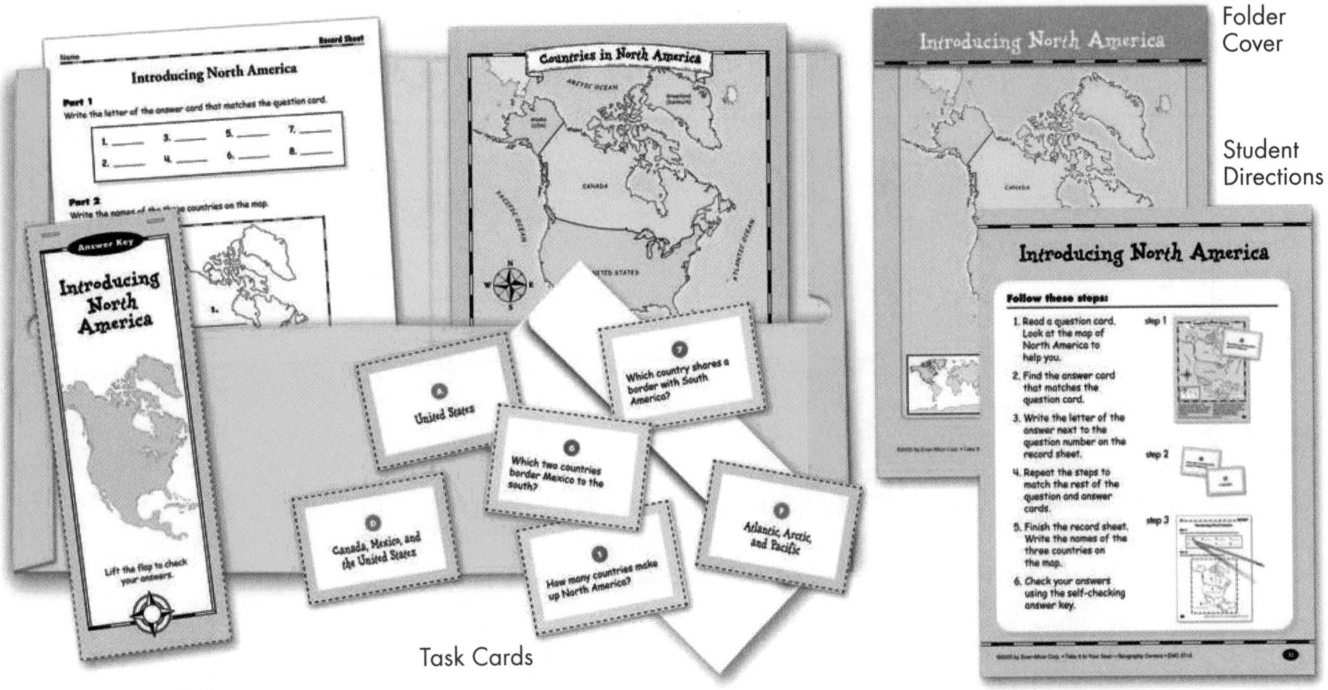

Folder Cover
Student Directions
Task Cards
Introducing North America
Countries in North America
Introducing North America
Introducing North America
Answer Key
Introducing North America

Preparing the Center

1. Prepare a folder following the directions on page 3.

   Cover—page 39

   Student Directions—page 41

   Task Cards—pages 45 and 47
   - Question Cards
   - Answer Cards

   Self-Checking Key—page 49

2. Laminate the map of North America on page 43. Place the map card in the folder for the student to use with the task cards.

3. Reproduce a supply of the record sheet on page 38. Place copies in the left-hand pocket of the folder.

Using the Center

1. The student reads a question card. The student uses the map of North America to help answer the question.
2. Next, the student matches the question card with the correct answer card. The cards are self-checking.
3. Then the student records the matching number and letter on the record sheet.
4. The student repeats the steps for the remaining cards.
5. The student completes the record sheet by labeling the map.
6. Finally, the student uses the self-checking key to check answers.

Name

Introducing North America

Part 1

Write the letter of the answer card that matches the question card.

1. ______	3. ______	5. ______	7. ______
2. ______	4. ______	6. ______	8. ______

Part 2

Write the names of the three countries on the map.

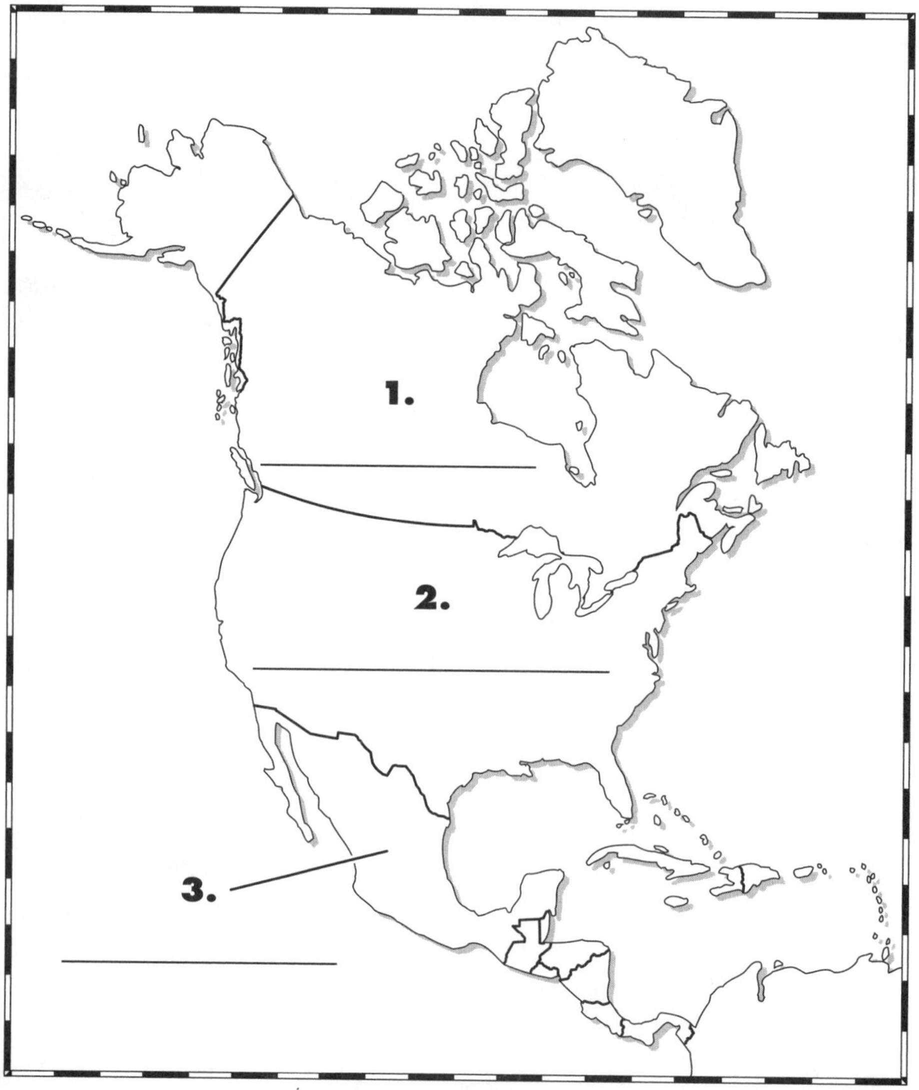
1.
2.
3.

Introducing North America

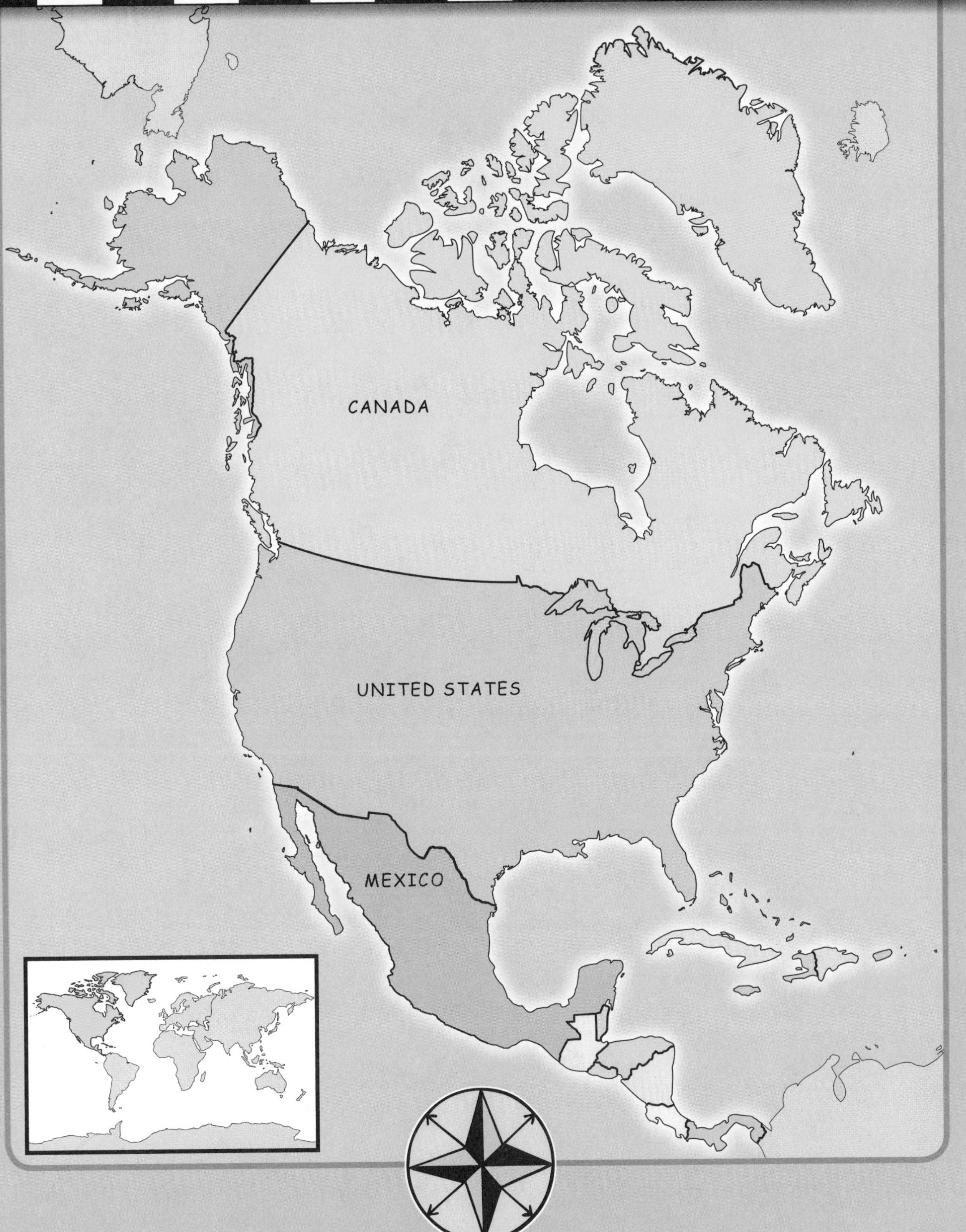
CANADA
UNITED STATES
MEXICO

W
S

N
E
S

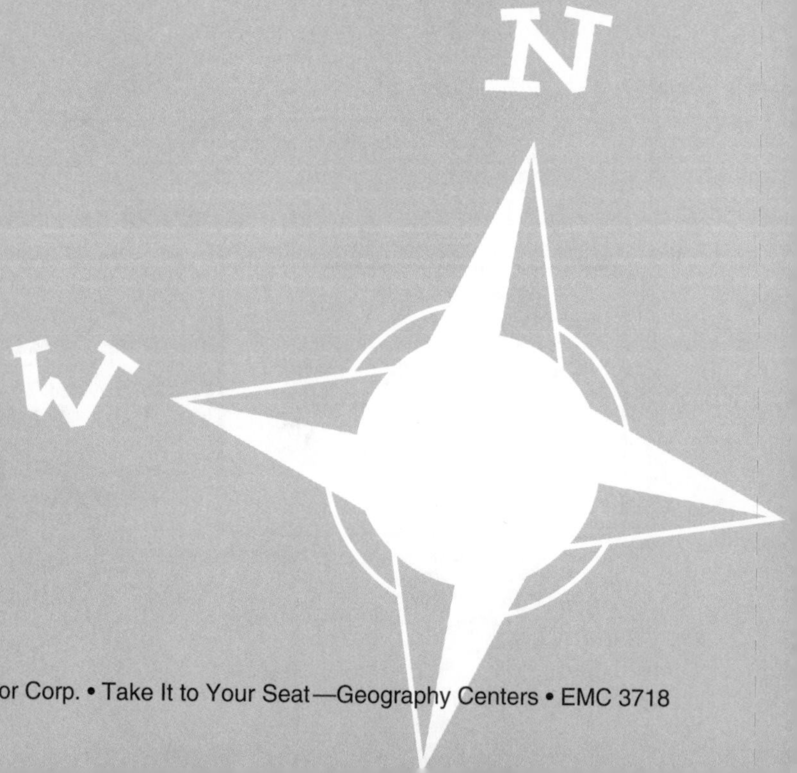
N
W

Introducing North America

Follow these steps:

1. Read a question card. Look at the map of North America to help you.
2. Find the answer card that matches the question card.
3. Write the letter of the answer next to the question number on the record sheet.
4. Repeat the steps to match the rest of the question and answer cards.
5. Finish the record sheet. Write the names of the three countries on the map.
6. Check your answers using the self-checking answer key.

step 1

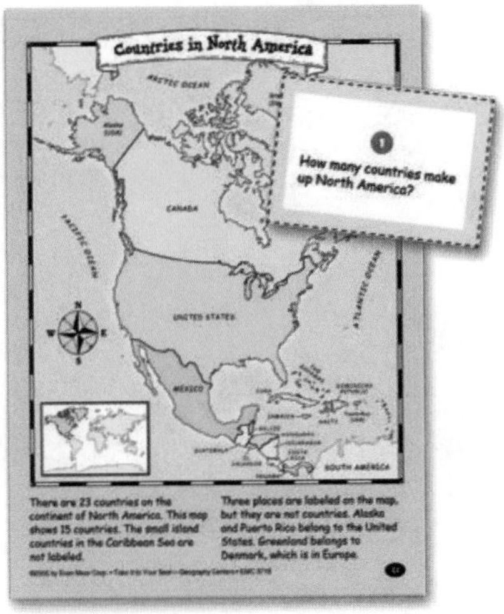
Countries in North America
How many countries make up North America?

step 2

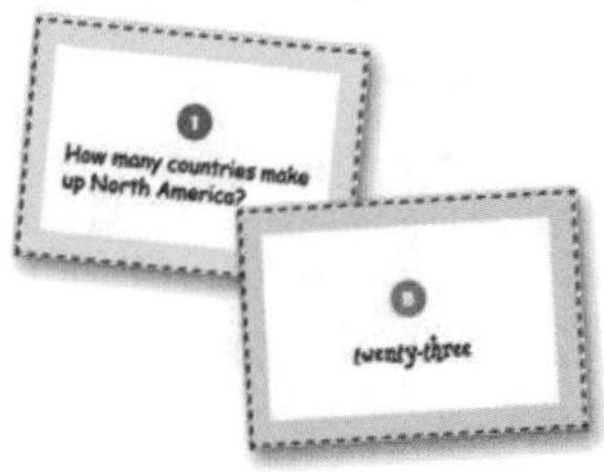
How many countries make up North America?
twenty-three

step 3

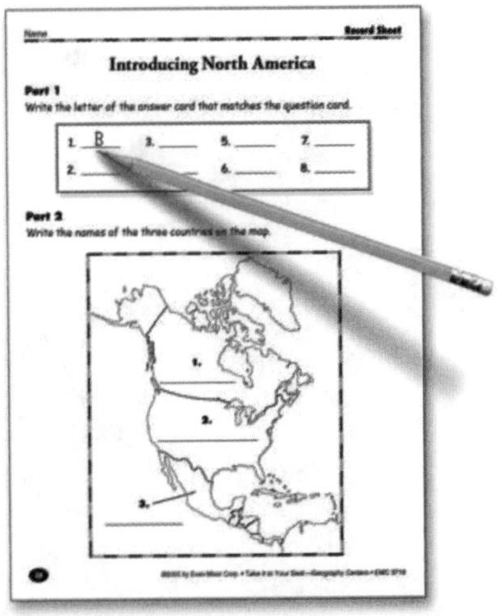
Introducing North America

W
S

N
E
S

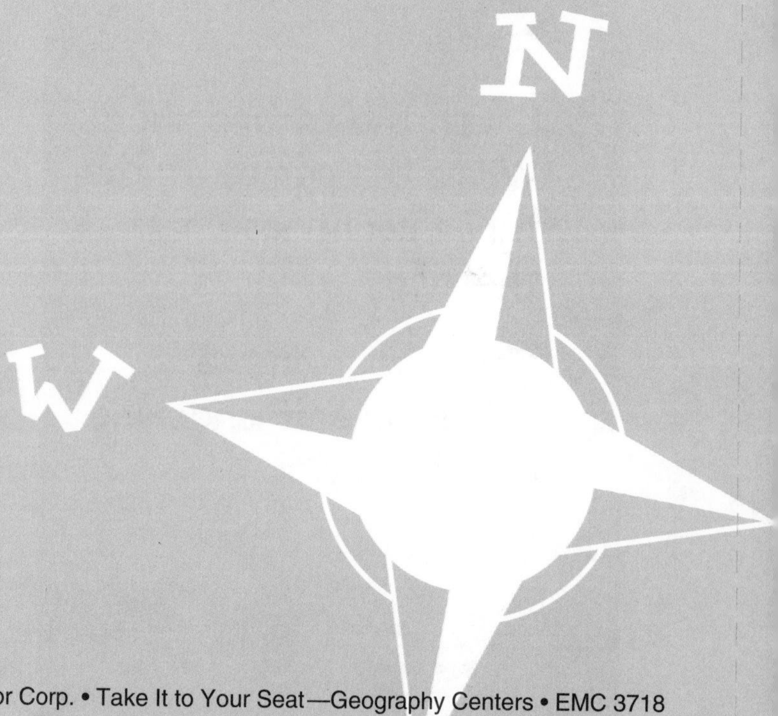
N
W

Countries in North America

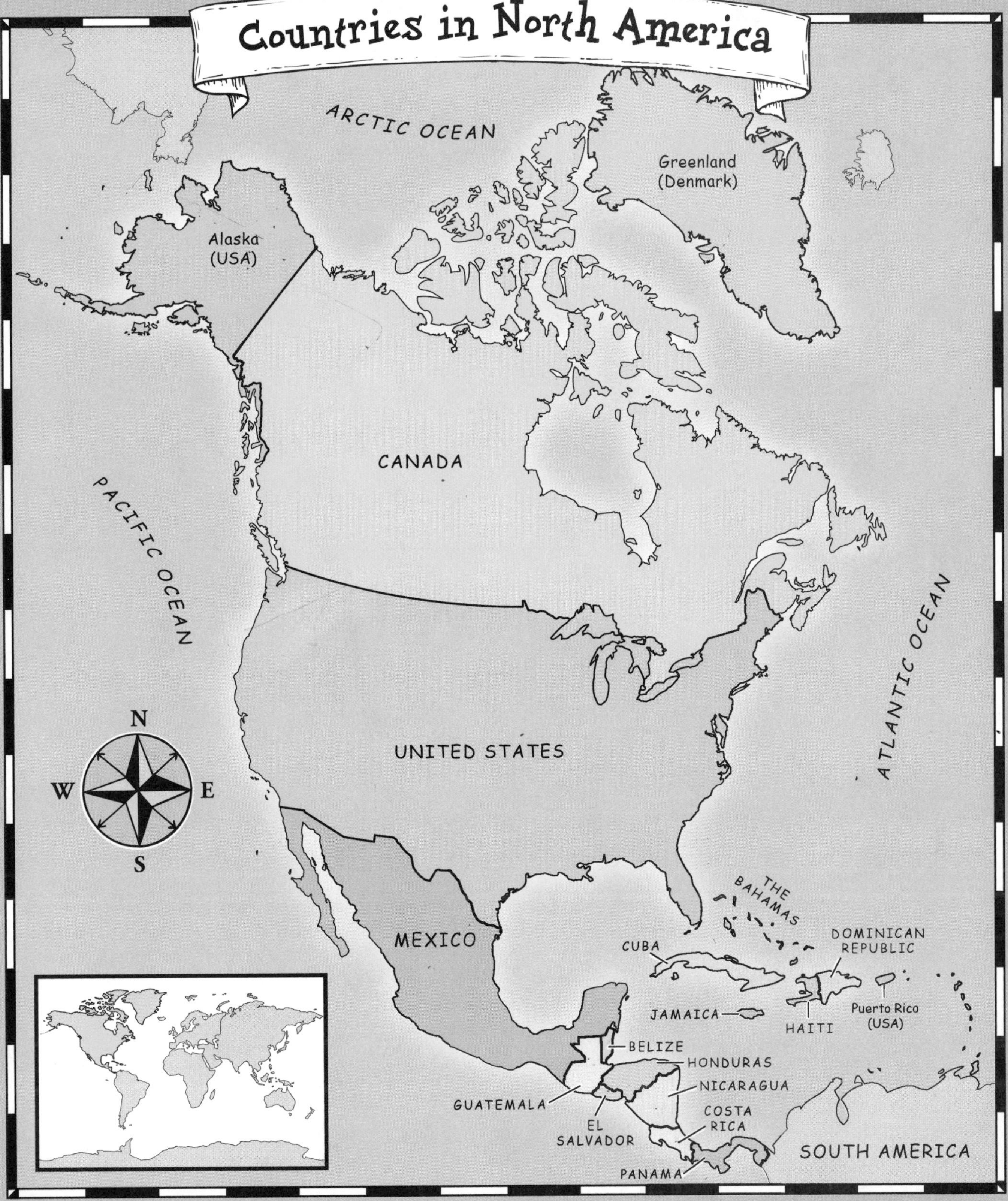
ARCTIC OCEAN
Greenland
(Denmark)
Alaska
(USA)
CANADA
PACIFIC OCEAN
ATLANTIC OCEAN
UNITED STATES
N
S
E
W
MEXICO
THE BAHAMAS
CUBA
DOMINICAN REPUBLIC
JAMAICA
HAITI
Puerto Rico
(USA)
BELIZE
HONDURAS
NICARAGUA
GUATEMALA
EL SALVADOR
COSTA RICA
PANAMA
SOUTH AMERICA

There are 23 countries on the continent of North America. This map shows 15 countries. The small island countries in the Caribbean Sea are not labeled.

Three places are labeled on the map, but they are not countries. Alaska and Puerto Rico belong to the United States. Greenland belongs to Denmark, which is in Europe.

W
S

N
E
S

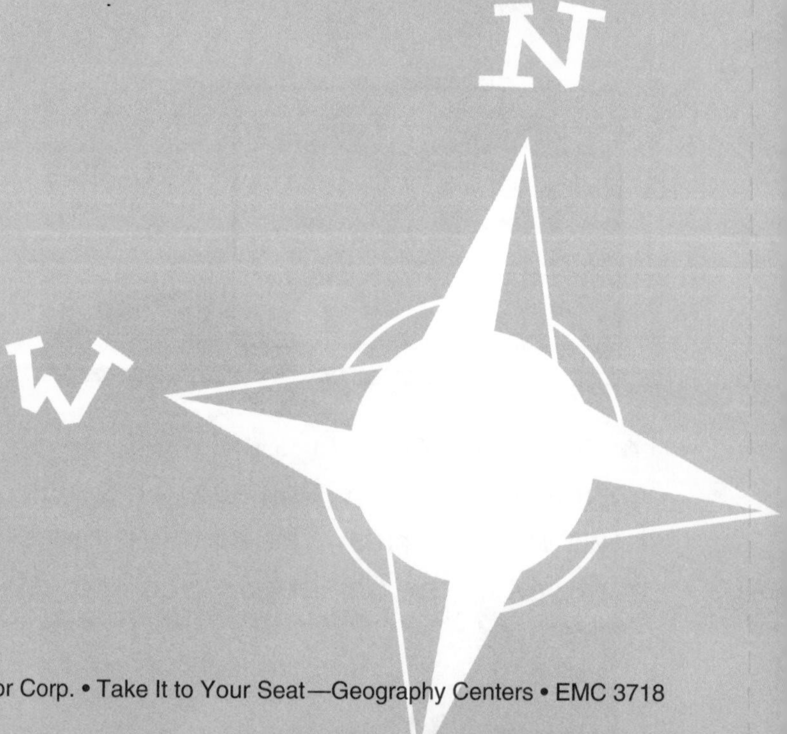
N
W

1

How many countries make up North America?

2

Which three oceans border North America?

3

Which three countries are the largest?

4

Which country is north of the United States?

5

Which country is directly north of Mexico?

6

Which two countries border Mexico to the south?

7

Which country shares a border with South America?

8

Which island country is the largest in size?

Introducing North America

Introducing North America

©2005 by Evan-Moor Corp. • EMC 3718

Introducing North America

©2005 by Evan-Moor Corp. • EMC 3718

Introducing North America

©2005 by Evan-Moor Corp. • EMC 3718

Introducing North America

©2005 by Evan-Moor Corp. • EMC 3718

Introducing North America

©2005 by Evan-Moor Corp. • EMC 3718

Introducing North America

©2005 by Evan-Moor Corp. • EMC 3718

Introducing North America

©2005 by Evan-Moor Corp. • EMC 3718

A

United States

E

Belize and Guatemala

B

twenty-three

F

Atlantic, Arctic, and Pacific

C

Cuba

G

Canada

D

Canada, Mexico, and the United States

H

Panama

Introducing North America

Introducing North America

©2005 by Evan-Moor Corp. • EMC 3718

Introducing North America

©2005 by Evan-Moor Corp. • EMC 3718

Introducing North America

©2005 by Evan-Moor Corp. • EMC 3718

Introducing North America

©2005 by Evan-Moor Corp. • EMC 3718

Introducing North America

©2005 by Evan-Moor Corp. • EMC 3718

Introducing North America

©2005 by Evan-Moor Corp. • EMC 3718

Introducing North America

©2005 by Evan-Moor Corp. • EMC 3718

Answer Key

Introducing North America

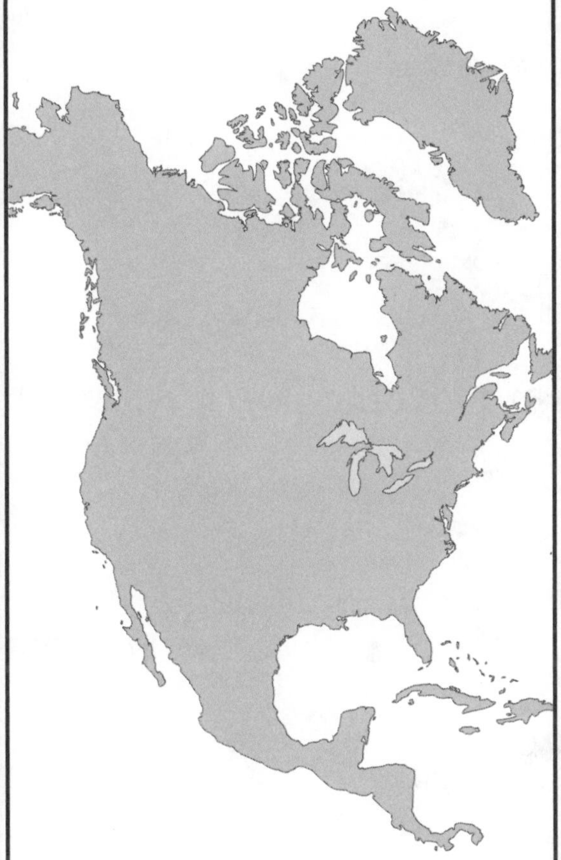

Lift the flap to check your answers.

Introducing North America

Part 1

1. B
2. F
3. D
4. G
5. A
6. E
7. H
8. C

Part 2

1. Canada
2. United States
3. Mexico

Introducing North America

Introducing North America

©2005 by Evan-Moor Corp. • EMC 3718

Regions of the United States

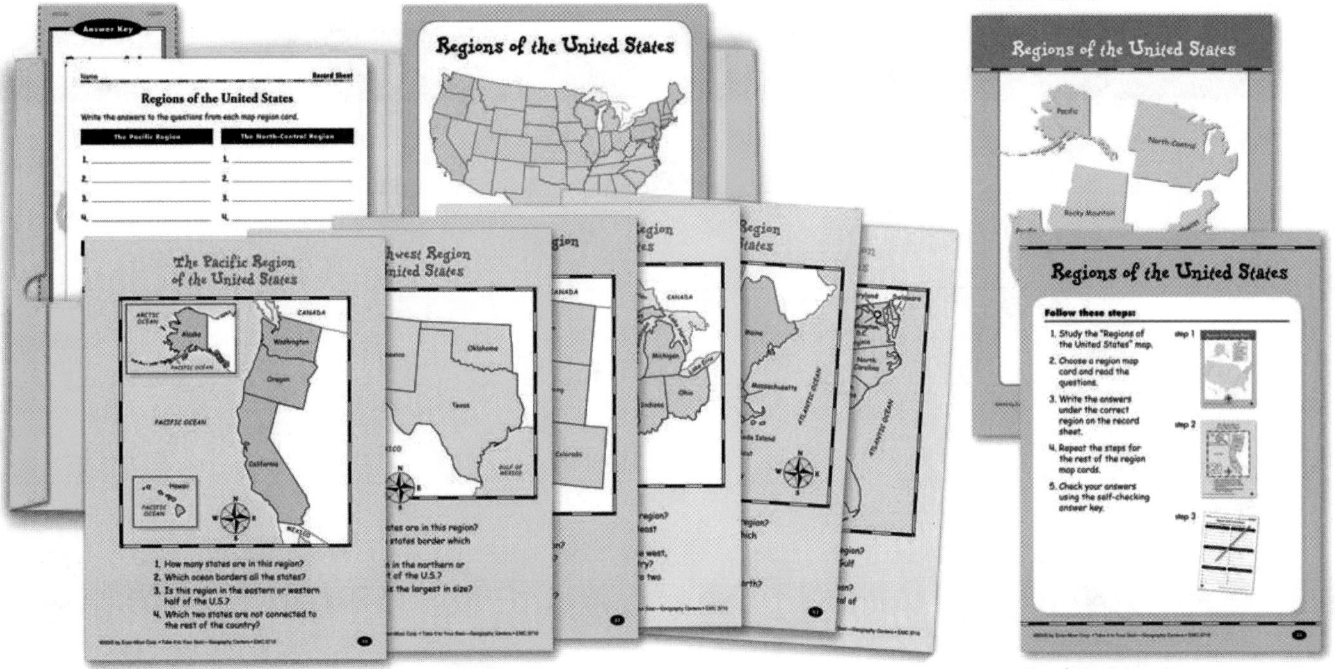
Regions of the United States
The Pacific Region of the United States
Regions of the United States
Regions of the United States

Folder Cover

Map Task Cards

Student Directions

Preparing the Center

1. Prepare a folder following the directions on page 3.

   Cover—page 53

   Student Directions—page 55

   Map Task Cards—pages 59–64

   Self-Checking Key—page 65

2. Laminate the "Regions of the United States" map on page 57. Place the map card in the pocket for student reference.

3. Reproduce a supply of the record sheet on page 52. Place copies in the left-hand pocket of the folder.

Using the Center

1. The student studies the "Regions of the United States" map.

2. Next, the student chooses a map region card and reads the questions on the card.

3. Then the student records the answers on the record sheet under the correct region heading.

4. The student repeats the steps for the remaining map region cards.

5. Finally, the student uses the self-checking key to check answers.

Regions of the United States

Write the answers to the questions from each map region card.

The Pacific Region

1. ______________________
2. ______________________
3. ______________________
4. ______________________

The North-Central Region

1. ______________________
2. ______________________
3. ______________________
4. ______________________

The Southwest Region

1. ______________________
2. ______________________
3. ______________________
4. ______________________

The Northeast Region

1. ______________________
2. ______________________
3. ______________________
4. ______________________

The Rocky Mountain Region

1. ______________________
2. ______________________
3. ______________________
4. ______________________

The Southeast Region

1. ______________________
2. ______________________
3. ______________________
4. ______________________

Regions of the United States

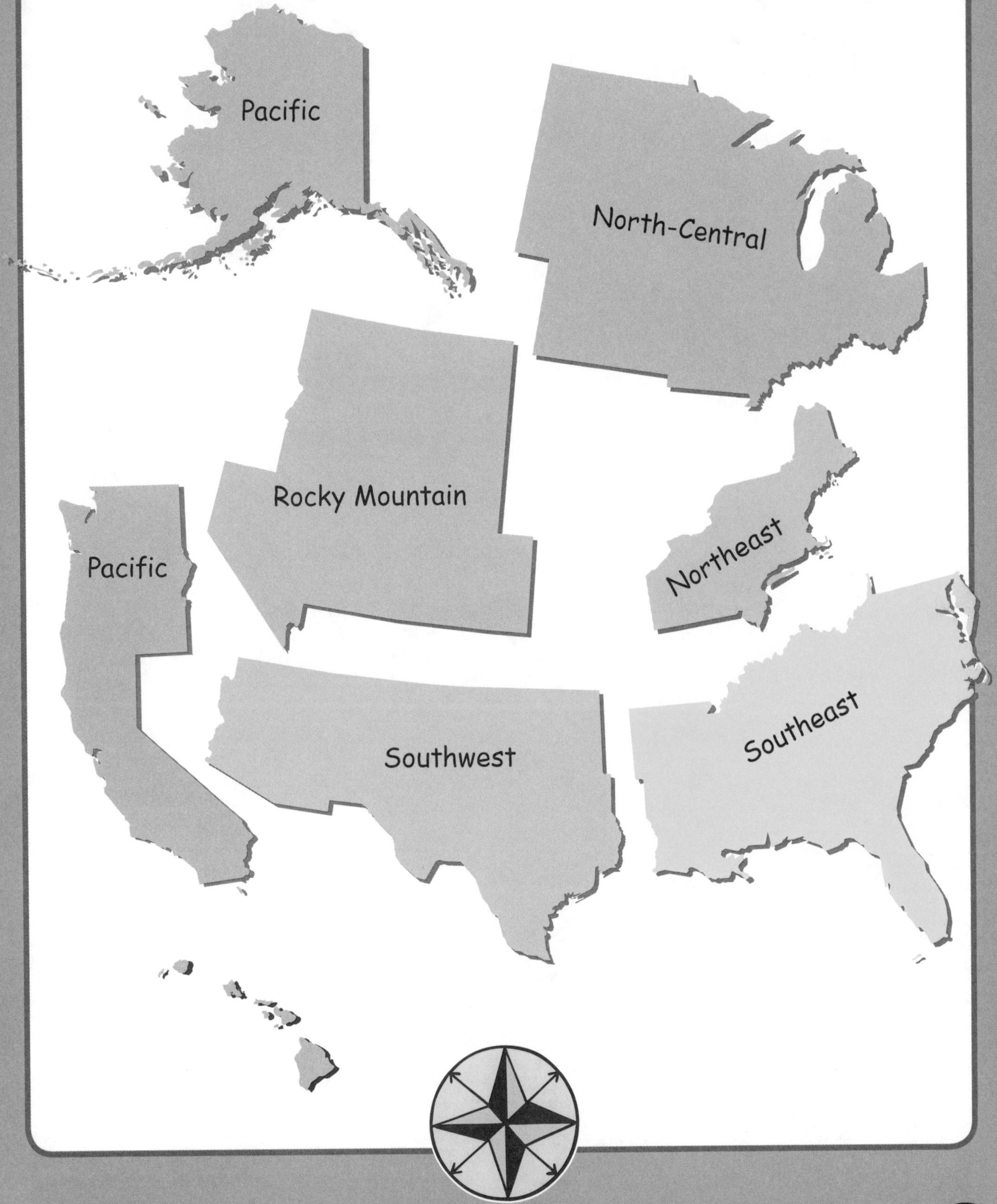
Pacific
North-Central
Rocky Mountain
Pacific
Northeast
Southwest
Southeast

W
S

N
E
S

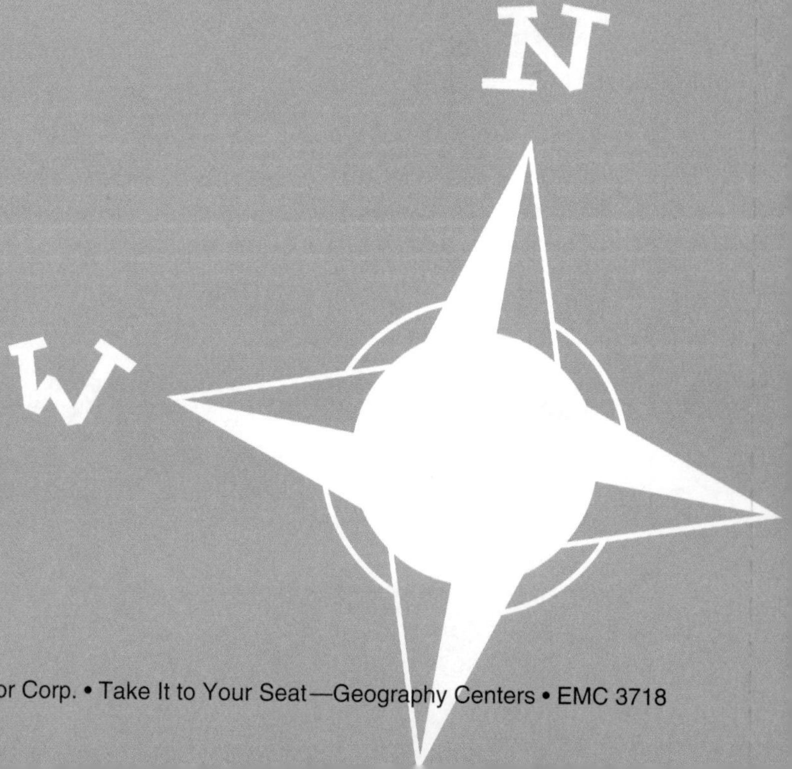
N
W

Regions of the United States

Follow these steps:

1. Study the "Regions of the United States" map.
2. Choose a region map card and read the questions.
3. Write the answers under the correct region on the record sheet.
4. Repeat the steps for the rest of the region map cards.
5. Check your answers using the self-checking answer key.

step 1

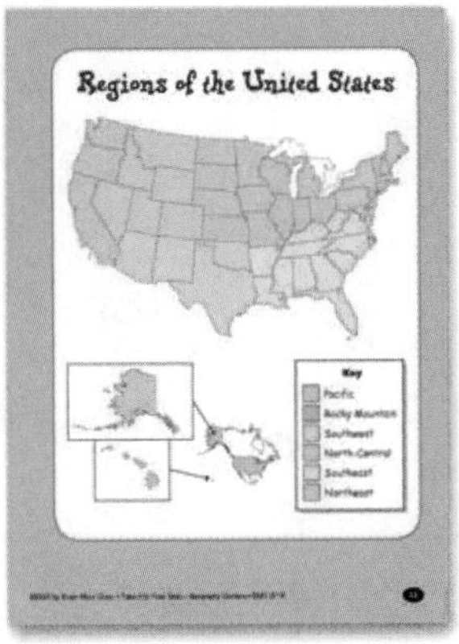
Regions of the United States

step 2

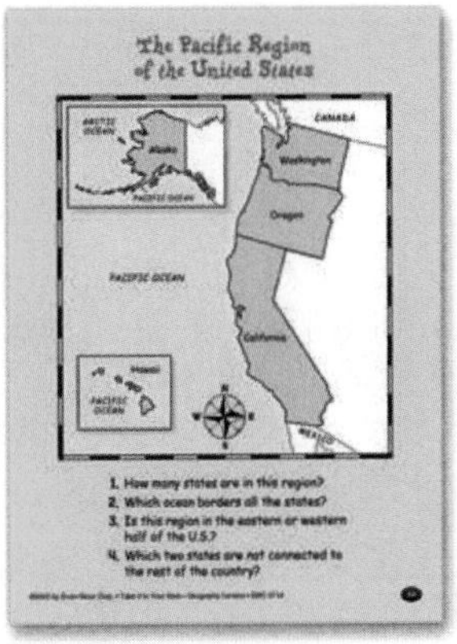
The Pacific Region of the United States

step 3

Regions of the United States

W
S

N
E
S

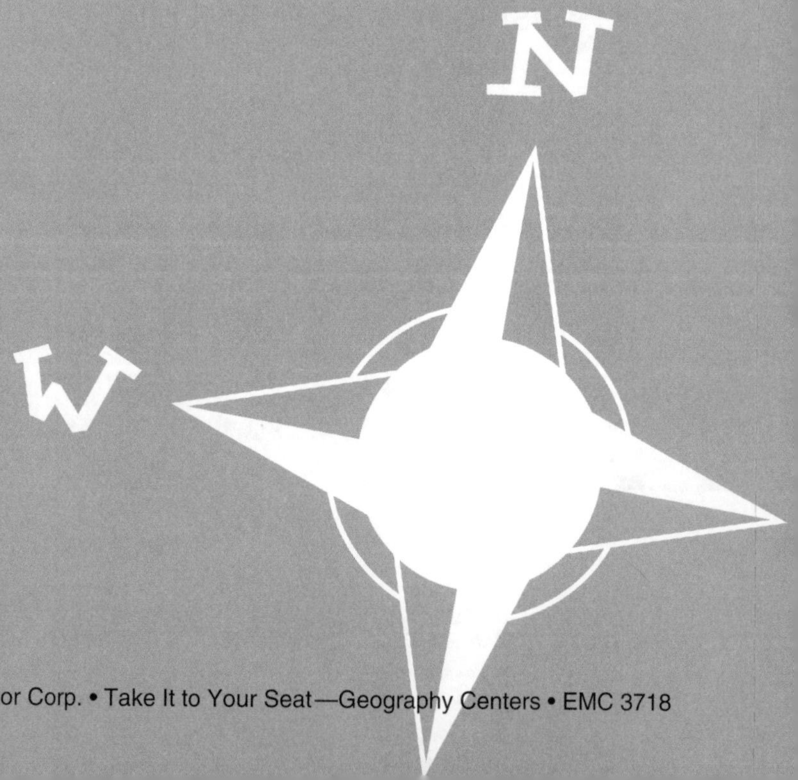
N
W

Regions of the United States

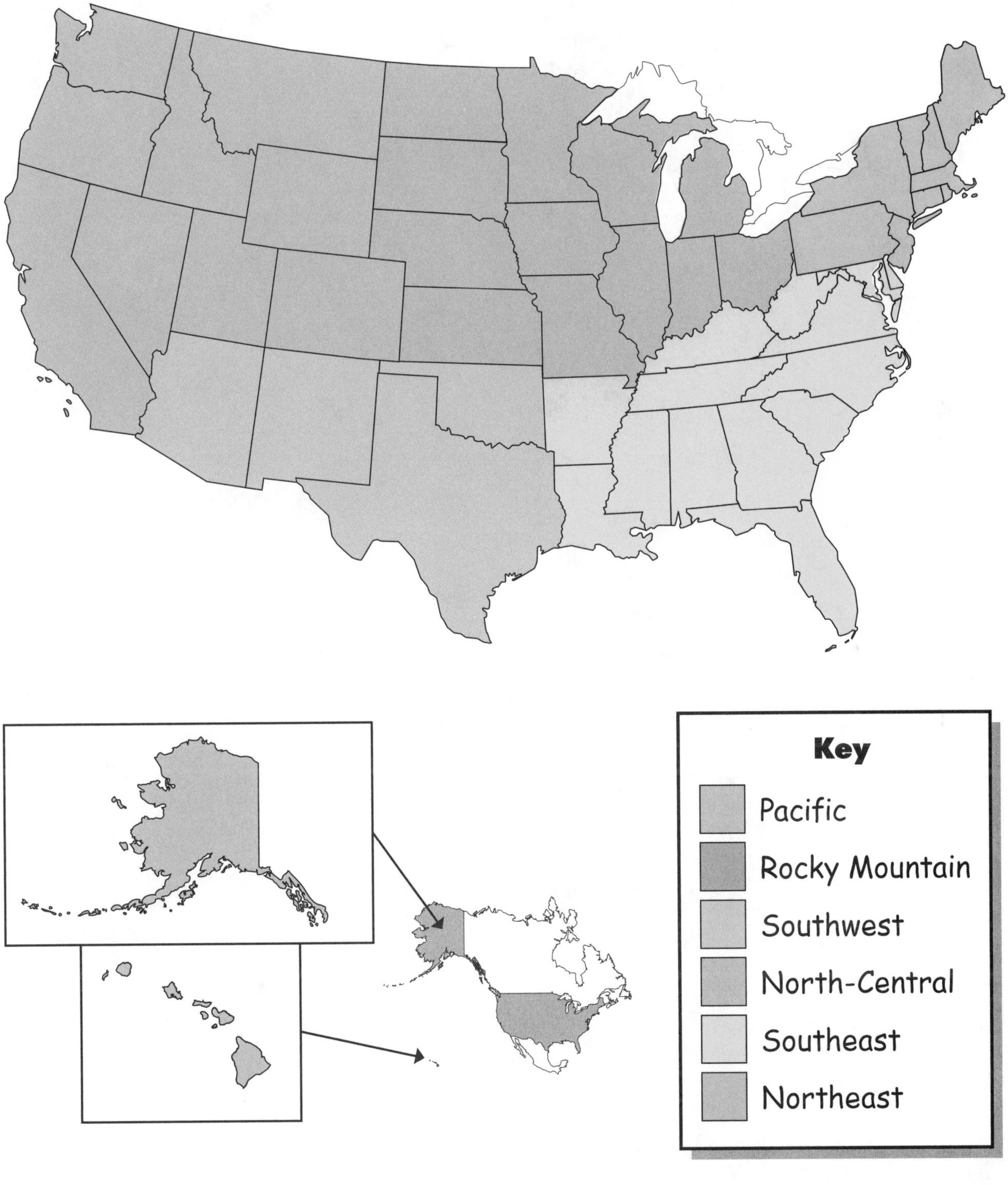
Key
Pacific
Rocky Mountain
Southwest
North-Central
Southeast
Northeast

W
S

N
E
S

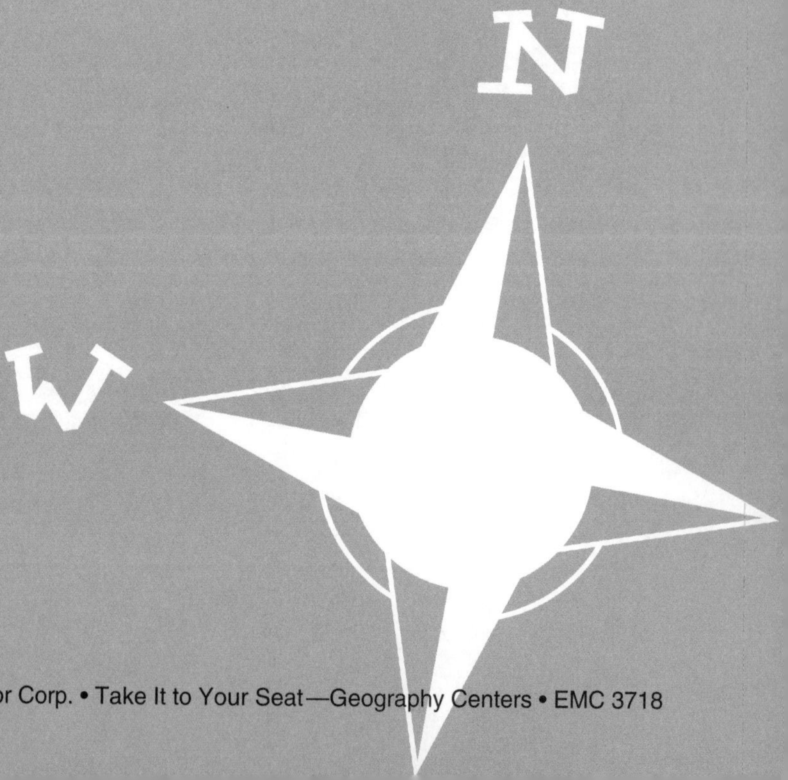
N
W

The Pacific Region of the United States

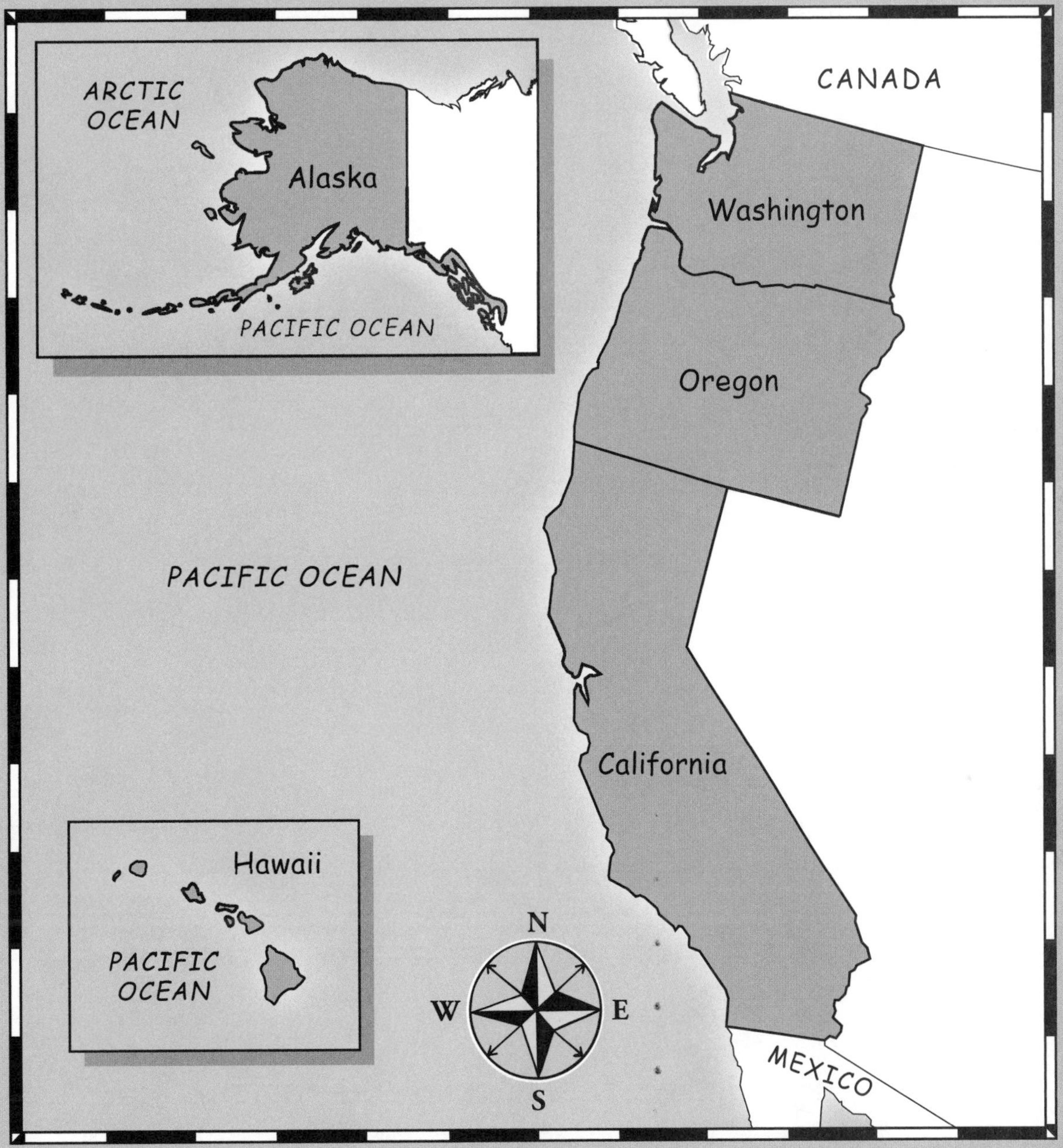

ARCTIC OCEAN
Alaska
PACIFIC OCEAN
CANADA
Washington
Oregon
PACIFIC OCEAN
California
Hawaii
PACIFIC OCEAN
N
W
E
S
MEXICO

1. How many states are in this region?
2. Which ocean borders all the states?
3. Is this region in the eastern or western half of the U.S.?
4. Which two states are not connected to the rest of the country?

The Southwest Region of the United States

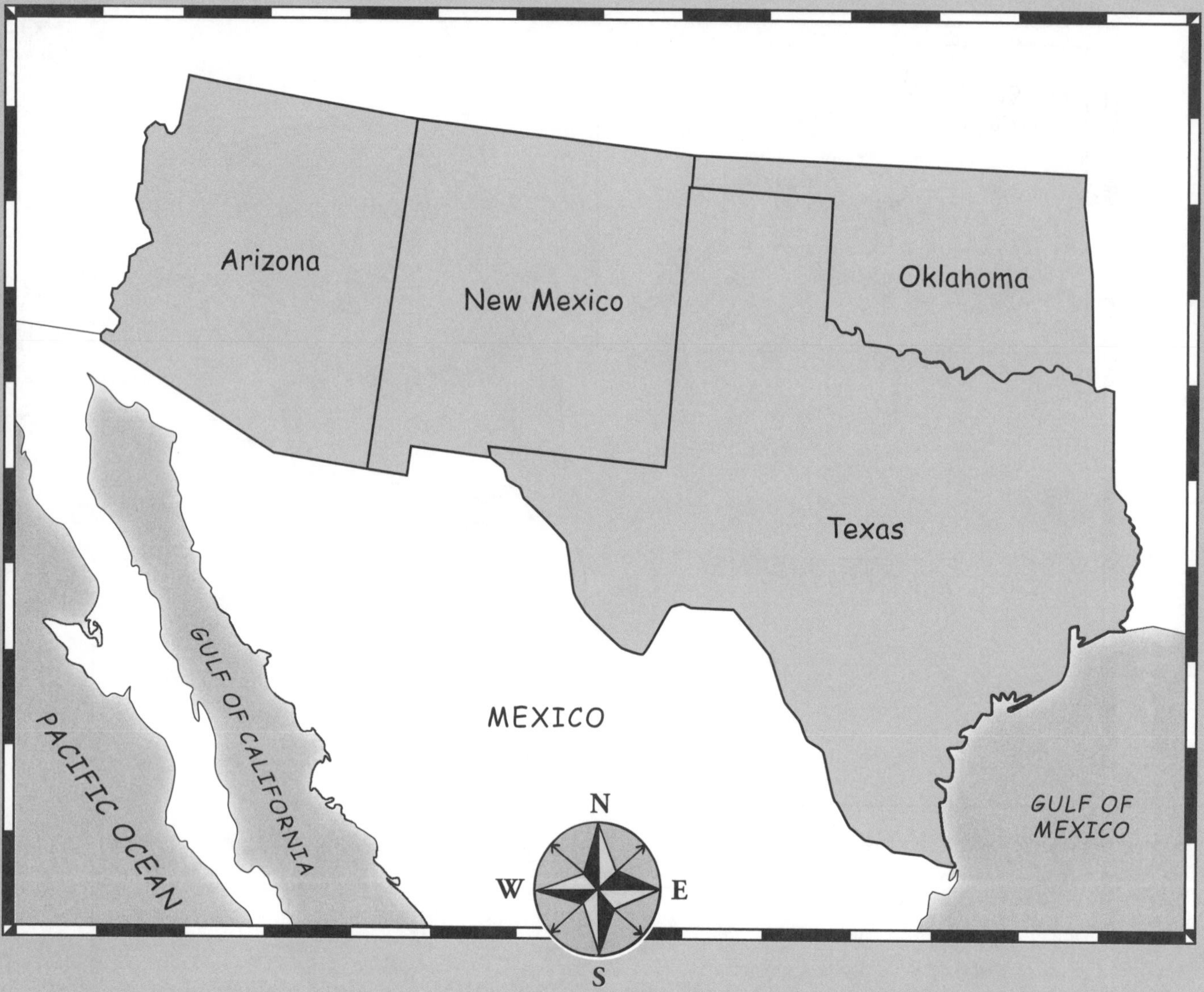
Arizona
New Mexico
Oklahoma
Texas
MEXICO
GULF OF CALIFORNIA
PACIFIC OCEAN
GULF OF MEXICO
N
W
E
S

1. How many states are in this region?
2. Three of the states border which country?
3. Is this region in the northern or southern part of the U.S.?
4. Which state is the largest in size?

The Rocky Mountain Region of the United States

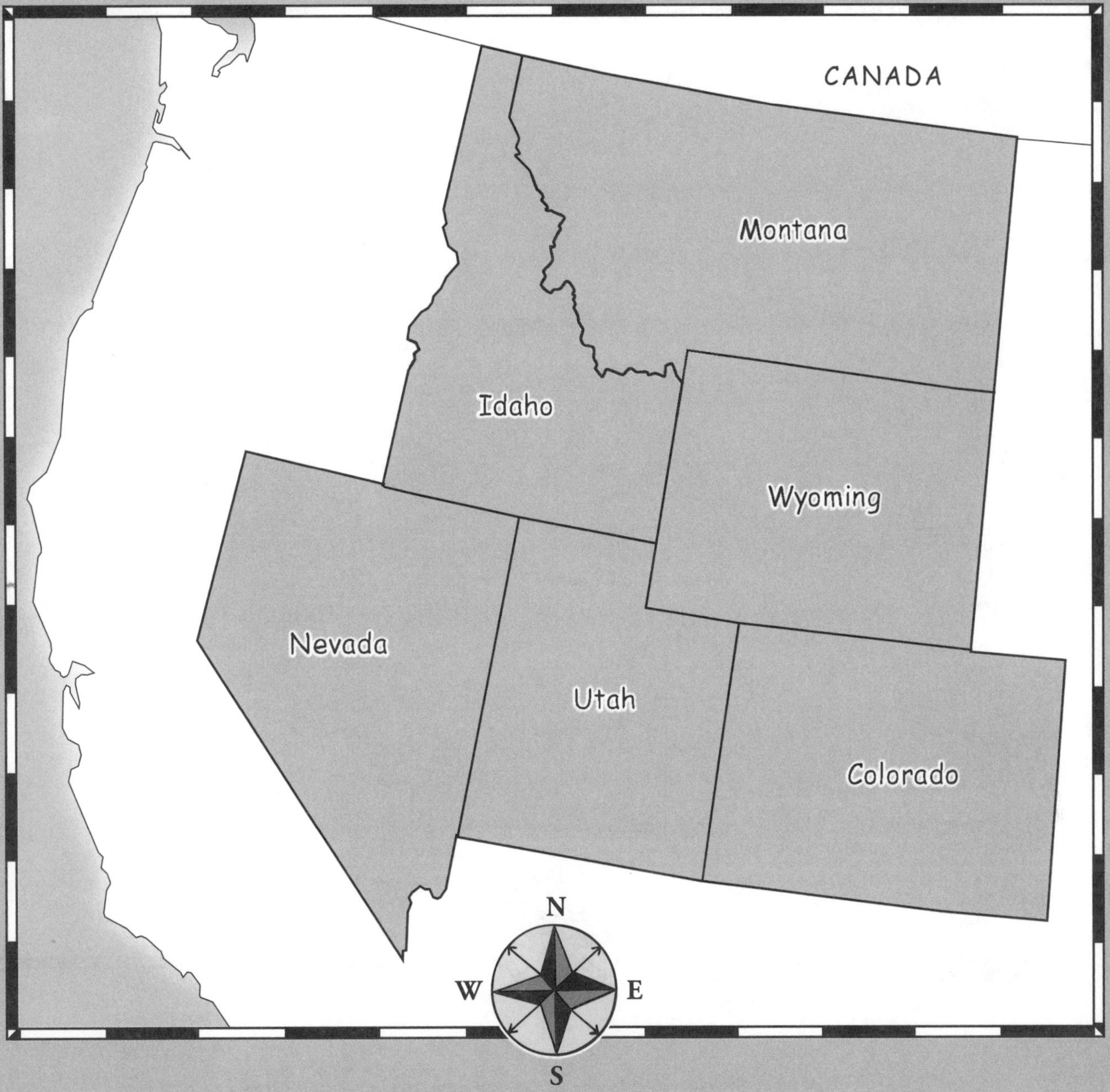
CANADA
Montana
Idaho
Wyoming
Nevada
Utah
Colorado
N
W
E
S

1. How many states are in this region?
2. Which two states border Canada?
3. Is this region in the eastern or western part of the U.S.?
4. Which state is the farthest west?

The North-Central Region of the United States

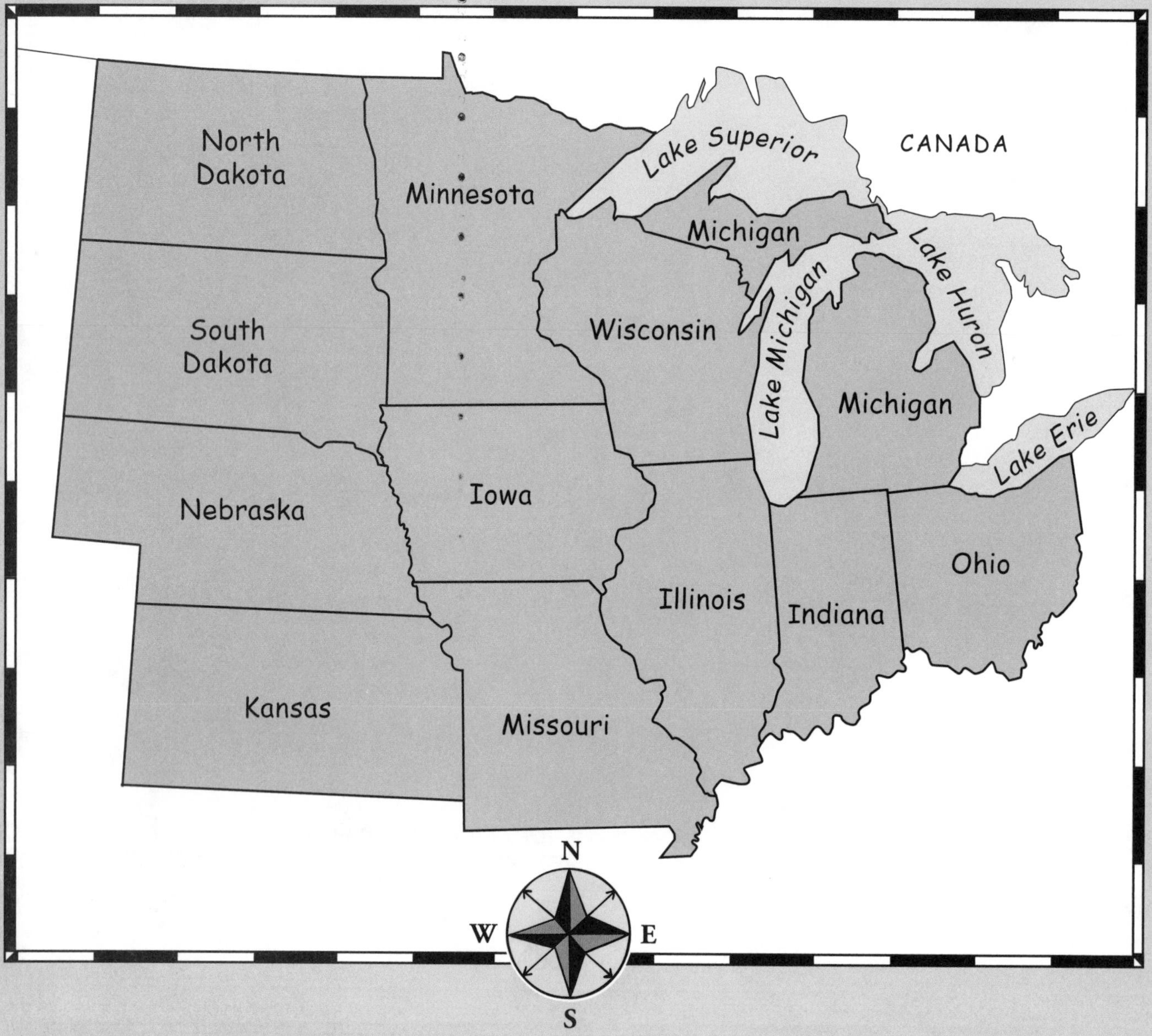

North Dakota
Minnesota
Lake Superior
CANADA
Michigan
South Dakota
Wisconsin
Lake Michigan
Lake Huron
Michigan
Lake Erie
Nebraska
Iowa
Ohio
Illinois
Indiana
Kansas
Missouri
N
W
E
S

1. How many states are in this region?
2. How many states border at least one of the Great Lakes?
3. Is this region in the east, the west, or the middle of the country?
4. Which state is separated into two parts by Lake Michigan?

The Northeast Region of the United States

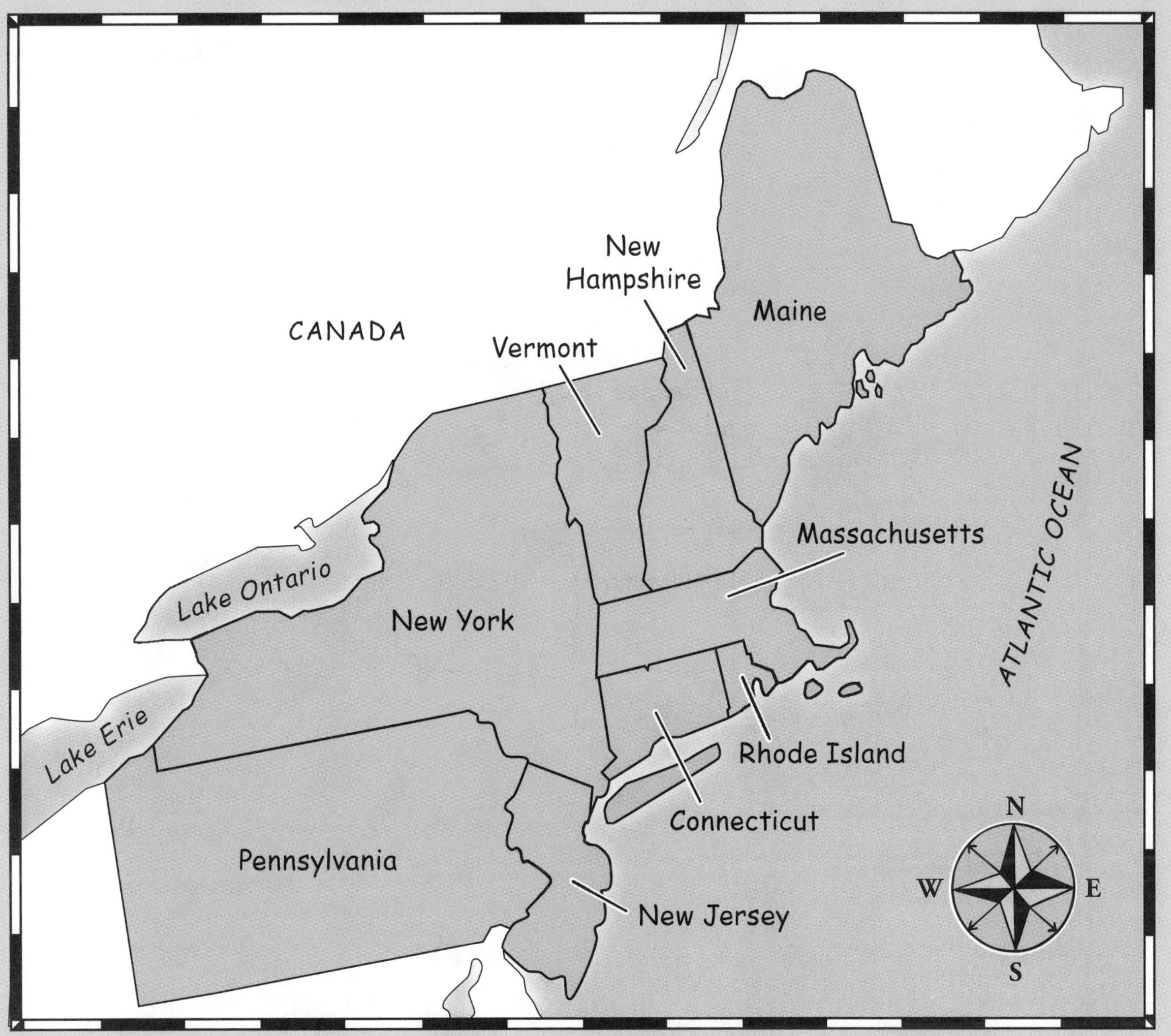

CANADA
New Hampshire
Maine
Vermont
Lake Ontario
New York
Massachusetts
ATLANTIC OCEAN
Lake Erie
Rhode Island
Connecticut
Pennsylvania
New Jersey
N
W
E
S

1. How many states are in this region?
2. Many of the states border which ocean?
3. Several states border which country?
4. Which state is the farthest north?

The Southeast Region of the United States

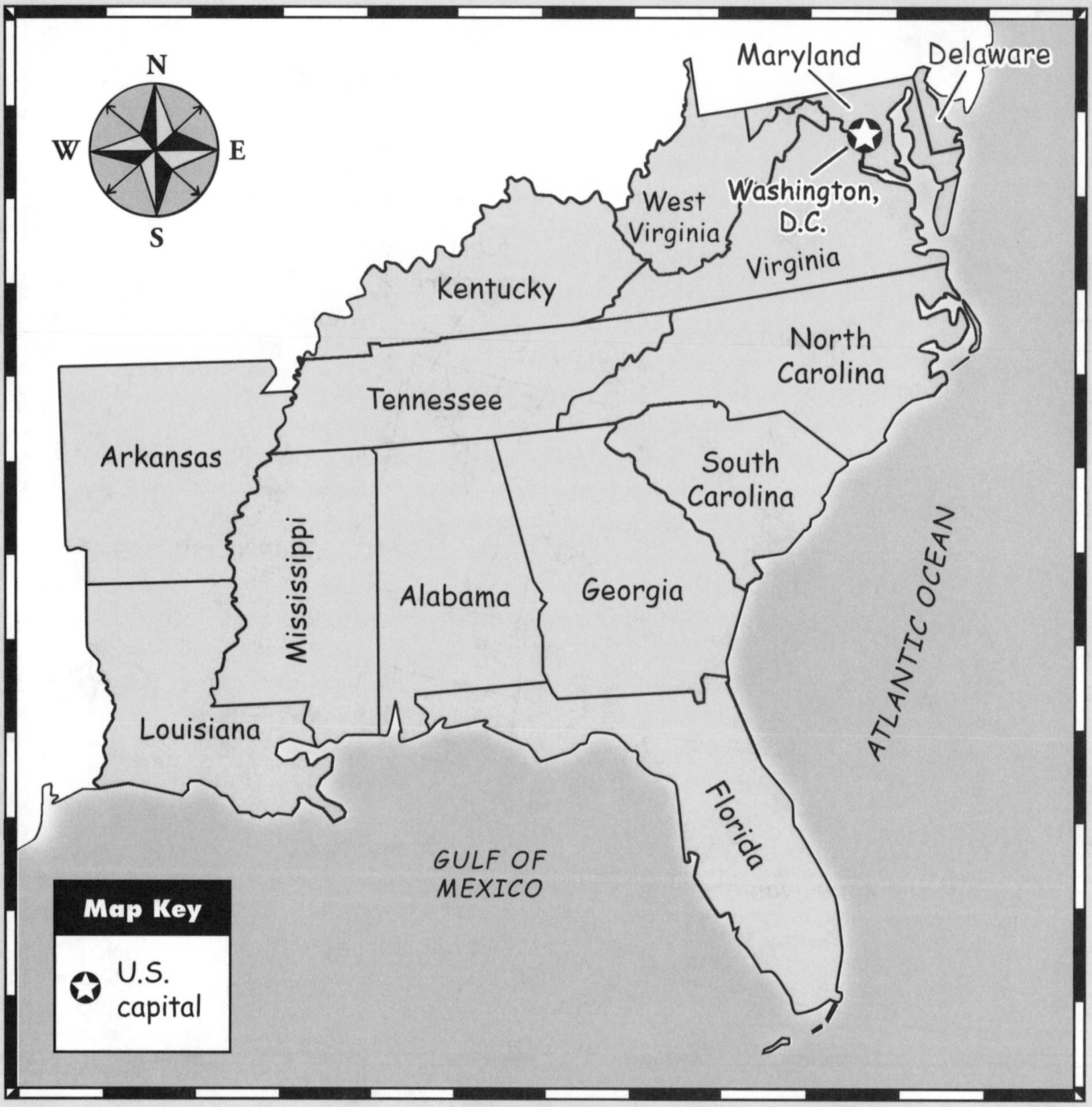

N
S
E
W
Maryland
Delaware
West Virginia
Washington, D.C.
Virginia
Kentucky
North Carolina
Tennessee
Arkansas
South Carolina
Mississippi
Alabama
Georgia
ATLANTIC OCEAN
Louisiana
Florida
GULF OF MEXICO
Map Key
U.S. capital

1. How many states are in this region?
2. How many states border the Gulf of Mexico?
3. Many states border which ocean?
4. What is the name of the capital of the U.S.?

Answer Key

Regions of the United States

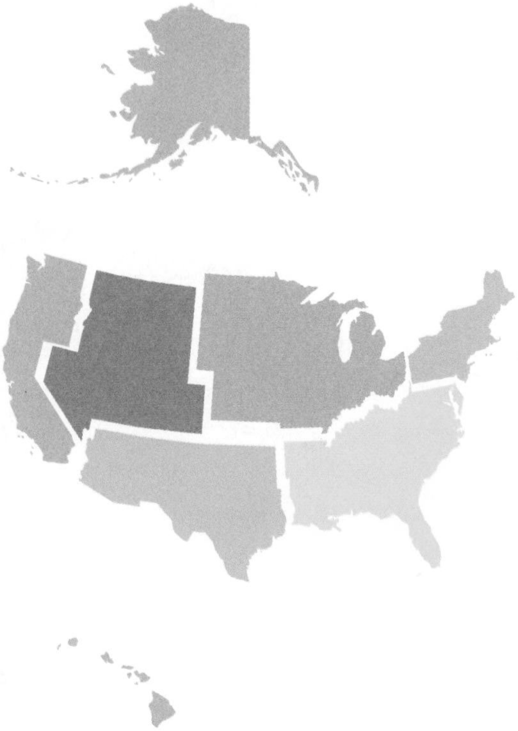

Lift the flap to check your answers.

Regions of the United States

Pacific Region

1. 5 states
2. Pacific Ocean
3. western
4. Alaska and Hawaii

Southwest Region

1. 4 states
2. Mexico
3. southern
4. Texas

Rocky Mountain Region

1. 6 states
2. Idaho and Montana
3. western
4. Nevada

North-Central Region

1. 12 states
2. 6 states
3. middle
4. Michigan

Northeast Region

1. 9 states
2. Atlantic Ocean
3. Canada
4. Maine

Southeast Region

1. 14 states
2. 4 states
3. Atlantic Ocean
4. Washington, D.C.

Regions of the United States

Regions of the United States

©2005 by Evan-Moor Corp. • EMC 3718

The Compass Rose

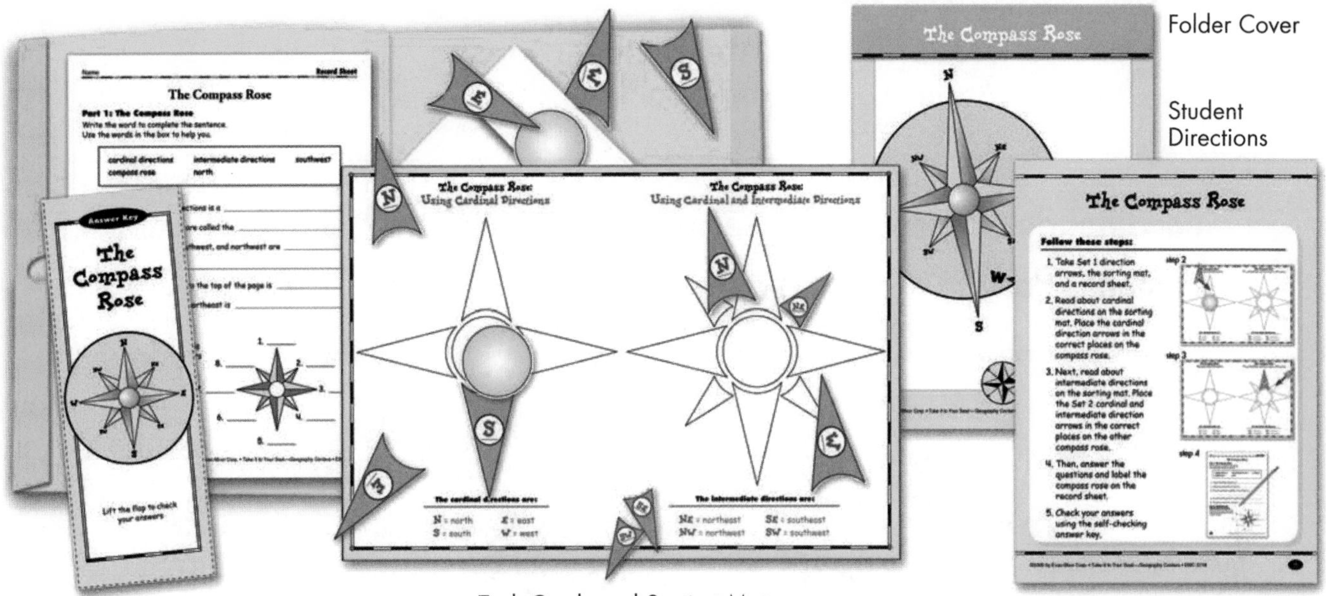
The Compass Rose
The Compass Rose
The Compass Rose

Folder Cover

Student Directions

Task Cards and Sorting Mat

Preparing the Center

1. Prepare a folder following the directions on page 3.

   Cover—page 69

   Student Directions—page 71

   Task Cards—pages 77 and 79
   - Set 1: Cardinal Direction Arrows
   - Set 2: Intermediate Direction Arrows

   Sorting Mat—pages 73 and 75

   Self-Checking Key—page 81

2. Reproduce a supply of the record sheet on page 68. Place copies in the left-hand pocket of the folder.

Using the Center

1. The student starts with Set 1 cardinal direction arrows, the sorting mat, and a record sheet.

2. The student reads about cardinal directions on the sorting mat. The student then places the cardinal direction arrows in the correct places to make a compass rose.

3. Next, the student reads about intermediate directions and then places Set 2 direction arrows to make the other compass rose.

4. Then the student answers the questions and labels the compass rose on the record sheet.

5. Finally, the student uses the self-checking key to check answers.

The Compass Rose

Part 1: The Compass Rose

Write the word or words to complete each sentence.
Use the words in the box to help you.

cardinal directions	intermediate directions	southwest
compass rose	north	

1. A symbol that shows directions is a ______________________.
2. The four main directions are called ______________________.
3. Northeast, southeast, southwest, and northwest are called

   ______________________.
4. The direction that points to the top of the page is ______________.
5. The opposite direction of northeast is ______________________.

Part 2: Cardinal and Intermediate Directions

Write the eight directions on this compass rose. You may use letters instead of words.

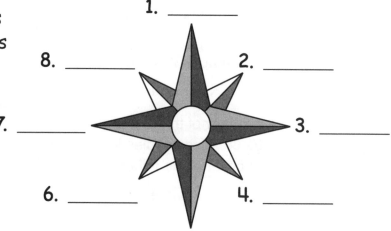

1. ________

8. ________ 2. ________

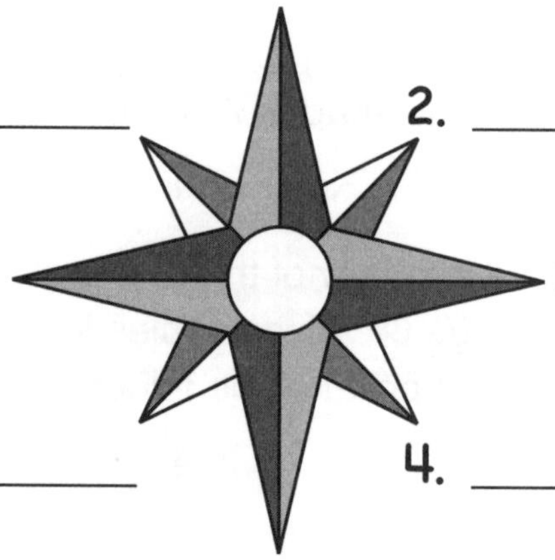

7. ________ 3. ________

6. ________ 4. ________

5. ________

The Compass Rose

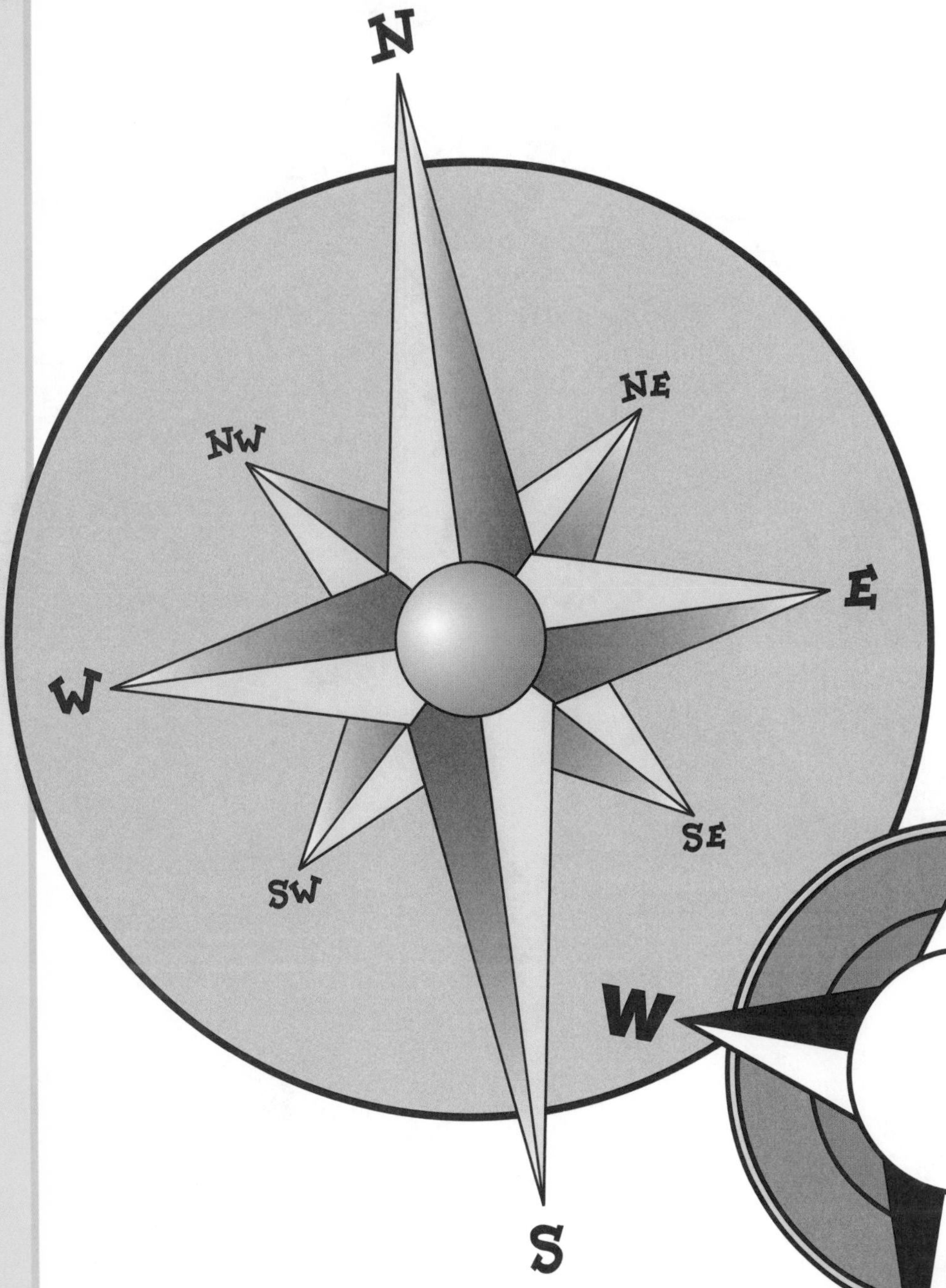
N
NE
NW
E
W
SE
SW
S

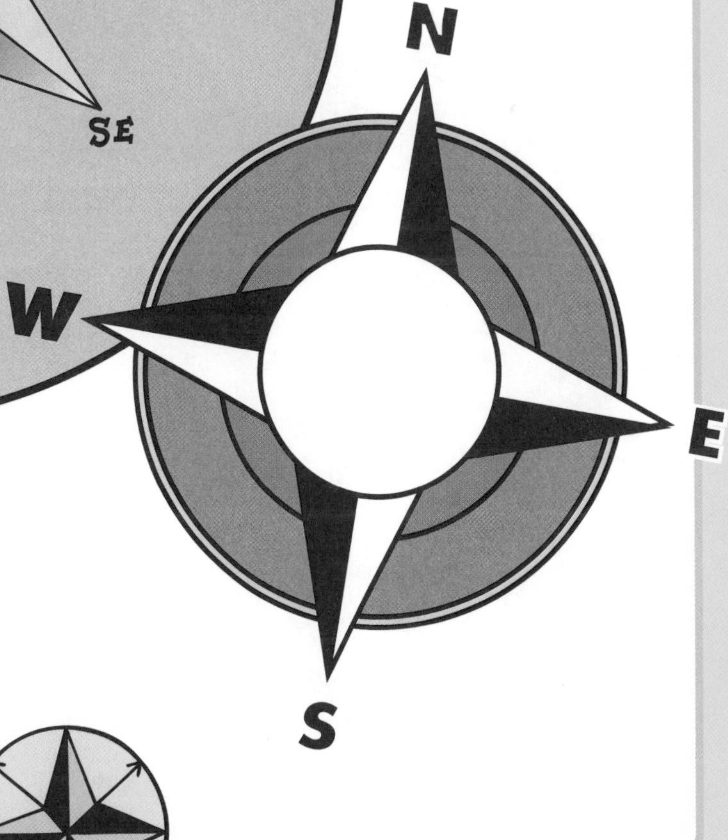
N
W
E
S

W
S

N
E
S

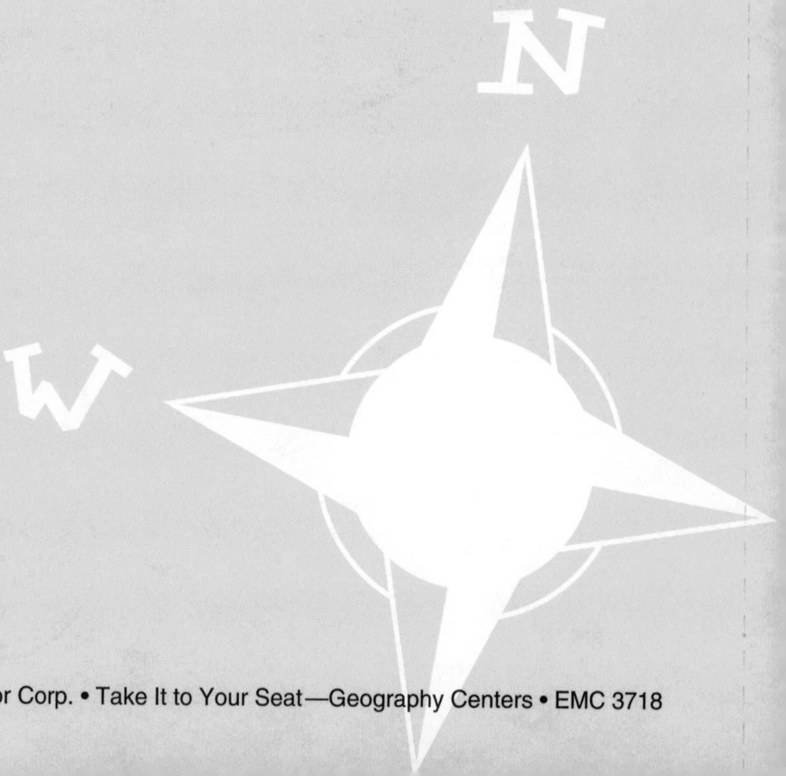
N
W

The Compass Rose

Follow these steps:

1. Take the Set 1 direction arrows, the sorting mat, and a record sheet.

2. Read about cardinal directions on the sorting mat. Place the cardinal direction arrows in the correct places on the compass rose.

3. Next, read about intermediate directions on the sorting mat. Place the Set 2 cardinal and intermediate direction arrows in the correct places on the other compass rose.

4. Then answer the questions and label the compass rose on the record sheet.

5. Check your answers using the self-checking answer key.

step 2

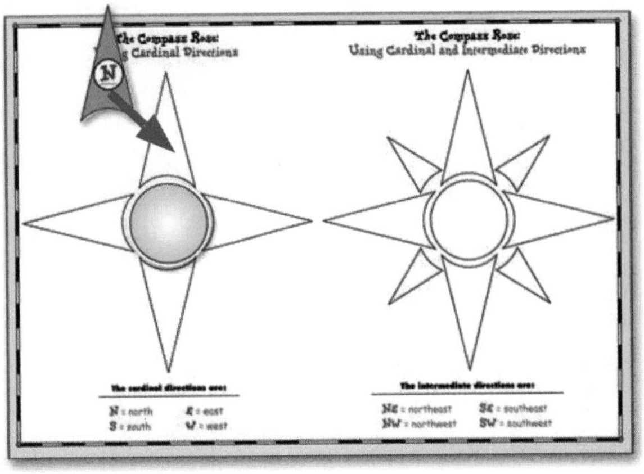
N
The Compass Rose:
Using Cardinal and Intermediate Directions

step 3

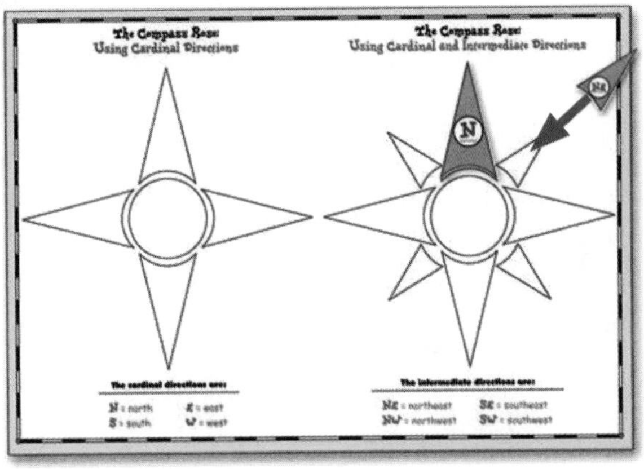
The Compass Rose:
Using Cardinal Directions
The Compass Rose:
Using Cardinal and Intermediate Directions
N
NE
The cardinal directions are:
N = north
E = east
S = south
W = west
The intermediate directions are:
NE = northeast
SE = southeast
NW = northwest
SW = southwest

step 4

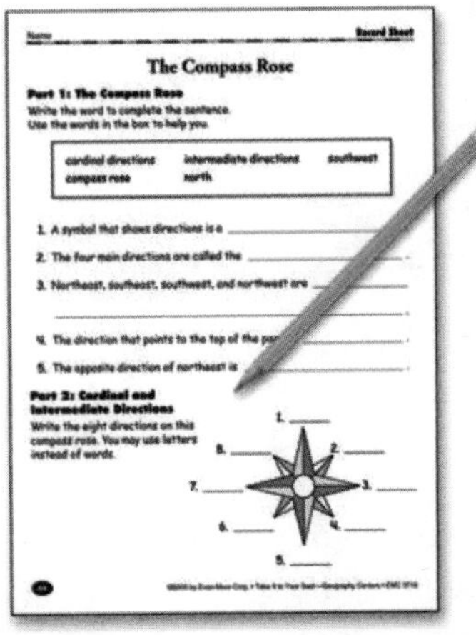
The Compass Rose

W
S

N
E
S

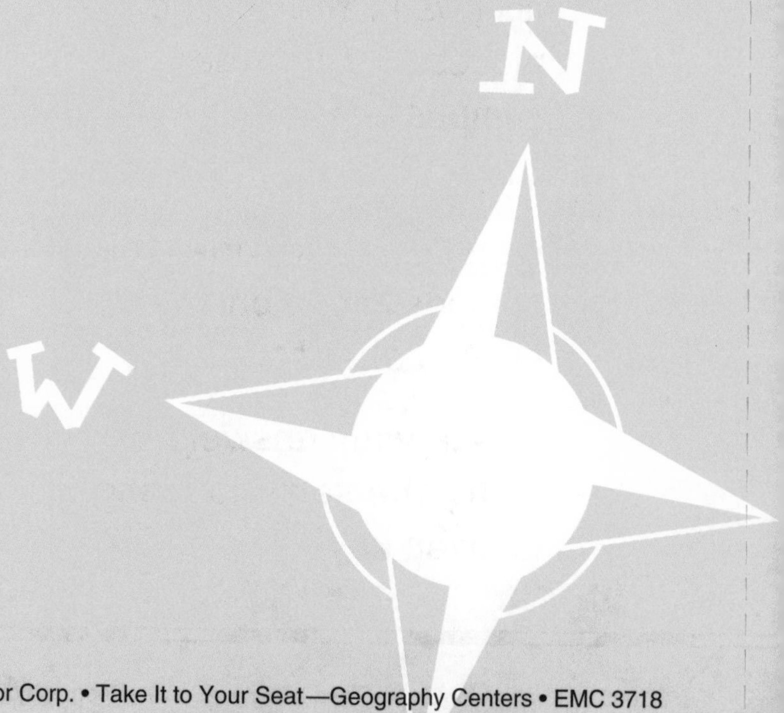
N
W

The Compass Rose: Using Cardinal Directions

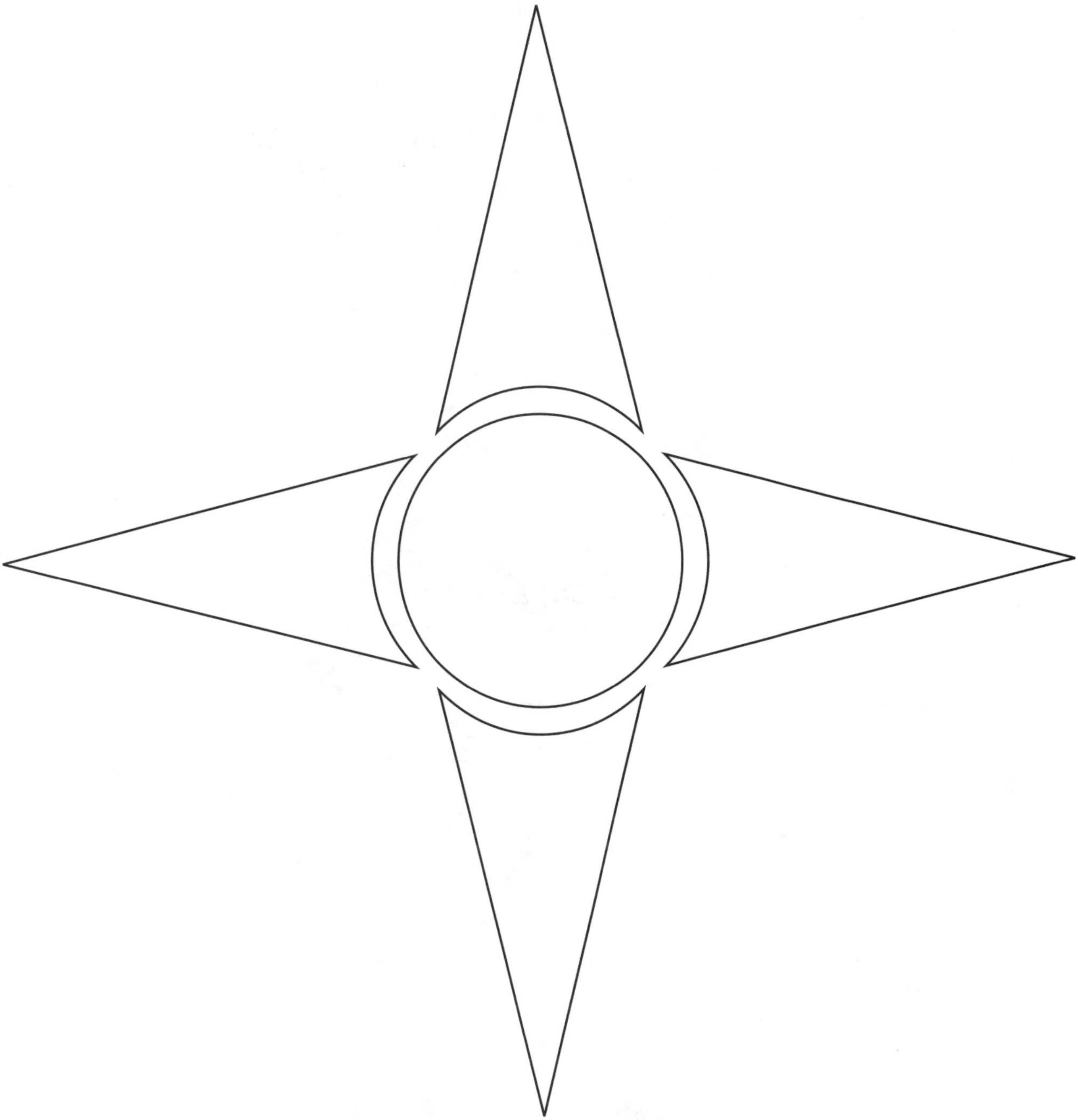

The cardinal directions are:

N = north **E** = east

S = south **W** = west

The Compass Rose

The Compass Rose:
Using Cardinal and Intermediate Directions

glue

The intermediate directions are:

NE = northeast **SE** = southeast
NW = northwest **SW** = southwest

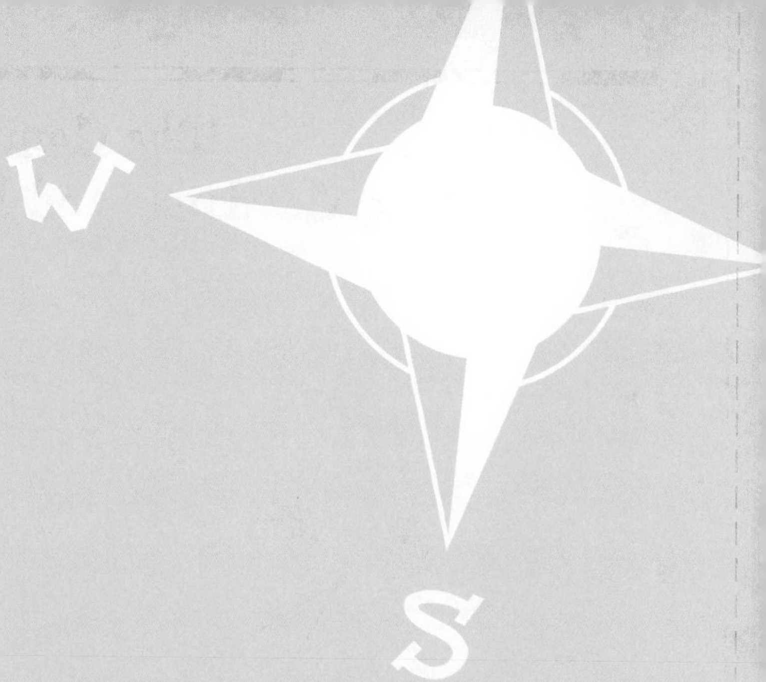
W
S

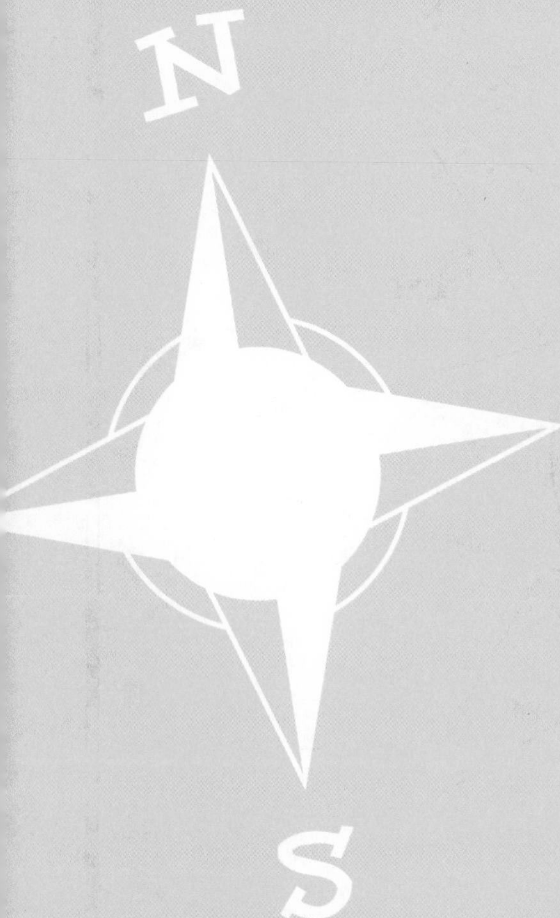
N
S

E

The Compass Rose

N
W

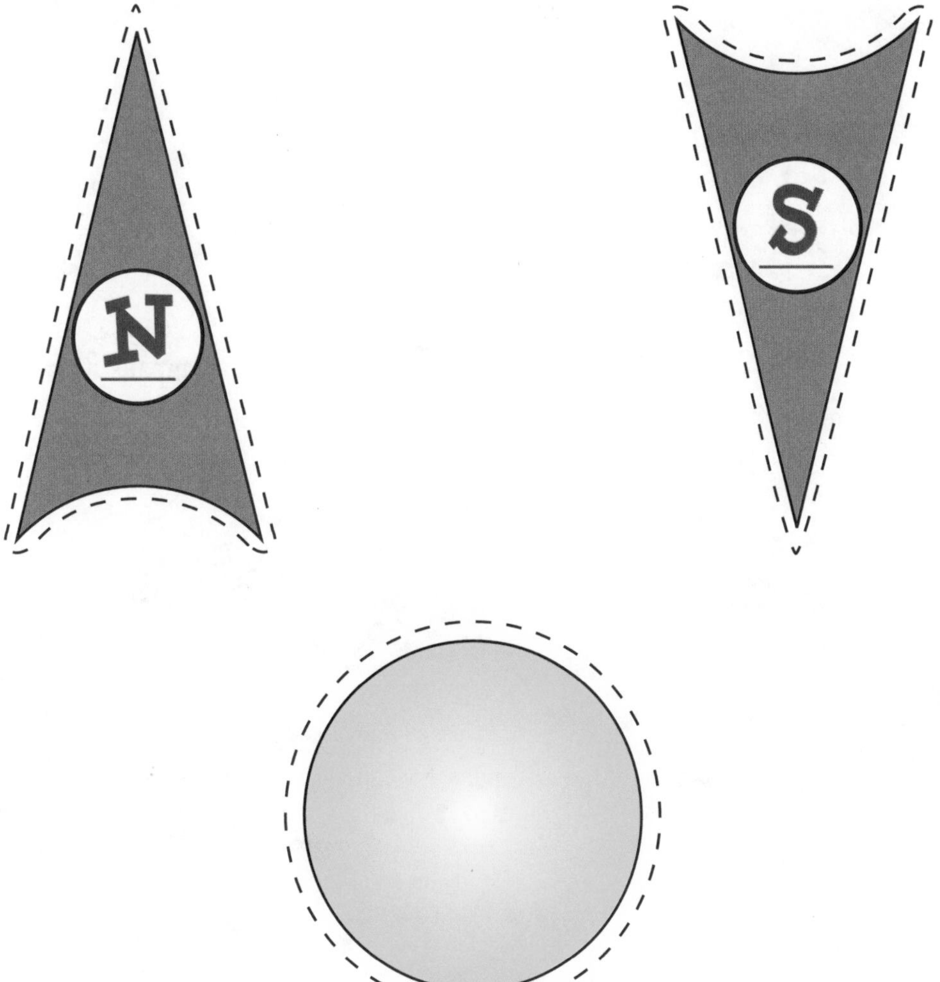
N
S
E
W

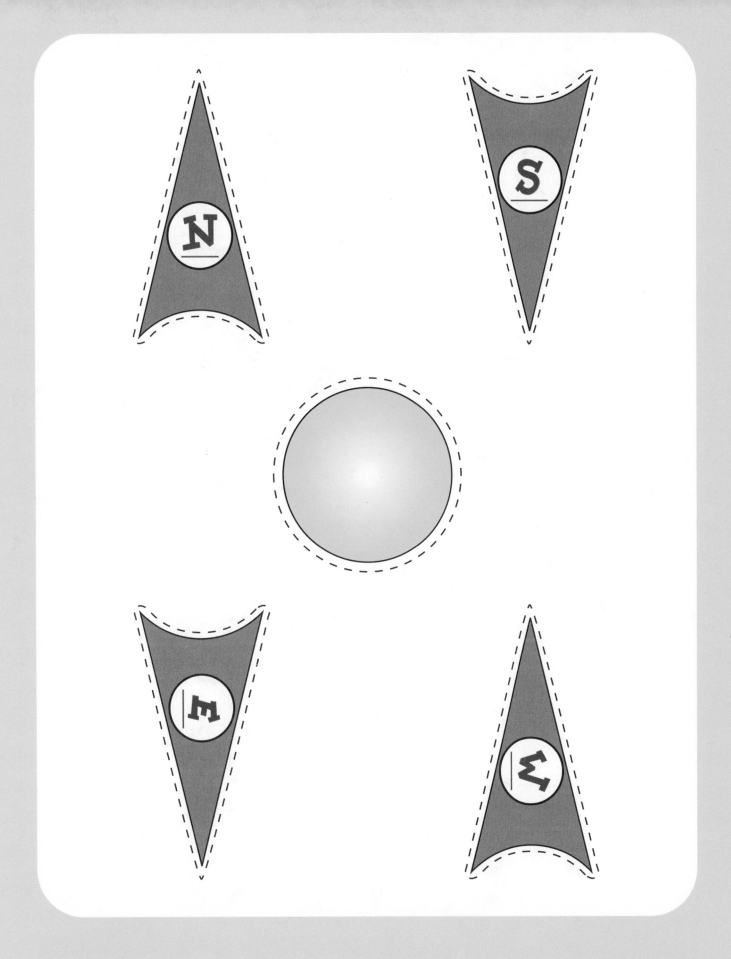

The
Compass Rose
Set 1

The
Compass Rose
Set 1
©2005
by Evan-Moor Corp.
EMC 3718

The
Compass Rose
Set 1
©2005
by Evan-Moor Corp.
EMC 3718

The
Compass Rose
Set 1
©2005
by Evan-Moor Corp.
EMC 3718

The
Compass Rose
Set 1
©2005
by Evan-Moor Corp.
EMC 3718

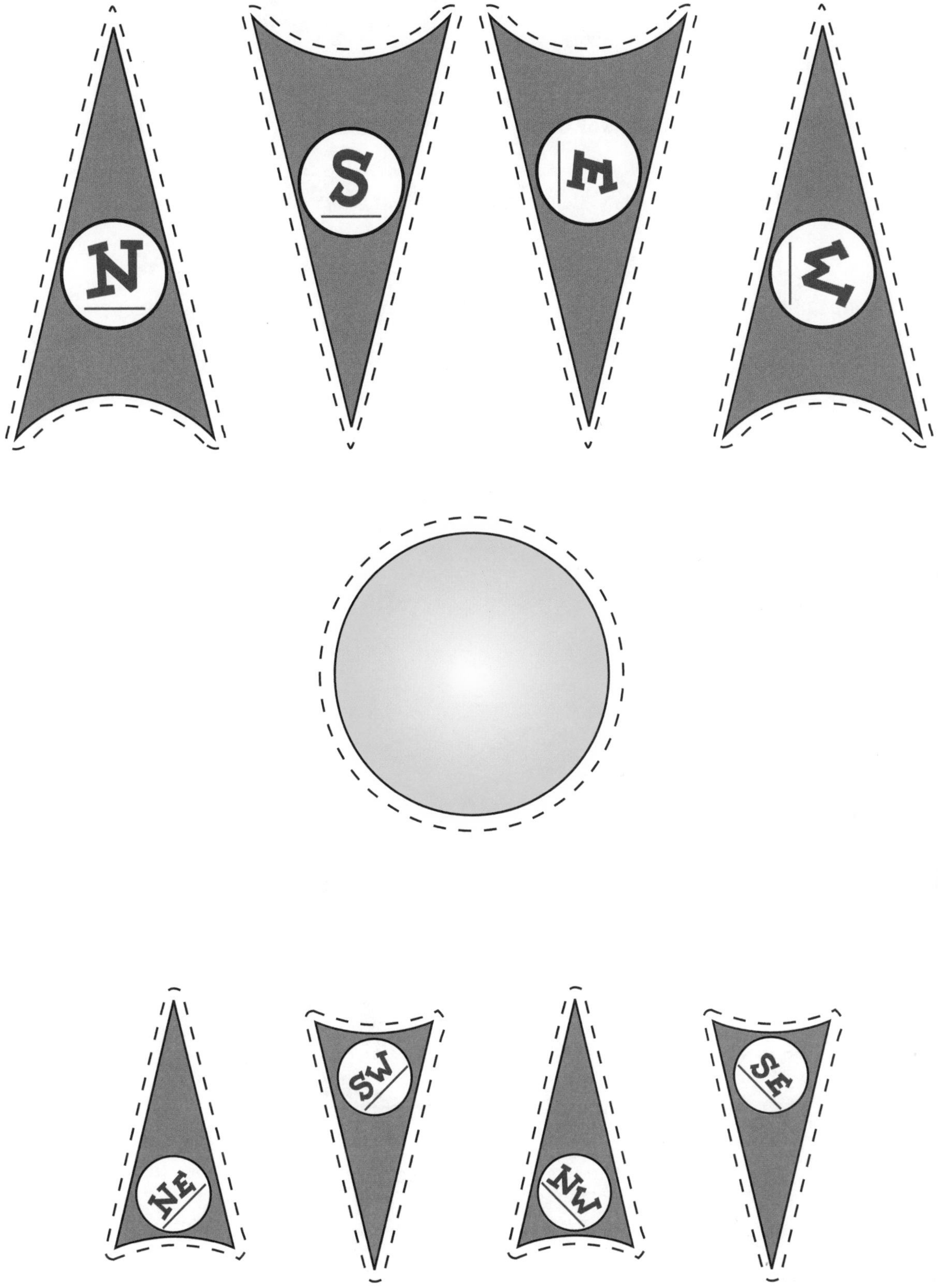
N
S
E
W
NE
SW
NW
SE

The Compass Rose
Set 2
©2005
by Evan-Moor Corp.
EMC 3718

The Compass Rose
Set 2
©2005
by Evan-Moor Corp.
EMC 3718

The Compass Rose
Set 2
©2005 by Evan-Moor Corp.
EMC 3718

The Compass Rose
Set 2
©2005 by Evan-Moor Corp.
EMC 3718

The Compass Rose
Set 2
©2005 by Evan-Moor Corp.
EMC 3718

The Compass Rose
Set 2
©2005
by Evan-Moor Corp.
EMC 3718

The Compass Rose
Set 2
©2005
by Evan-Moor Corp.
EMC 3718

The Compass Rose
Set 2
©2005
by Evan-Moor Corp.
EMC 3718

The Compass Rose
Set 2
©2005
by Evan-Moor Corp.
EMC 3718

Answer Key

The Compass Rose

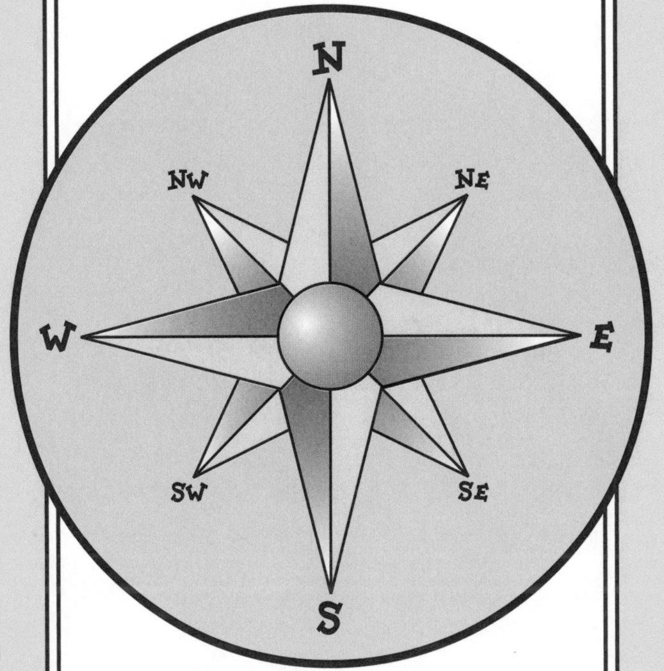
N
NW
NE
W
E
SW
SE
S

Lift the flap to check your answers.

The Compass Rose

Part 1

1. compass rose
2. cardinal directions
3. intermediate directions
4. north
5. southwest

Part 2

1. N
2. NE
3. E
4. SE
5. S
6. SW
7. W
8. NW

The Compass Rose

The Compass Rose

Using a Map Key

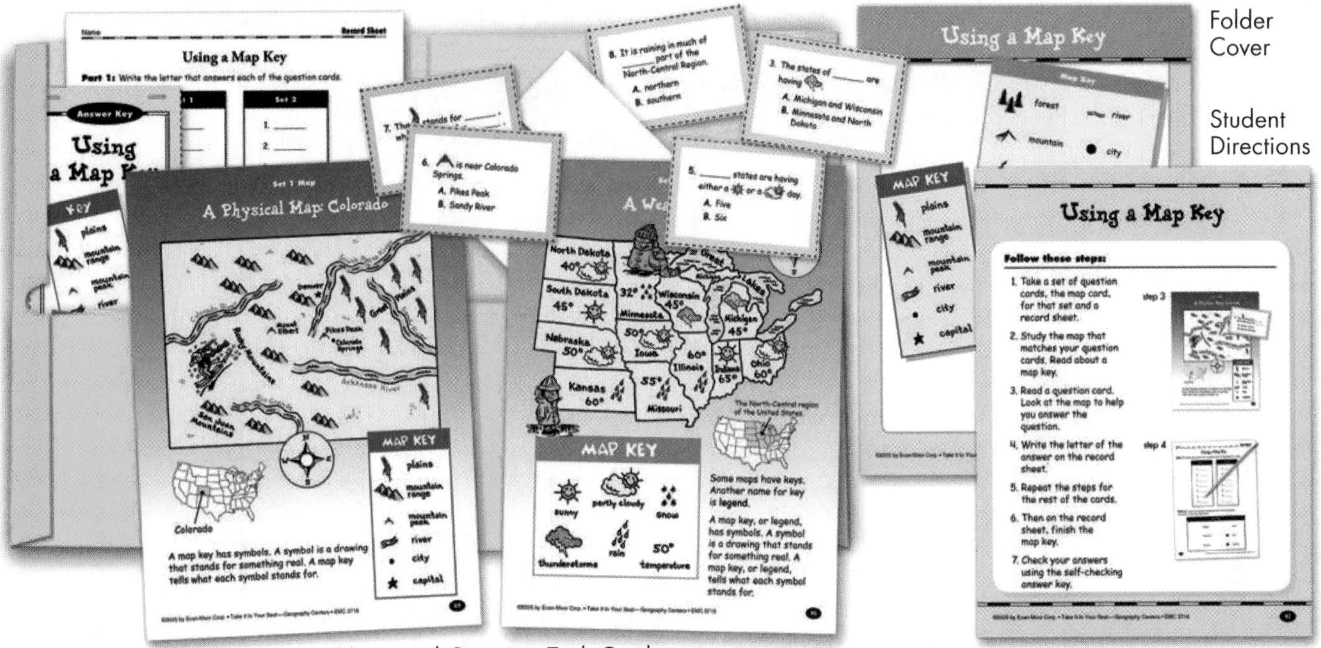
Using a Map Key
Answer Key
A Physical Map: Colorado
MAP KEY
Using a Map Key
Follow these steps:

Folder Cover

Student Directions

Maps and Question Task Cards

Preparing the Center

1. Prepare a folder following the directions on page 3.

   Cover—page 85

   Student Directions—page 87

   Question Task Cards—pages 91 and 93
   - Set 1—purple
   - Set 2—blue

   Self-Checking Key—page 95

2. Laminate the maps on pages 89 and 90. Place the two-sided map card in the pocket for the student to use with the question cards.

3. Reproduce a supply of the record sheet on page 84. Place copies in the left-hand pocket of the folder.

Using the Center

1. The student takes a set of question cards, the map card, and a record sheet.
2. The student reads about a map key and studies the map.
3. Next, the student reads a question card and uses the appropriate map to help find the answer.
4. The student then records the answer on the record sheet.
5. The student repeats the steps for the remaining cards.
6. On the record sheet, the student completes a map key.
7. Finally, the student uses the self-checking key to check answers.

Using a Map Key

Part 1: Write the letter that answers each of the question cards.

Set 1	Set 2
1. ______	1. ______
2. ______	2. ______
3. ______	3. ______
4. ______	4. ______
5. ______	5. ______
6. ______	6. ______
7. ______	7. ______
8. ______	8. ______

Part 2: Finish the map key. Draw symbols to show forests, mountains, volcanoes, and rivers.

Map Key			
	forest		river
	mountain	●	city
	volcano	★	capital

Using a Map Key

Map Key
forest
river
mountain
city
volcano
capital

MAP KEY
plains
mountain range
mountain peak
river
city
capital

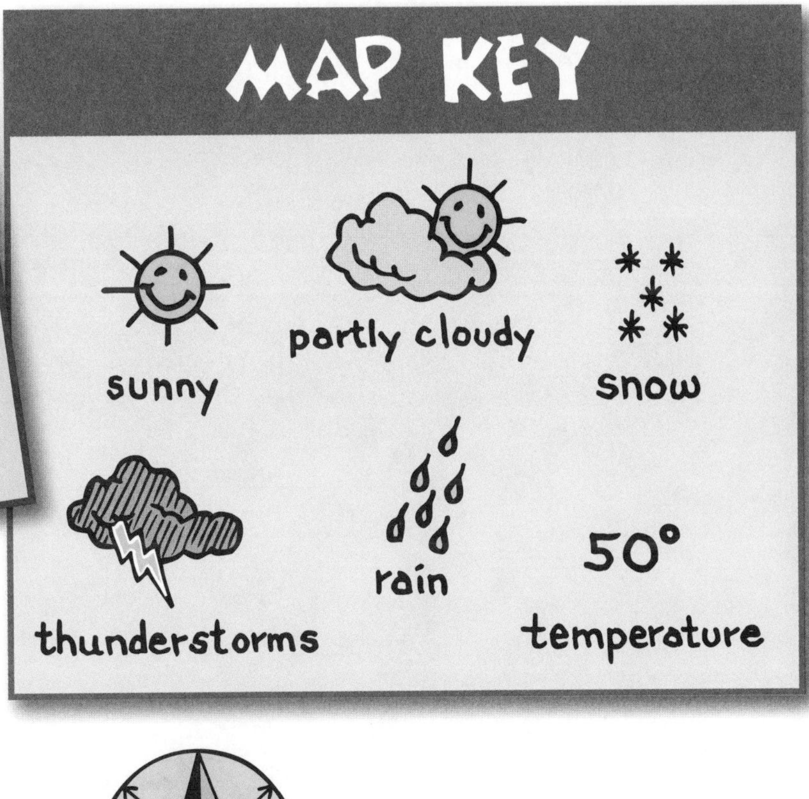
MAP KEY
sunny
partly cloudy
snow
thunderstorms
rain
50°
temperature

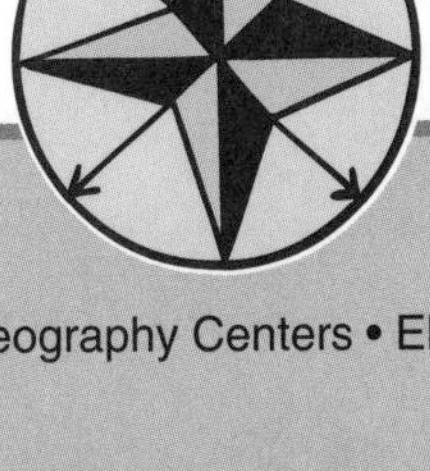

W
S

N
E
S

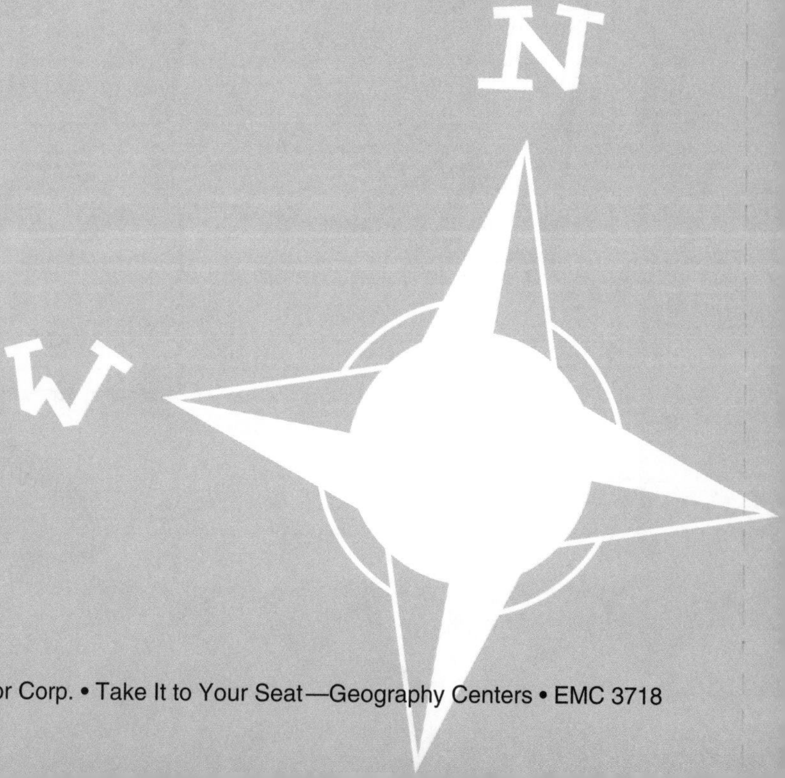
N
W

Using a Map Key

Follow these steps:

1. Take a set of question cards, the map card, and a record sheet.
2. Study the map that matches your question cards. Read about a map key.
3. Read a question card. Look at the map to help you answer the question.
4. Write the letter of the answer on the record sheet.
5. Repeat the steps for the rest of the cards.
6. Then finish the map key on the record sheet.
7. Check your answers using the self-checking answer key.

step 3

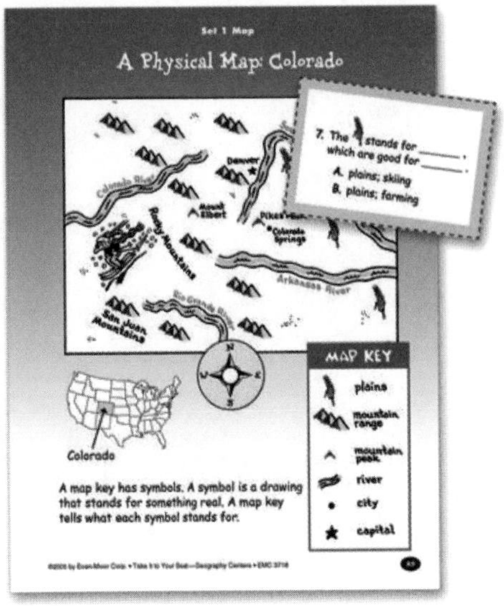
Set 1 Map
A Physical Map: Colorado
MAP KEY
plains
mountain range
mountain peak
river
city
capital
Colorado
A map key has symbols. A symbol is a drawing that stands for something real. A map key tells what each symbol stands for.

step 4

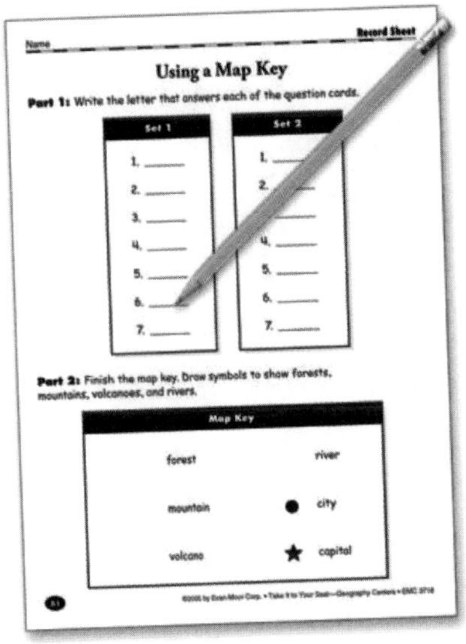
Record Sheet
Using a Map Key
Part 1: Write the letter that answers each of the question cards.
Set 1
Set 2
Part 2: Finish the map key. Draw symbols to show forests, mountains, volcanoes, and rivers.
Map Key
forest
river
mountain
city
volcano
capital

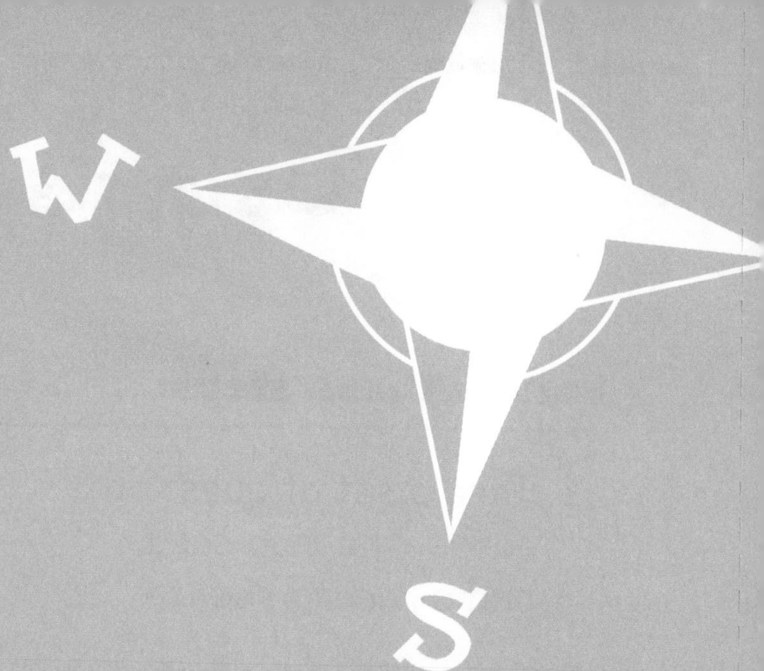
W
S

N
E
S

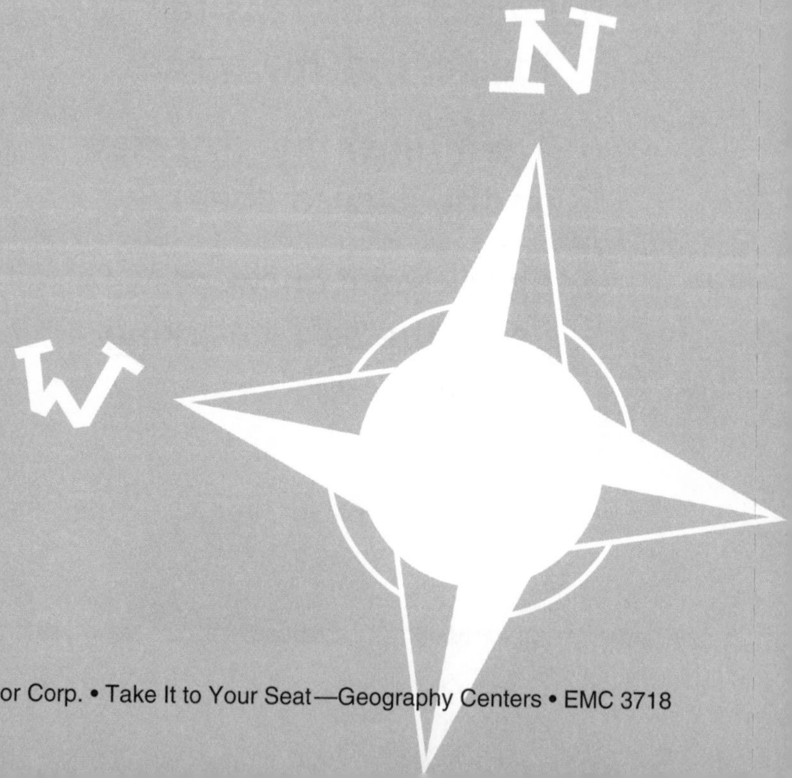
N
W

A Physical Map: Colorado

South Platte River
Denver
Colorado River
Great Plains
Sandy River
Mount Elbert
Pikes Peak
Colorado Springs
Rocky Mountains
Arkansas River
Rio Grande
San Juan Mountains
N
W
E
S

Colorado

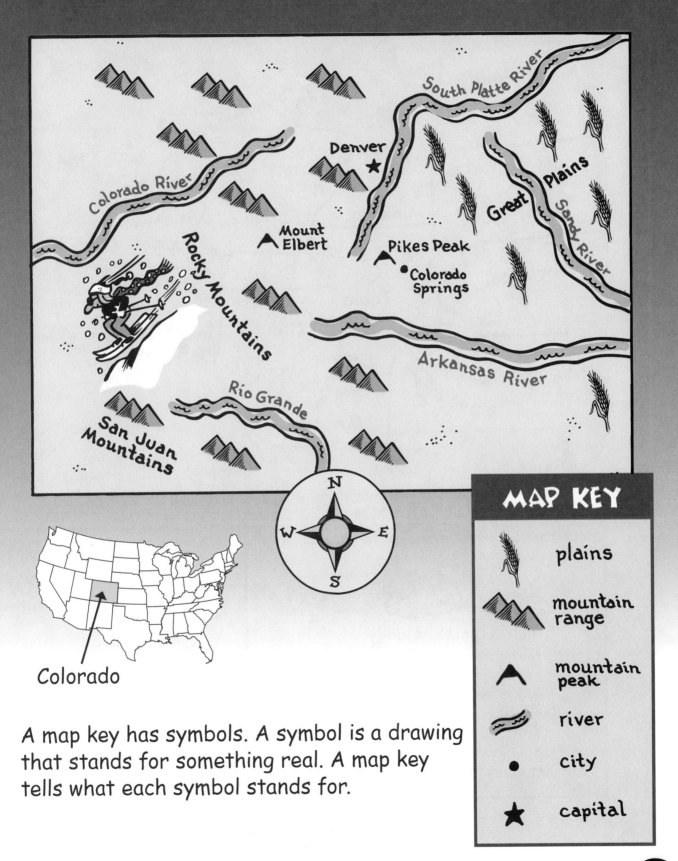

MAP KEY
plains
mountain range
mountain peak
river
city
capital

A map key has symbols. A symbol is a drawing that stands for something real. A map key tells what each symbol stands for.

A Weather Map

N
W
E
S
North Dakota
40°
South Dakota
45°
32°
Minnesota
Wisconsin
45°
Great
Michigan
Lakes
Michigan
45°
Nebraska
50°
50°
Iowa
60°
Illinois
Indiana
65°
Ohio
60°
Kansas
60°
55°
Missouri

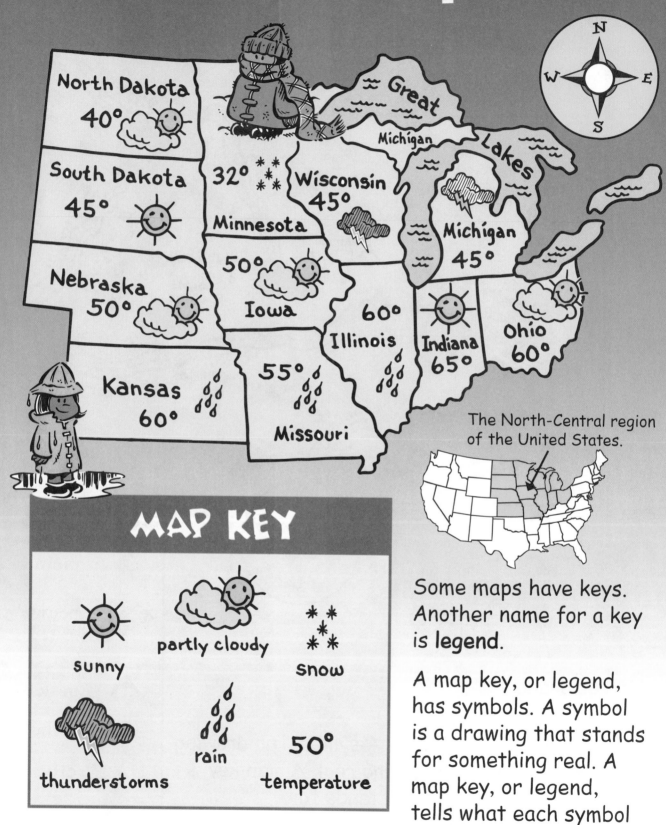

The North-Central region of the United States.

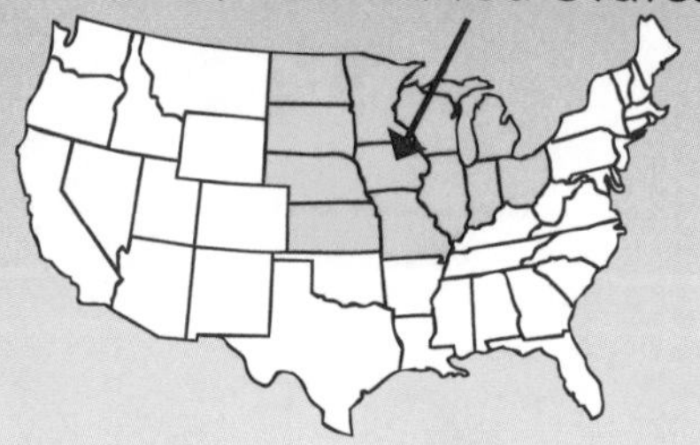

MAP KEY
sunny
partly cloudy
snow
thunderstorms
rain
50°
temperature

Some maps have keys. Another name for a key is **legend**.

A map key, or legend, has symbols. A symbol is a drawing that stands for something real. A map key, or legend, tells what each symbol stands for.

1. A map key has _______ .

   A. arrows that stand for directions

   B. symbols that stand for real things

5. The _______ is east of the San Juan Mountains.

   A. Colorado River

   B. Rio Grande

2. The map shows _______ .

   A. landforms and waterways of Colorado

   B. major cities and highways of Colorado

6.  is near Colorado Springs.

   A. Pikes Peak

   B. Sandy River

3. The capital of Colorado is _______ .

   A. Colorado Springs

   B. Denver

7. The  stands for _______ , which are good for _______ .

   A. plains; skiing

   B. plains; farming

4. Mount Elbert is a _______ .

   A. mountain peak

   B. mountain range

8. A large range west of Denver is the _______ .

   A. Great Plains

   B. Rocky Mountains

Using a Map Key
Set 1

Using a Map Key
Set 1

©2005 by Evan-Moor Corp. • EMC 3718

Using a Map Key
Set 1

©2005 by Evan-Moor Corp. • EMC 3718

Using a Map Key
Set 1

©2005 by Evan-Moor Corp. • EMC 3718

Using a Map Key
Set 1

©2005 by Evan-Moor Corp. • EMC 3718

Using a Map Key
Set 1

©2005 by Evan-Moor Corp. • EMC 3718

Using a Map Key
Set 1

©2005 by Evan-Moor Corp. • EMC 3718

Using a Map Key
Set 1

©2005 by Evan-Moor Corp. • EMC 3718

1. The map shows the weather in _______ states.
   - A. 12
   - B. 13

2. Another name for a **key** on a map is a _______ .
   - A. compass rose
   - B. legend

3. The states of _______ are having .
   - A. Michigan and Wisconsin
   - B. Minnesota and North Dakota

4. _______ is the warmest and _______ is the coldest.
   - A. Indiana; Minnesota
   - B. Minnesota; Indiana

5. _______ states are having either a  or a  day.
   - A. Five
   - B. Six

6. The weather near the Great Lakes is mostly _______ .
   - A. cold and stormy
   - B. warm and calm

7. It is snowing in _______ and the temperature is _______ .
   - A. Kansas, 60°
   - B. Minnesota, 32°

8. It is raining in much of the _______ part of the North-Central Region.
   - A. northern
   - B. southern

Using a Map Key
Set 2

Using a Map Key
Set 2

Using a Map Key
Set 2

Using a Map Key
Set 2

Using a Map Key
Set 2

Using a Map Key
Set 2

Using a Map Key
Set 2

Using a Map Key
Set 2

Answer Key

Using a Map Key

Key
plains
mountain range
mountain peak
river
MAP KEY
sunny
partly cloudy
snow
thunderstorms
rain
50°
temperature

Lift the flap to check your answers.

Using a Map Key

Part 1

Set 1	Set 2
1. B	1. A
2. A	2. B
3. B	3. A
4. A	4. A
5. B	5. B
6. A	6. A
7. B	7. B
8. B	8. B

Part 2

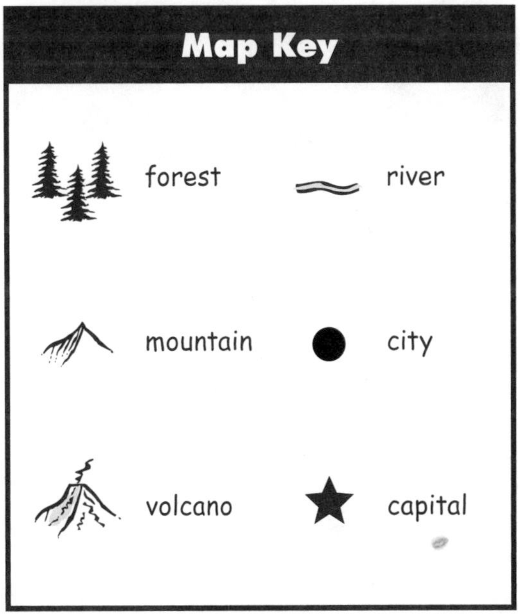
Map Key
forest
river
mountain
city
volcano
capital

W
S

N
E
S

Using a Map Key

Using a Map Key

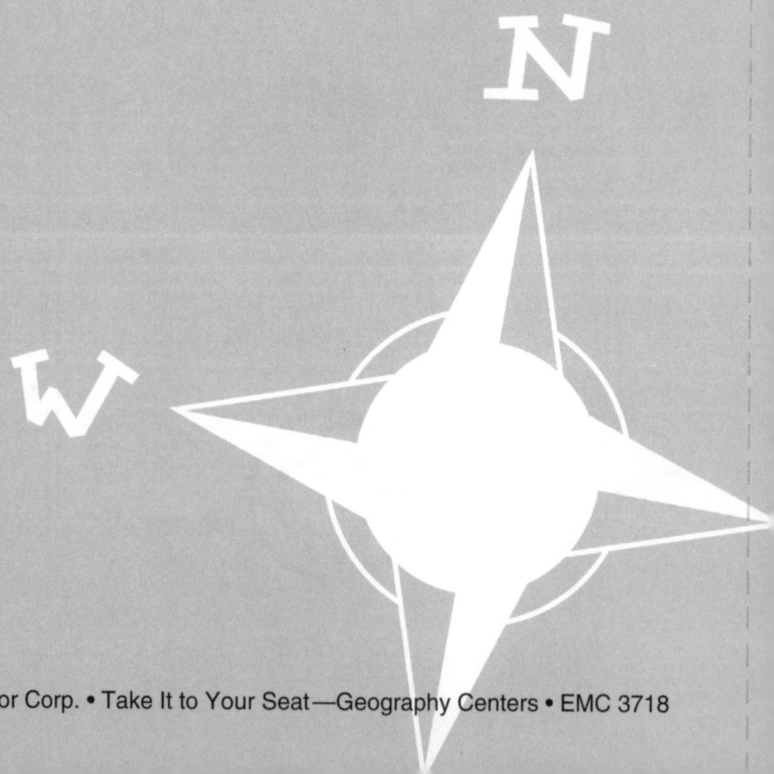
N
W

A Map Grid

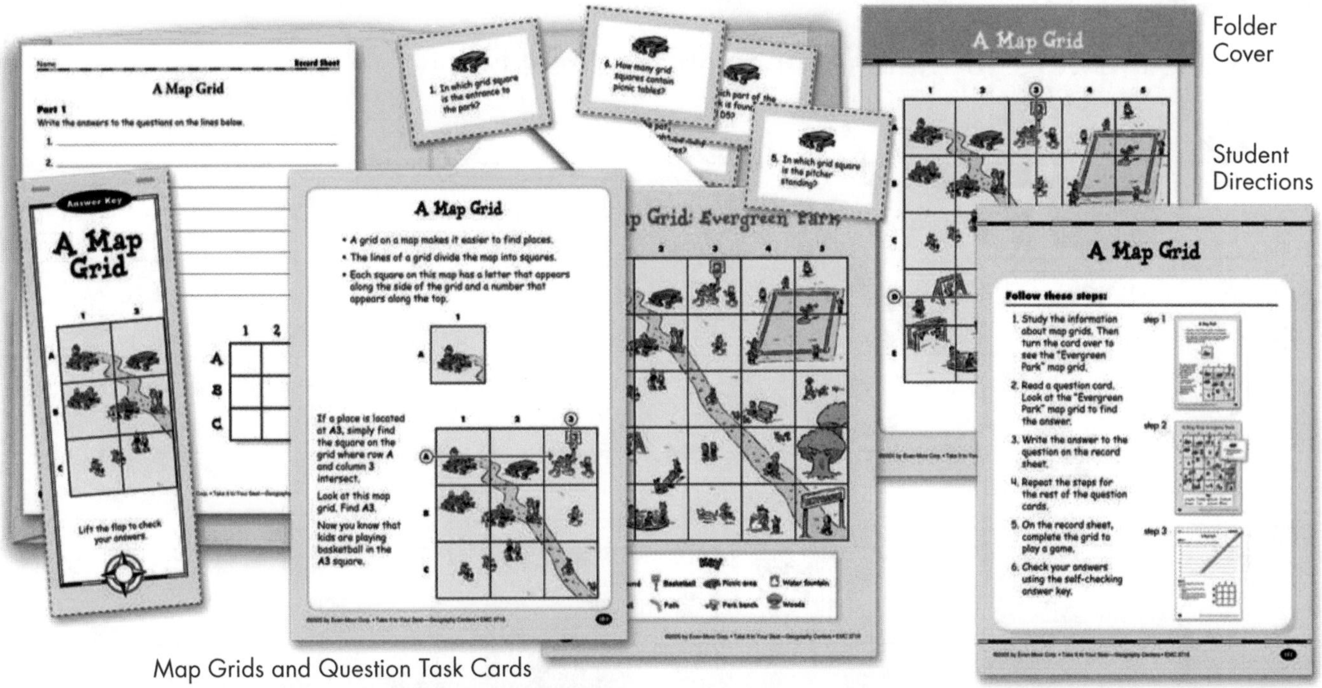
A Map Grid
A Map Grid
A Map Grid
A Map Grid
A Map Grid

Folder Cover

Student Directions

Map Grids and Question Task Cards

Preparing the Center

1. Prepare a folder following the directions on page 3.

   Cover—page 99

   Student Directions—page 101

   Question Task Cards—page 105

   Self-Checking Key—page 107

2. Laminate the map grids on pages 103 and 104. Place the two-sided map grid card in the folder for the student to use with the question cards.
3. Reproduce a supply of the record sheet on page 98. Place copies in the left-hand pocket of the folder.

Using the Center

1. The student studies the map grid information. Then the student turns the card over to see the “Evergreen Park” map grid.
2. Next, the student reads a question card. The student looks at the map grid to find the answer.
3. Then the student records the answer on the record sheet.
4. The student repeats the steps for the remaining cards.
5. On the record sheet, the student also completes a tick-tack-toe game.
6. Finally, the student uses the self-checking key to check answers.

A Map Grid

Part 1

Write the answers to the questions on the lines below.

1. ______
2. ______
3. ______
4. ______
5. ______
6. ______
7. ______
8. ______
9. ______

Part 2

Follow these directions to fill in the map grid:

1. Draw a circle in A1, A2, B2, C1, and C3.
2. Draw an **X** in A3, B1, B3, and C2.
3. Draw a line through the squares that make tick tack toe.

	1	2	3
A			
B			
C			

A Map Grid

1
2
3
4
5
A
B
C
D
E
ENTRANCE

W
S

N
E
S

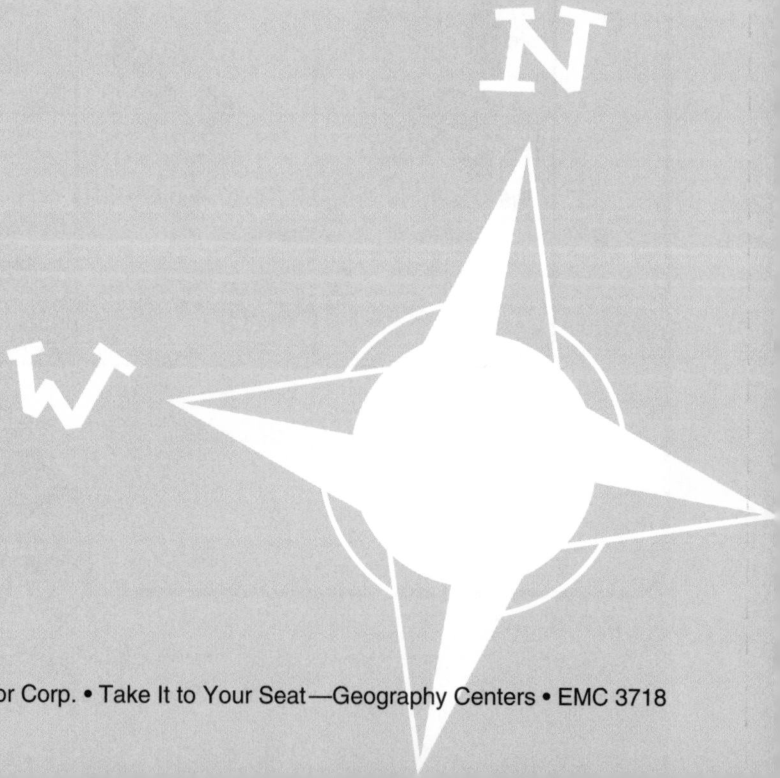
N
W

A Map Grid

Follow these steps:

1. Study the information about map grids. Then turn the card over to see the "Evergreen Park" map grid.
2. Read a question card. Look at the "Evergreen Park" map grid to find the answer.
3. Write the answer to the question on the record sheet.
4. Repeat the steps for the rest of the question cards.
5. On the record sheet, complete the grid to play a game.
6. Check your answers using the self-checking answer key.

step 1

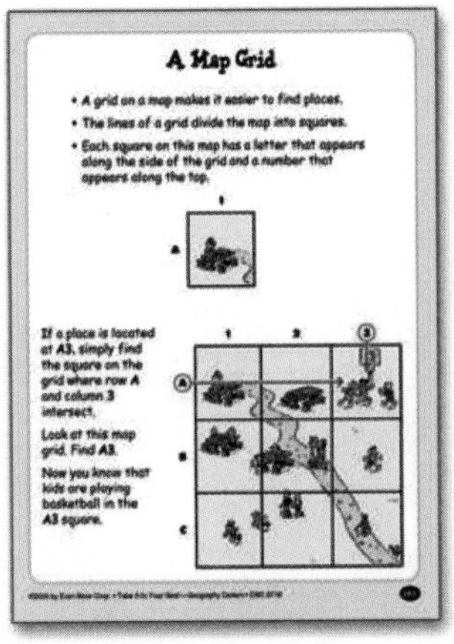
A Map Grid

step 2

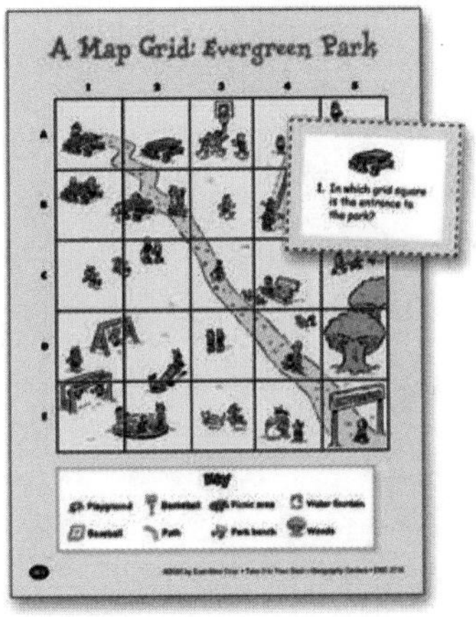
A Map Grid: Evergreen Park

step 3

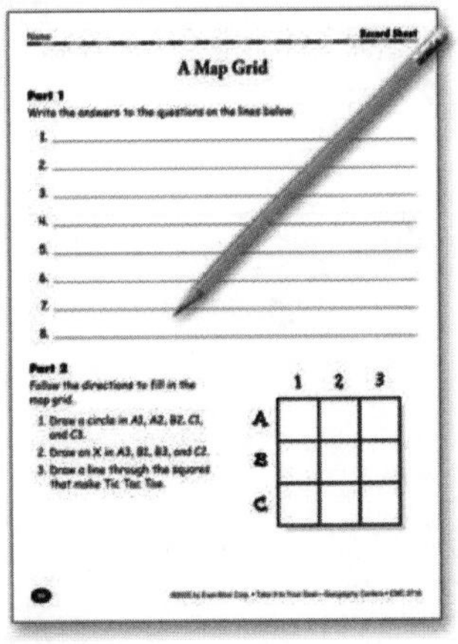
A Map Grid

W
S

N
E
S

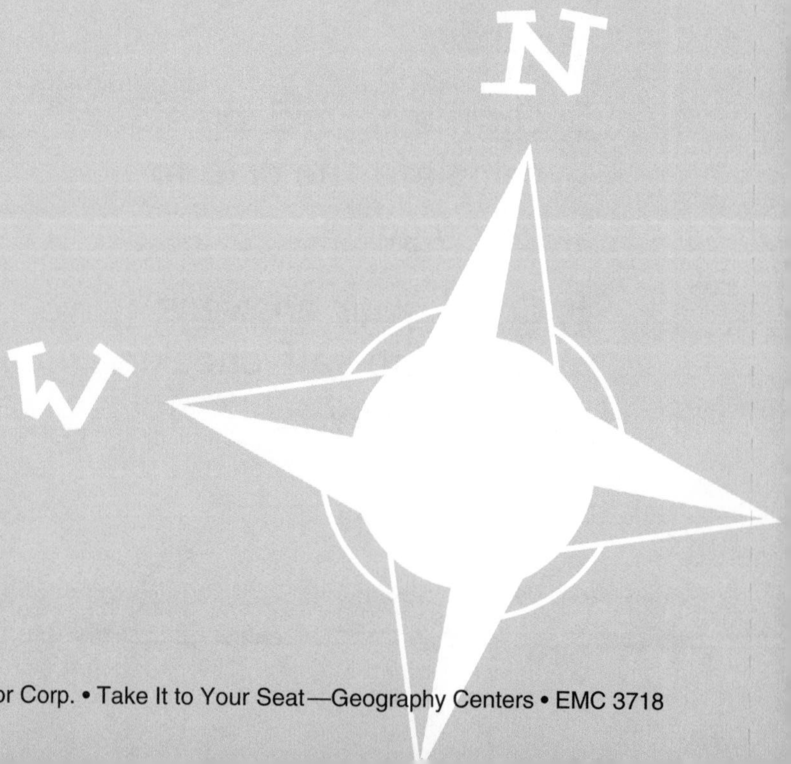
N
W

A Map Grid

- A grid on a map makes it easier to find places.
- The lines of a grid divide the map into squares.
- Each square on this map has a letter that appears along the side of the grid and a number that appears along the top.

1
A

If a place is located at **A3**, simply find the square on the grid where row ***A*** and column **3** intersect.

Look at this map grid. Find **A3**.

Now you know that kids are playing basketball in the **A3** square.

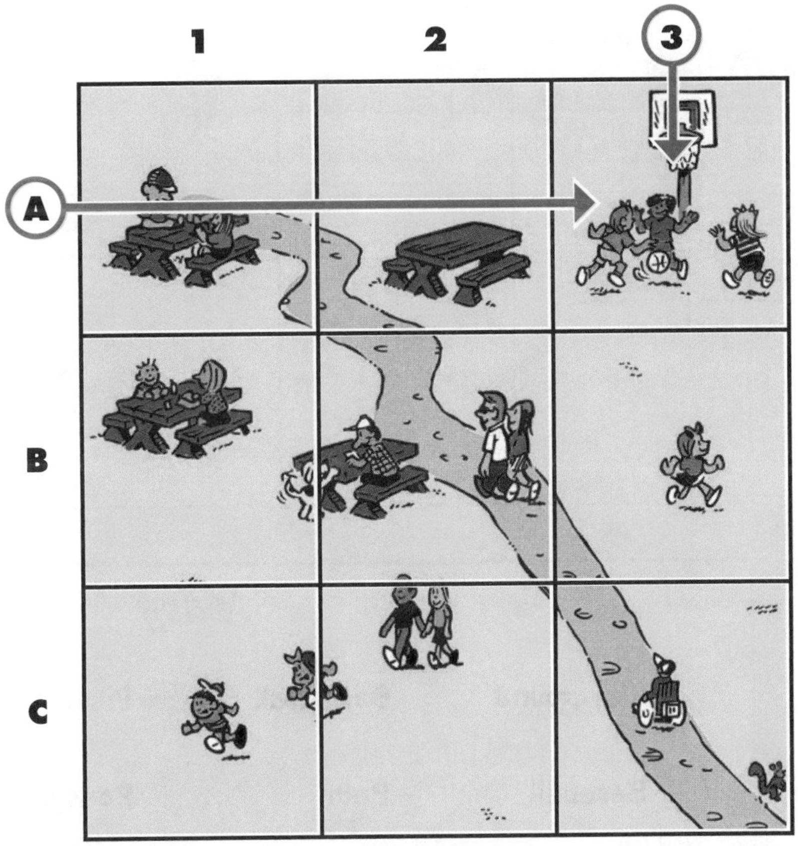
1
2
3
A
B
C

A Map Grid: Evergreen Park

1
2
3
4
5
A
B
C
D
E
ENTRANCE

Key
Playground
Basketball
Picnic area
Water fountain
Baseball
Path
Park bench
Woods

1. In which grid square is the entrance to the park?

2. What is happening in E3?

3. Which part of the park is found at C5 and D5?

4. The baseball diamond is in which grid squares?

5. In which grid square is the pitcher standing?

6. How many grid squares contain picnic tables?

7. The water fountain is in which grid square?

8. The path crosses through how many grid squares?

9. Which area of the park is at D1, D2, E1, and E2?

A Map Grid

A Map Grid

A Map Grid

A Map Grid

A Map Grid

A Map Grid

A Map Grid

A Map Grid

A Map Grid

Answer Key

A Map Grid

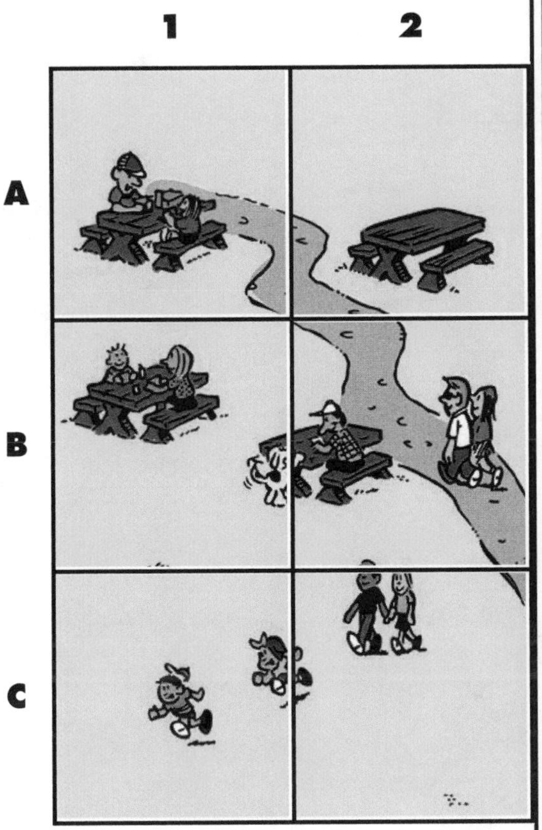
1
2
A
B
C

Lift the flap to check your answers.

A Map Grid

Part 1

1. E5
2. A girl is running with her dog.
3. the woods
4. A4, A5, B4, and B5
5. B5
6. 4
7. E4
8. 10
9. playground

Part 2

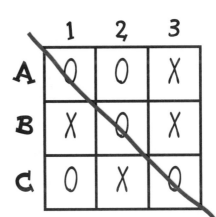

	1	2	3
A	O	O	X
B	X	O	X
C	O	X	O

A Map Grid

A Map Grid

©2005 by Evan-Moor Corp. • EMC 3718

Parts of a Map

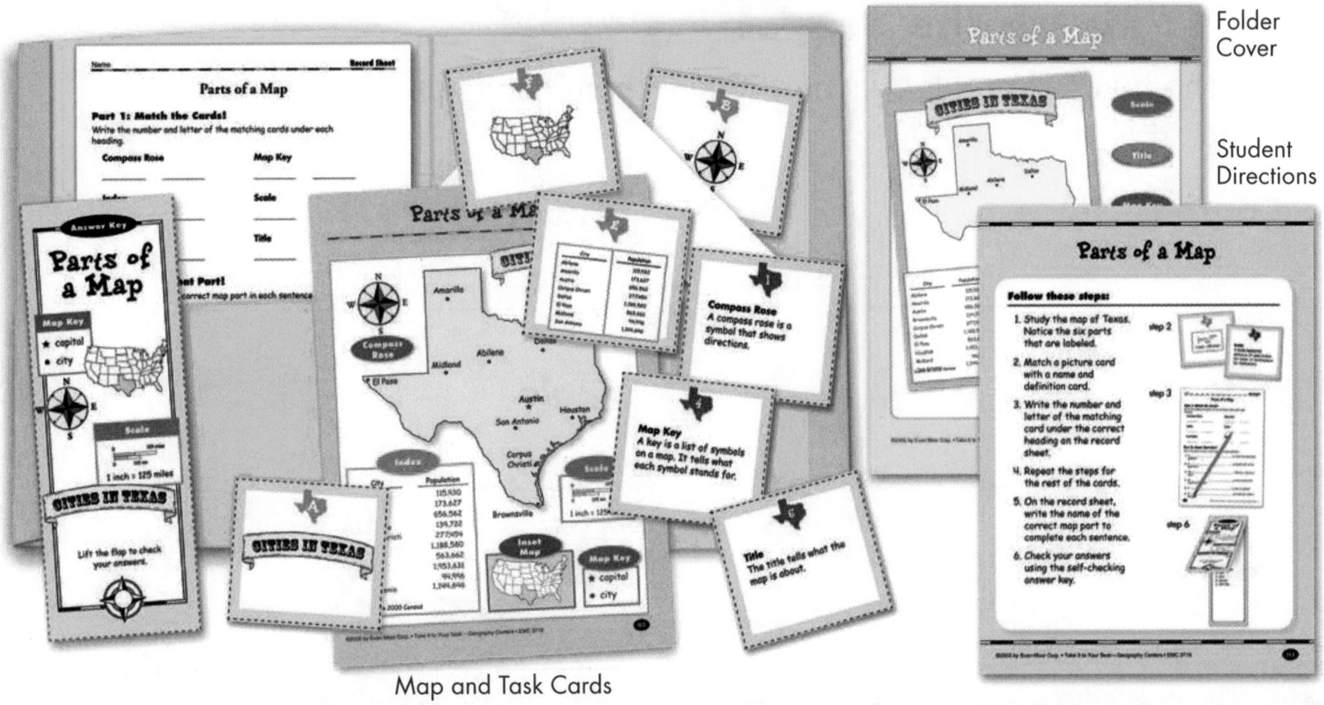

Folder Cover
Student Directions
Map and Task Cards

Preparing the Center

1. Prepare a folder following the directions on page 3.

    Cover—page 111

    Student Directions—page 113

    Task Cards—pages 117 and 119
    - Name and Definition Cards
    - Picture Cards

    Self-Checking Key—page 121

2. Laminate the map of Texas on page 115. Place the map in the folder for the student to use as a reference.
3. Reproduce a supply of the record sheet on page 110. Place copies in the left-hand pocket of the folder.

Using the Center

1. The student reads and locates the six parts labeled on the Texas map.
2. Next, the student matches the picture of the map part with its name and definition. The student uses the Texas map as a reference.
3. The student then records the matching number and letter on the record sheet.
4. The student repeats the steps for the remaining cards.
5. The student completes the record sheet by naming the parts of a map.
6. Finally, the student uses the self-checking key to check answers.

Parts of a Map

Part 1: Match the Cards!

Write the number and letter of the matching cards under each heading.

Compass Rose

__________ __________

Map Key

__________ __________

Index

__________ __________

Scale

__________ __________

Inset Map

__________ __________

Title

__________ __________

Part 2: Name That Part!

Write the name of the correct map part in each sentence.

1. A ____________________ is a ruler that measures distance.
2. A ____________________ is a symbol that shows directions.
3. The ____________________ tells what the map is about.
4. An ____________________ is a list of facts with names and numbers.
5. A ____________________ is a list of symbols.
6. An ____________________ is a small map inside a large one.

Parts of a Map

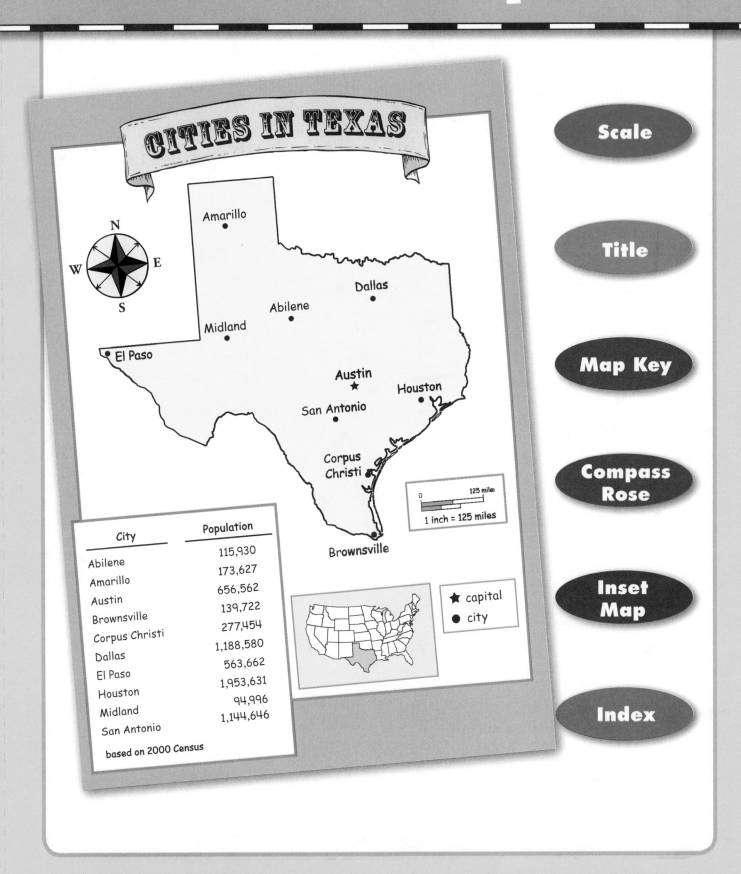

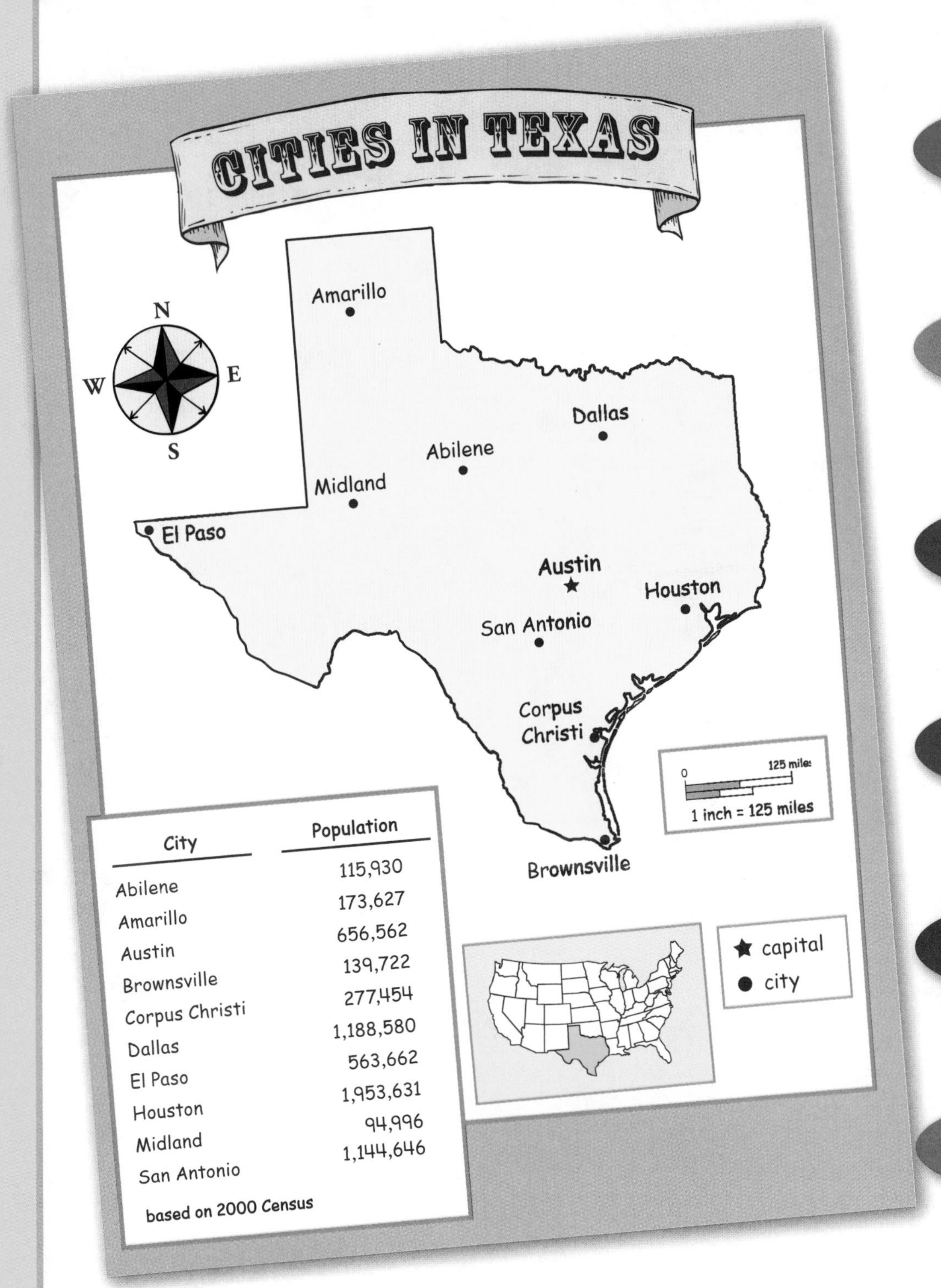
CITIES IN TEXAS
N
S
E
W
Amarillo
Dallas
Abilene
Midland
El Paso
Austin
Houston
San Antonio
Corpus Christi
Brownsville
0
1 inch = 125 miles
capital
city
City | Population
Abilene 115,930
Amarillo 173,627
Austin 656,562
Brownsville 139,722
Corpus Christi 277,454
Dallas 1,188,580
El Paso 563,662
Houston 1,953,631
Midland 94,996
San Antonio 1,144,646
based on 2000 Census

Scale

Title

Map Key

Compass Rose

Inset Map

Index

W
S
N
E
S
N
W

Parts of a Map

Follow these steps:

1. Study the map of Texas. Notice the six parts that are labeled.
2. Match a picture card with a name and definition card.
3. Write the number and letter of the matching card under the correct heading on the record sheet.
4. Repeat the steps for the rest of the cards.
5. On the record sheet, write the name of the correct map part to complete each sentence.
6. Check your answers using the self-checking answer key.

step 2

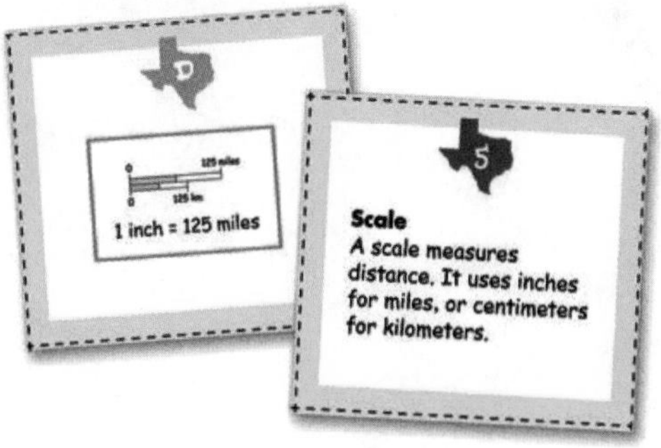

1 inch = 125 miles
5
Scale
A scale measures distance. It uses inches for miles, or centimeters for kilometers.

step 3

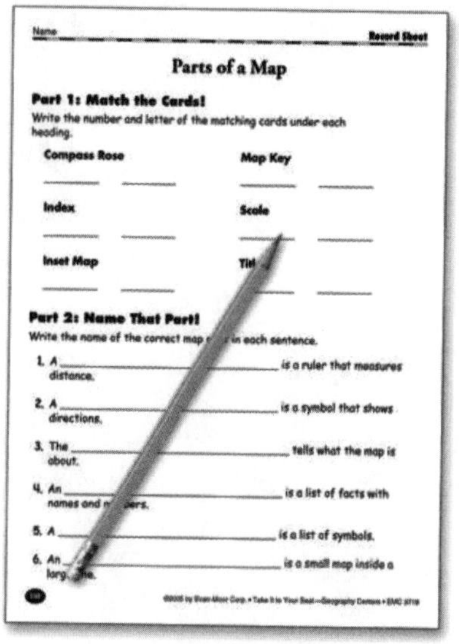

Parts of a Map
Part 1: Match the Cards!
Compass Rose
Map Key
Index
Scale
Inset Map
Part 2: Name That Part!

step 6

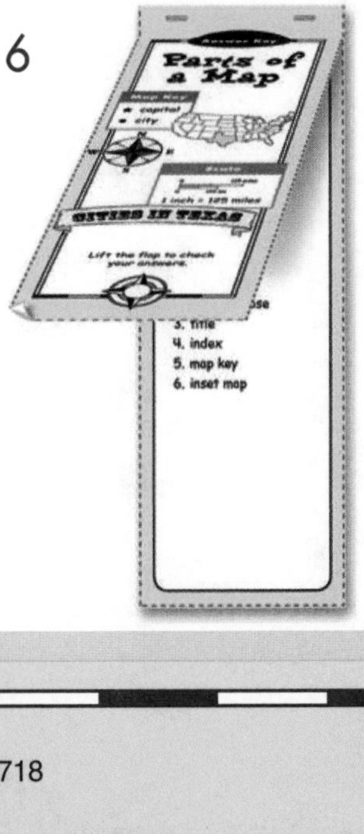

Parts of a Map
4. index
5. map key
6. inset map

W
S

N
E
S

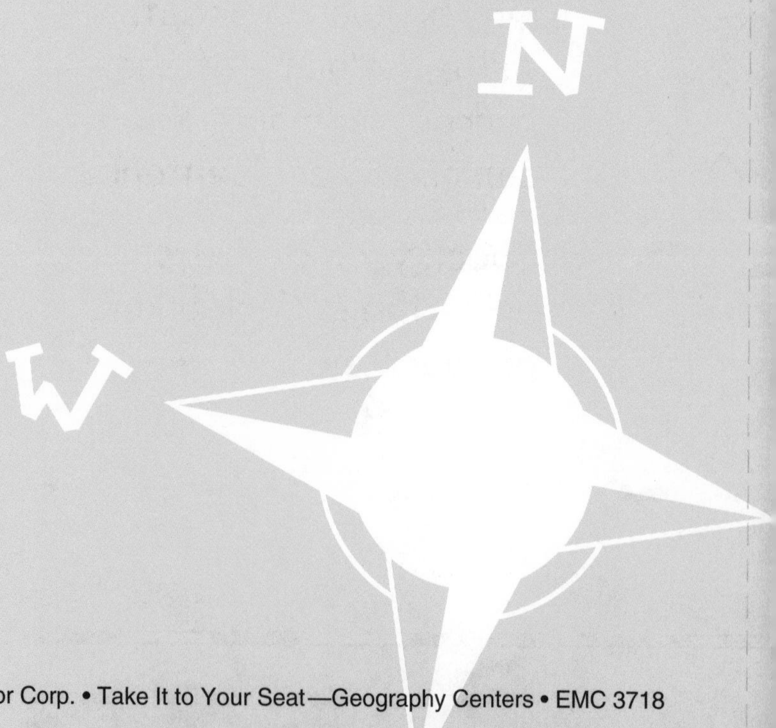
N
W

Parts of a Map

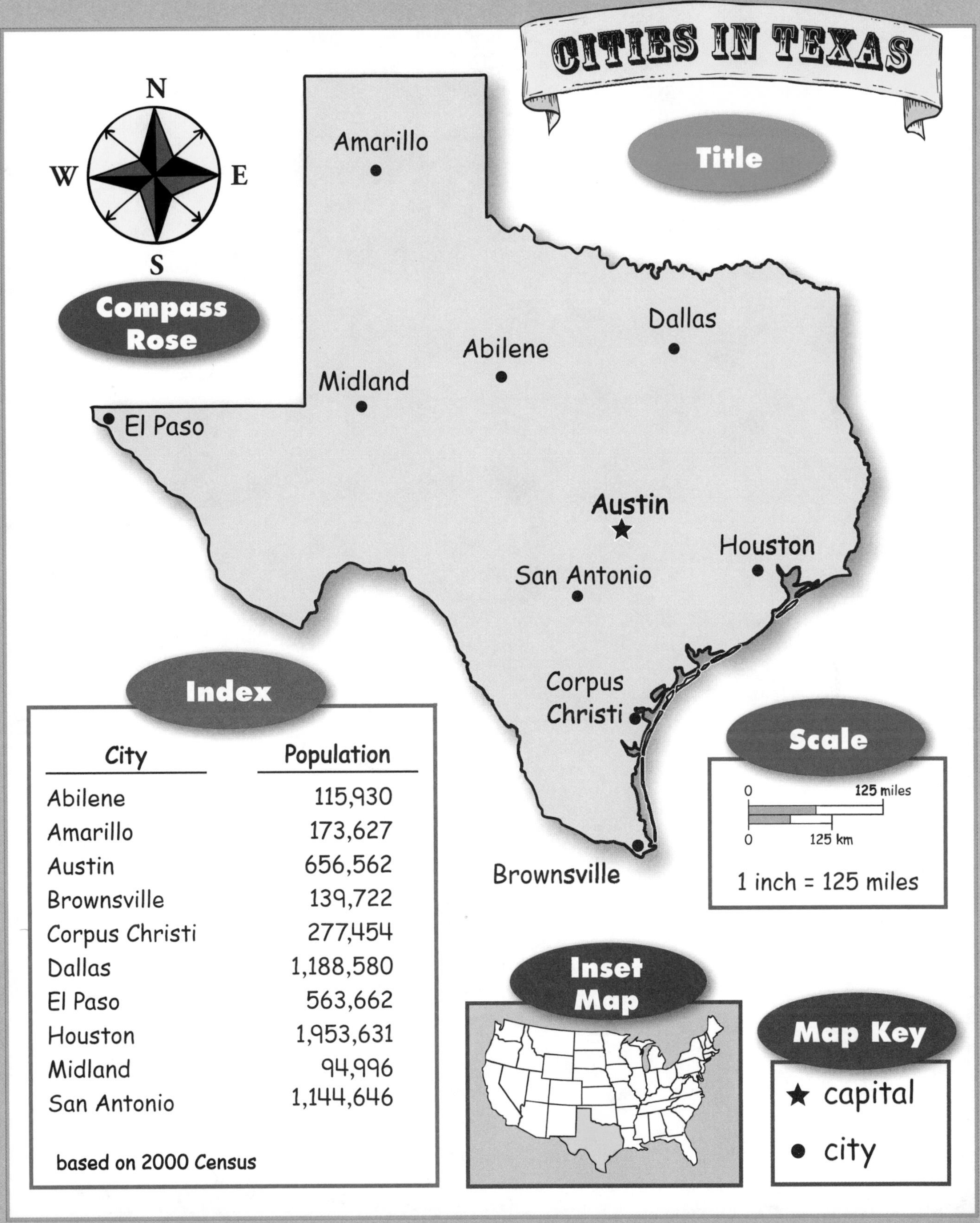
CITIES IN TEXAS
Title
N
W
E
S
Compass Rose
Amarillo
Dallas
Abilene
Midland
El Paso
Austin
Houston
San Antonio
Corpus Christi
Brownsville
Index
Scale
0
125 miles
0
125 km
1 inch = 125 miles
Inset Map
Map Key
capital
city

City	Population
Abilene	115,930
Amarillo	173,627
Austin	656,562
Brownsville	139,722
Corpus Christi	277,454
Dallas	1,188,580
El Paso	563,662
Houston	1,953,631
Midland	94,996
San Antonio	1,144,646

based on 2000 Census

W
S

N
E
S

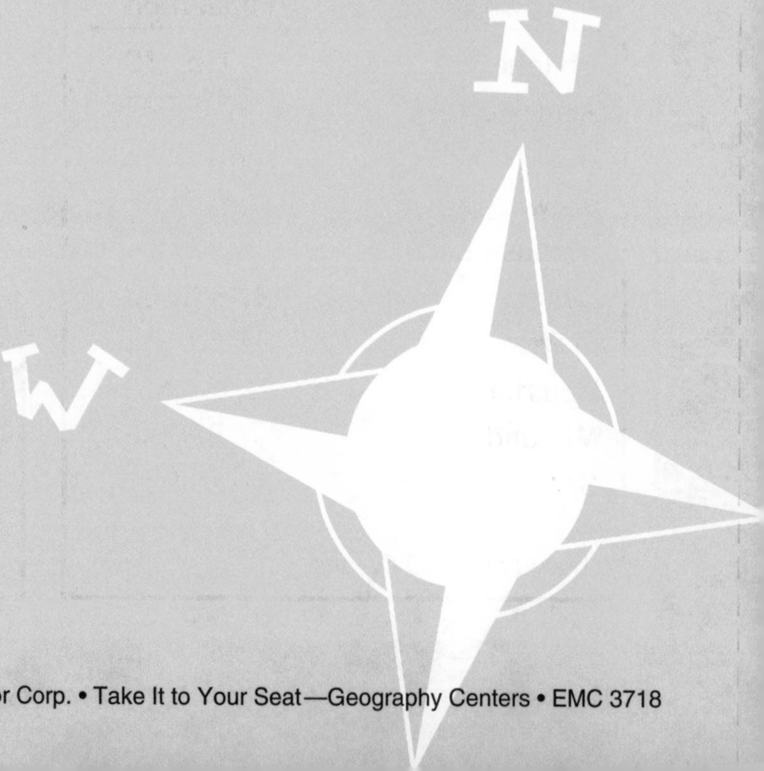
N
W

1

Compass Rose
A compass rose is a symbol that shows directions.

2

Index
An index is a list of facts. An index includes names and numbers.

3

Inset Map
An inset map is a small map inside a large one.

4

Map Key
A key is a list of symbols on a map. It tells what each symbol stands for.

5

Scale
A scale measures distance. It uses inches for miles, or centimeters for kilometers.

6

Title
The title tells what the map is about.

Parts of a Map

Parts of a Map

Parts of a Map

Parts of a Map

Parts of a Map

Parts of a Map

A

CITIES IN TEXAS

D

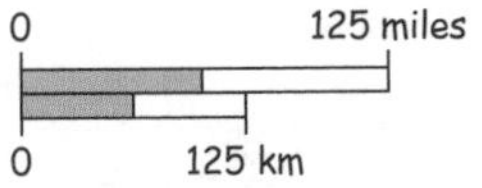

0
125 miles
0
125 km

1 inch = 125 miles

B

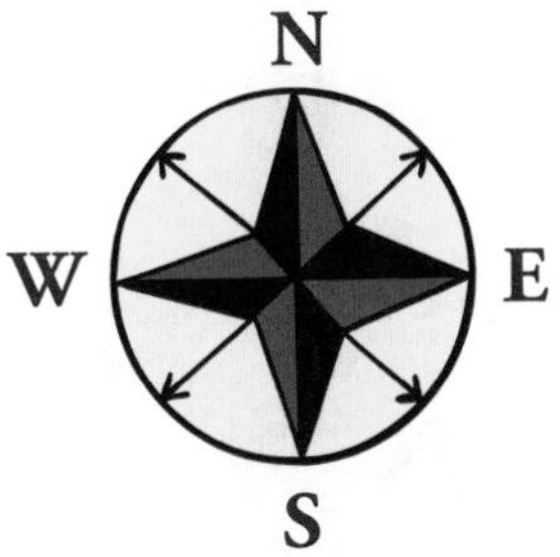

N
W
E
S

E

City	Population
Abilene	115,930
Amarillo	173,627
Austin	656,562
Brownsville	139,722
Corpus Christi	277,454
Dallas	1,188,580
El Paso	563,662
Houston	1,953,631
Midland	94,996
San Antonio	1,144,646

C

★ capital

● city

F

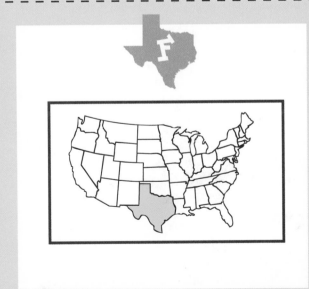

Parts of a Map

Parts of a Map
©2005 by Evan-Moor Corp. • EMC 3718

Parts of a Map
©2005 by Evan-Moor Corp. • EMC 3718

Parts of a Map
©2005 by Evan-Moor Corp. • EMC 3718

Parts of a Map
©2005 by Evan-Moor Corp. • EMC 3718

Parts of a Map
©2005 by Evan-Moor Corp. • EMC 3718

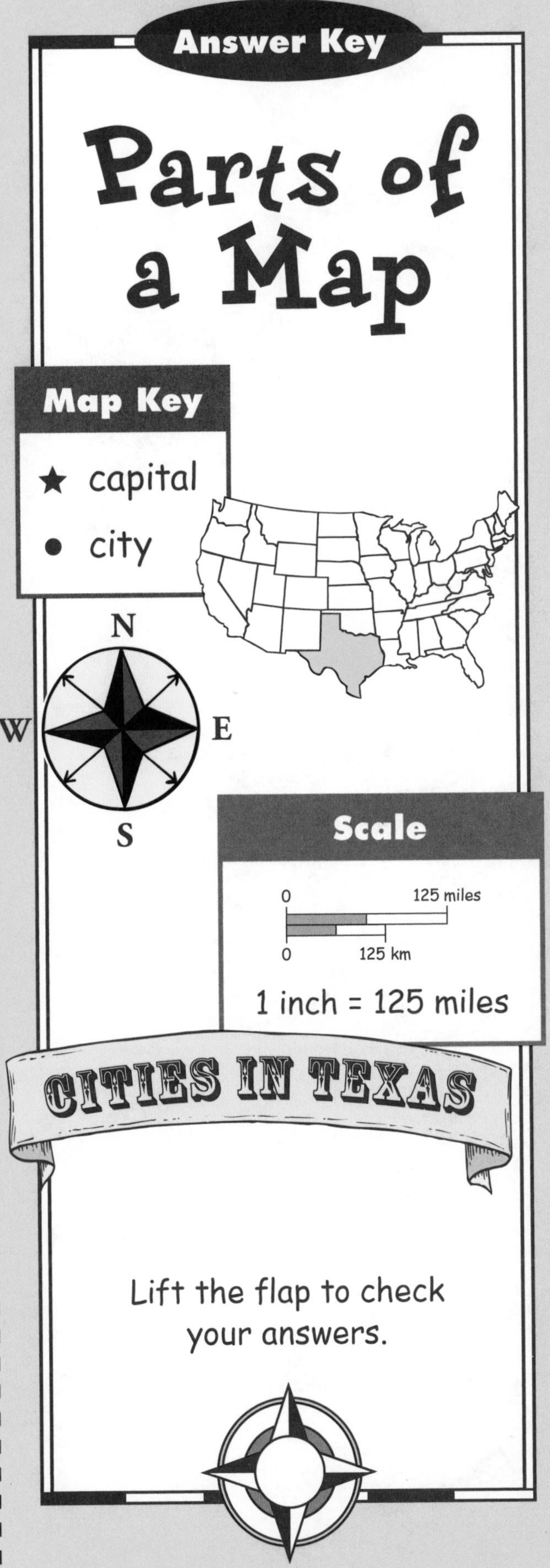
Answer Key
Parts of a Map
Map Key
★ capital
• city
N
W
E
S
Scale
0
125 miles
0
125 km
1 inch = 125 miles
CITIES IN TEXAS
Lift the flap to check your answers.

Parts of a Map

Part 1

Compass Rose: 1, B

Index: 2, E

Inset Map: 3, F

Map Key: 4, C

Scale: 5, D

Title: 6, A

Part 2

1. scale
2. compass rose
3. title
4. index
5. map key
6. inset map

Parts of a Map

Parts of a Map

©2005 by Evan-Moor Corp. • EMC 3718

Types of Maps

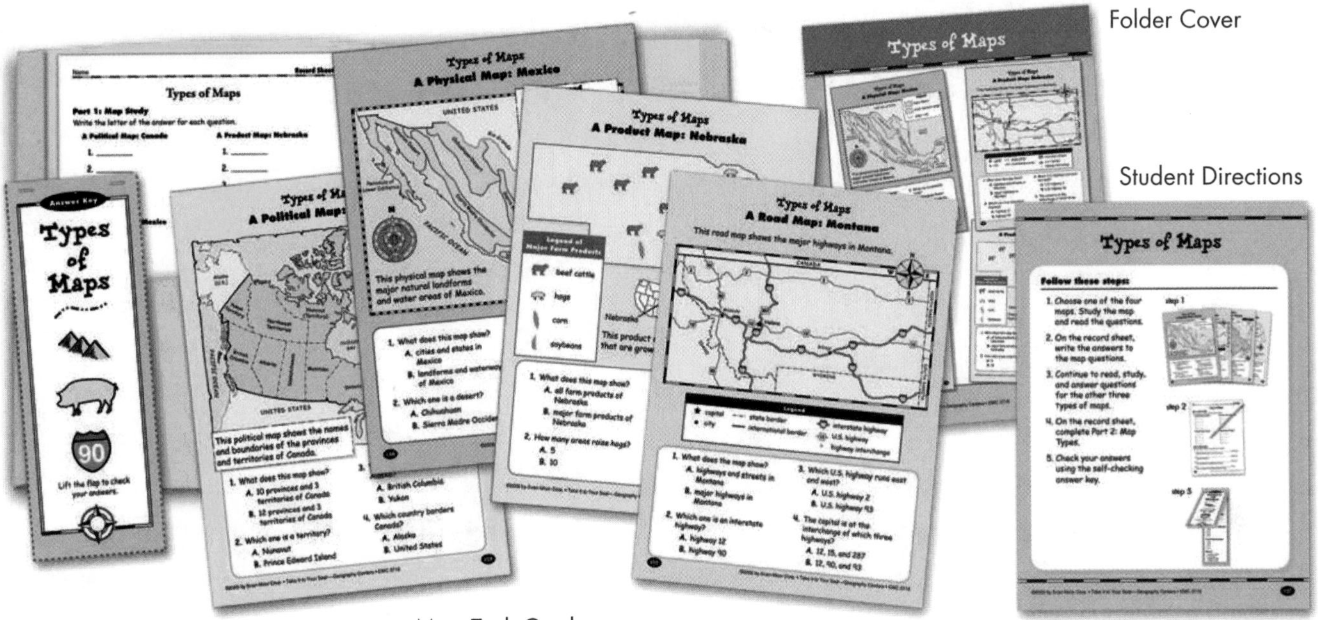
Types of Maps
A Physical Map: Mexico
A Product Map: Nebraska
A Road Map: Montana
Types of Maps
90

Folder Cover

Student Directions

Map Task Cards

Preparing the Center

1. Prepare a folder following the directions on page 3.

   Cover—page 125

   Student Directions—page 127

   Map Task Cards—pages 129–132

   Self-Checking Key—page 133

2. Reproduce a supply of the record sheet on page 124. Place copies in the left-hand pocket of the folder.

Using the Center

1. The student chooses one of the four maps to study. The student reads the questions on the map card.
2. Next, the student answers the questions about the map on the record sheet.
3. The student repeats the steps using the remaining maps.
4. On the record sheet, the student also matches each type of map with its definition.
5. Finally, the student uses the self-checking key to check answers.

Types of Maps

Part 1: Map Study

Write the letter of the answer for each question.

A Political Map: Canada

1. ________
2. ________
3. ________
4. ________

A Product Map: Nebraska

1. ________
2. ________
3. ________
4. ________

A Physical Map: Mexico

1. ________
2. ________
3. ________
4. ________

A Road Map: Montana

1. ________
2. ________
3. ________
4. ________

Part 2: Map Types

Write the type of map that completes the sentence.

1. A ______________________ shows major products that are grown or raised in an area.
2. A ______________________ shows the highways of an area.
3. A ______________________ shows the natural landforms and waterways of an area.
4. A ______________________ shows human-made features and boundaries of an area.

Types of Maps

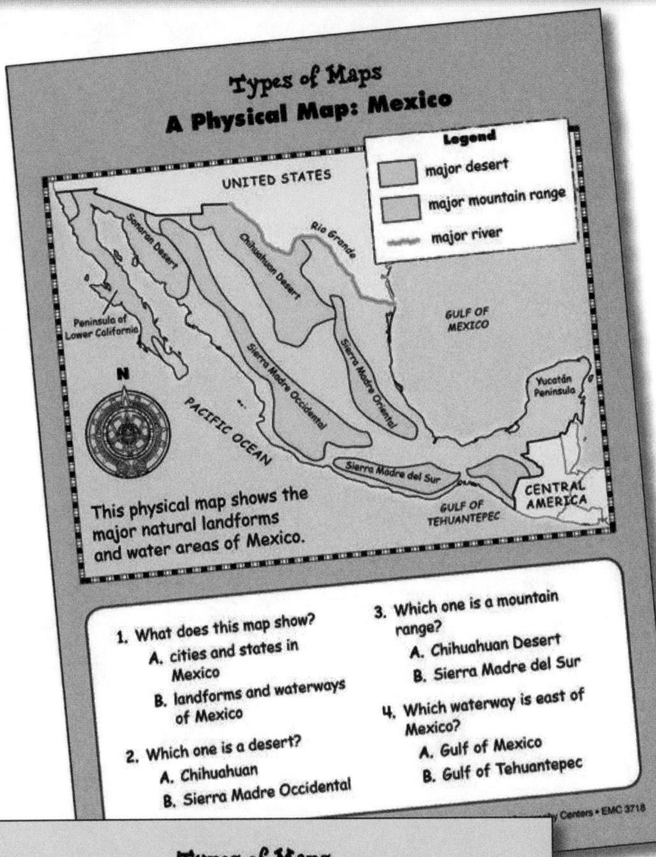

Types of Maps

A Physical Map: Mexico

Legend
major desert
major mountain range
major river
UNITED STATES
Rio Grande
Sonoran Desert
Chihuahuan Desert
Peninsula of Lower California
GULF OF MEXICO
Sierra Madre Occidental
Sierra Madre Oriental
Yucatán Peninsula
N
PACIFIC OCEAN
Sierra Madre del Sur
CENTRAL AMERICA
GULF OF TEHUANTEPEC

This physical map shows the major natural landforms and water areas of Mexico.

1. What does this map show?
   - A. cities and states in Mexico
   - B. landforms and waterways of Mexico
2. Which one is a desert?
   - A. Chihuahuan
   - B. Sierra Madre Occidental
3. Which one is a mountain range?
   - A. Chihuahuan Desert
   - B. Sierra Madre del Sur
4. Which waterway is east of Mexico?
   - A. Gulf of Mexico
   - B. Gulf of Tehuantepec

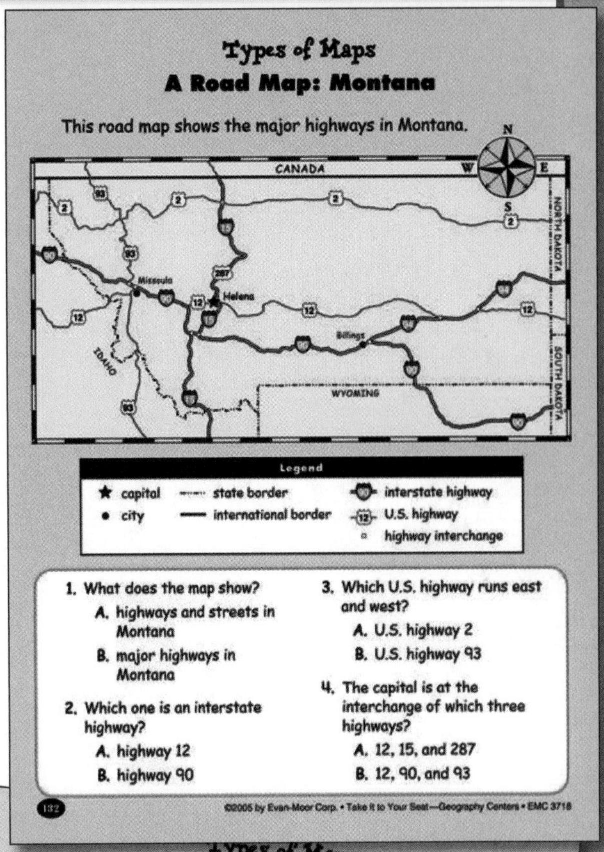

Types of Maps

A Road Map: Montana

This road map shows the major highways in Montana.

CANADA
N
W
E
S
NORTH DAKOTA
SOUTH DAKOTA
Missoula
Helena
Billings
IDAHO
WYOMING
Legend
capital
city
state border
international border
interstate highway
U.S. highway
highway interchange

1. What does the map show?
   - A. highways and streets in Montana
   - B. major highways in Montana
2. Which one is an interstate highway?
   - A. highway 12
   - B. highway 90
3. Which U.S. highway runs east and west?
   - A. U.S. highway 2
   - B. U.S. highway 93
4. The capital is at the interchange of which three highways?
   - A. 12, 15, and 287
   - B. 12, 90, and 93

132 ©2005 by Evan-Moor Corp. • Take It to Your Seat—Geography Centers • EMC 3718

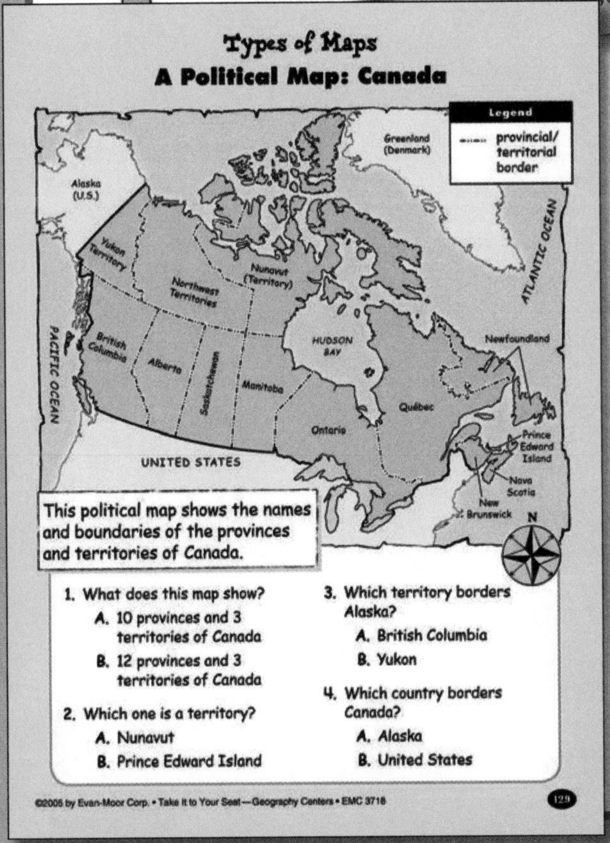

Types of Maps

A Political Map: Canada

Legend
provincial/territorial border
Greenland (Denmark)
Alaska (U.S.)
Yukon Territory
Northwest Territories
Nunavut (Territory)
ATLANTIC OCEAN
PACIFIC OCEAN
British Columbia
Alberta
Saskatchewan
Manitoba
HUDSON BAY
Newfoundland
Québec
Ontario
Prince Edward Island
Nova Scotia
New Brunswick
UNITED STATES
N

This political map shows the names and boundaries of the provinces and territories of Canada.

1. What does this map show?
   - A. 10 provinces and 3 territories of Canada
   - B. 12 provinces and 3 territories of Canada
2. Which one is a territory?
   - A. Nunavut
   - B. Prince Edward Island
3. Which territory borders Alaska?
   - A. British Columbia
   - B. Yukon
4. Which country borders Canada?
   - A. Alaska
   - B. United States

©2005 by Evan-Moor Corp. • Take It to Your Seat—Geography Centers • EMC 3718 129

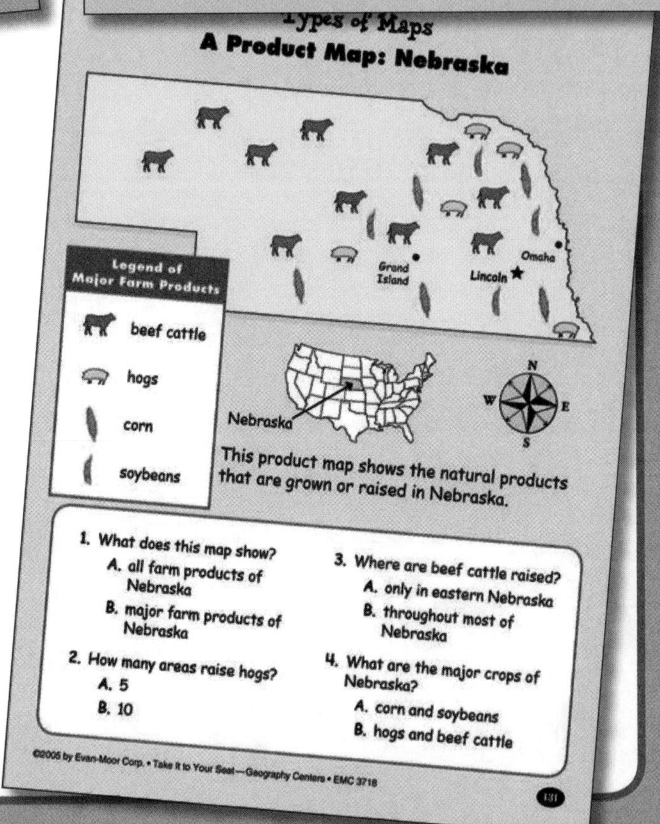

Types of Maps

A Product Map: Nebraska

Grand Island
Lincoln
Omaha
Legend of Major Farm Products
beef cattle
hogs
corn
soybeans
Nebraska
N
W
E
S

This product map shows the natural products that are grown or raised in Nebraska.

1. What does this map show?
   - A. all farm products of Nebraska
   - B. major farm products of Nebraska
2. How many areas raise hogs?
   - A. 5
   - B. 10
3. Where are beef cattle raised?
   - A. only in eastern Nebraska
   - B. throughout most of Nebraska
4. What are the major crops of Nebraska?
   - A. corn and soybeans
   - B. hogs and beef cattle

©2005 by Evan-Moor Corp. • Take It to Your Seat—Geography Centers • EMC 3718 131

W
S

N
E
S

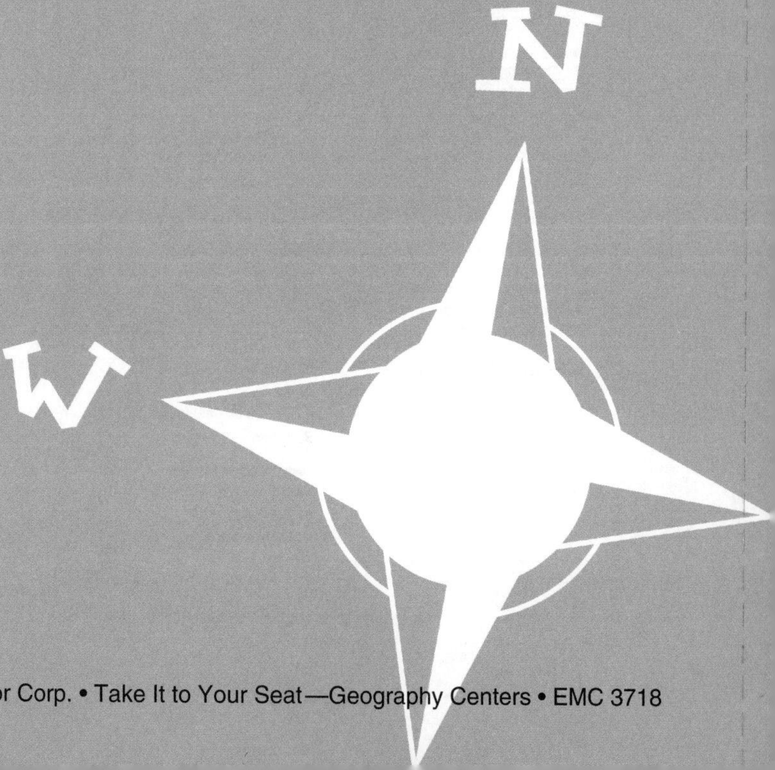
N
W

Types of Maps

Follow these steps:

1. Choose one of the four maps. Study the map and read the questions.
2. On the record sheet, write the answers to the map questions.
3. Continue to read, study, and answer questions for the other three types of maps.
4. On the record sheet, complete Part 2: Map Types.
5. Check your answers using the self-checking answer key.

step 1

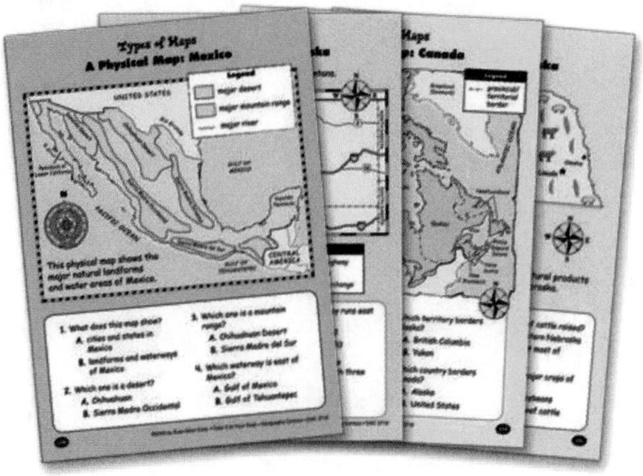
Types of Maps
A Physical Map: Mexico

step 2

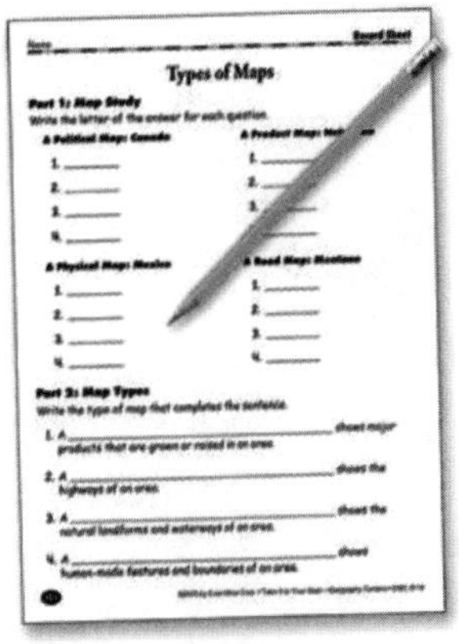
Types of Maps

step 5

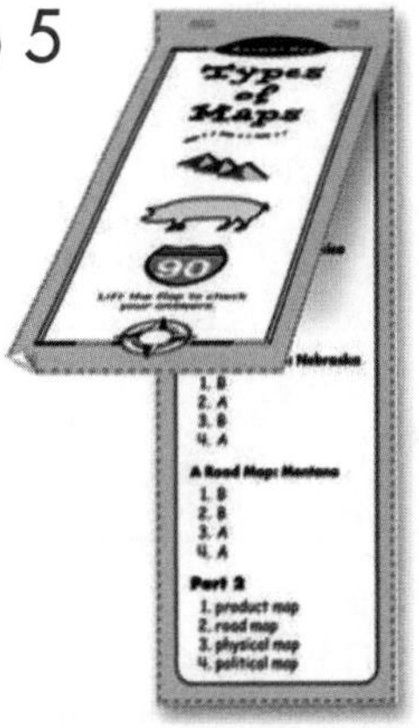
Types of Maps
Part 2
1. product map
2. road map
3. physical map
4. political map

W
S

N
E
S

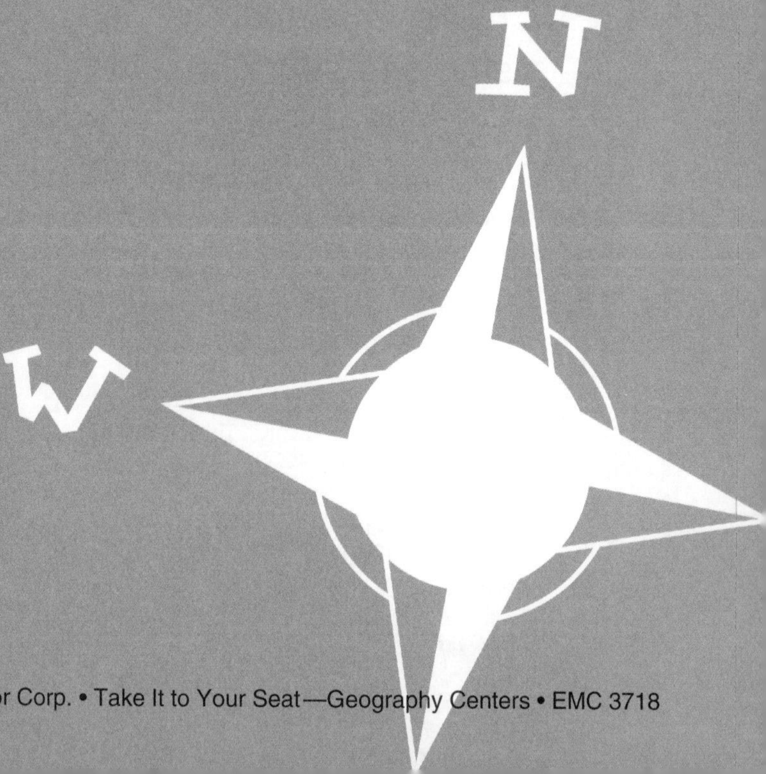
N
W

Types of Maps

A Political Map: Canada

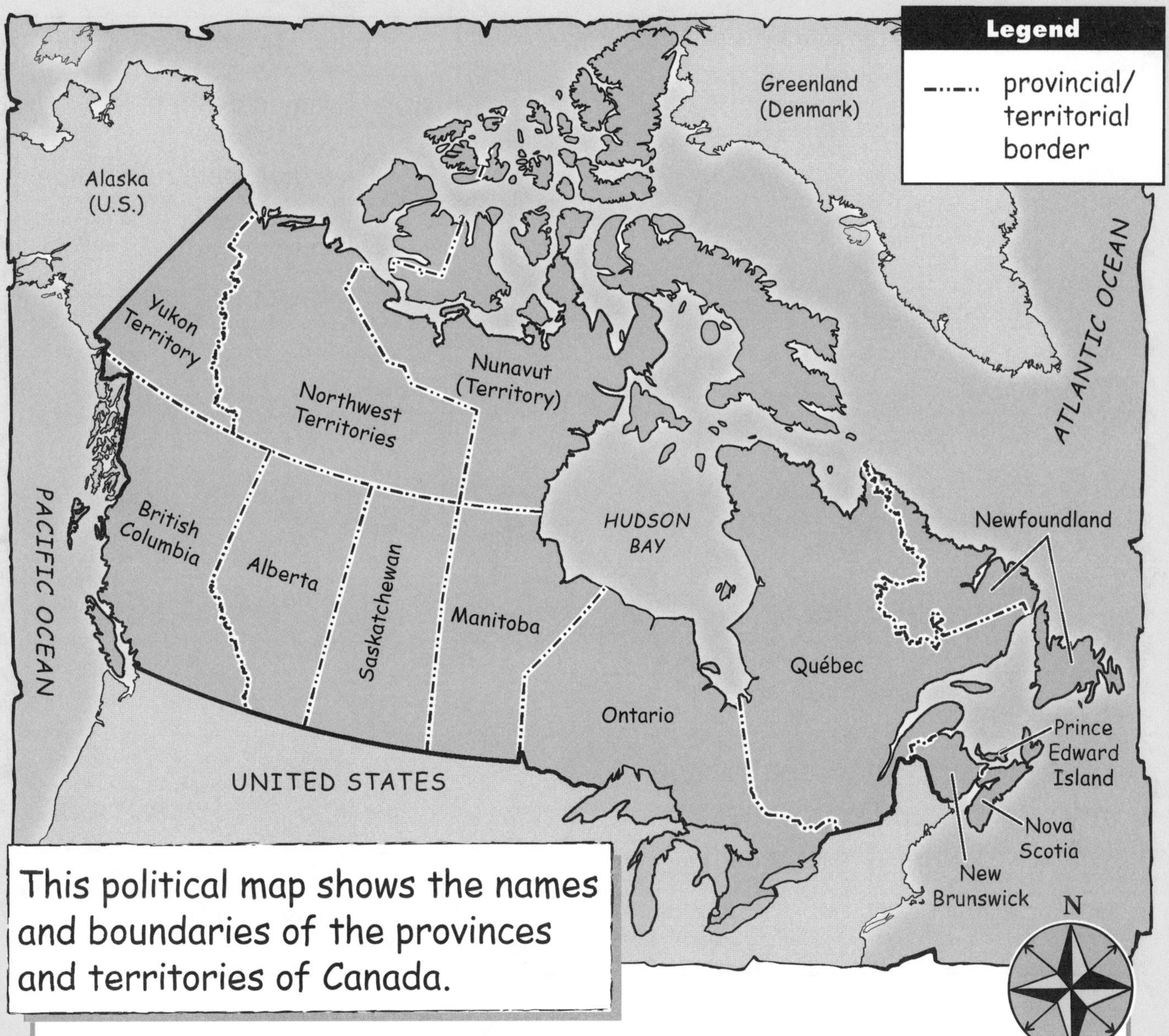
Legend
provincial/ territorial border
Greenland (Denmark)
Alaska (U.S.)
Yukon Territory
Northwest Territories
Nunavut (Territory)
ATLANTIC OCEAN
PACIFIC OCEAN
British Columbia
Alberta
Saskatchewan
Manitoba
HUDSON BAY
Ontario
Québec
Newfoundland
Prince Edward Island
Nova Scotia
New Brunswick
UNITED STATES
N

This political map shows the names and boundaries of the provinces and territories of Canada.

1. What does this map show?
   - A. 10 provinces and 3 territories of Canada
   - B. 12 provinces and 3 territories of Canada
2. Which one is a territory?
   - A. Nunavut
   - B. Prince Edward Island
3. Which territory borders Alaska?
   - A. British Columbia
   - B. Yukon
4. Which country borders Canada?
   - A. Alaska
   - B. United States

Types of Maps

A Physical Map: Mexico

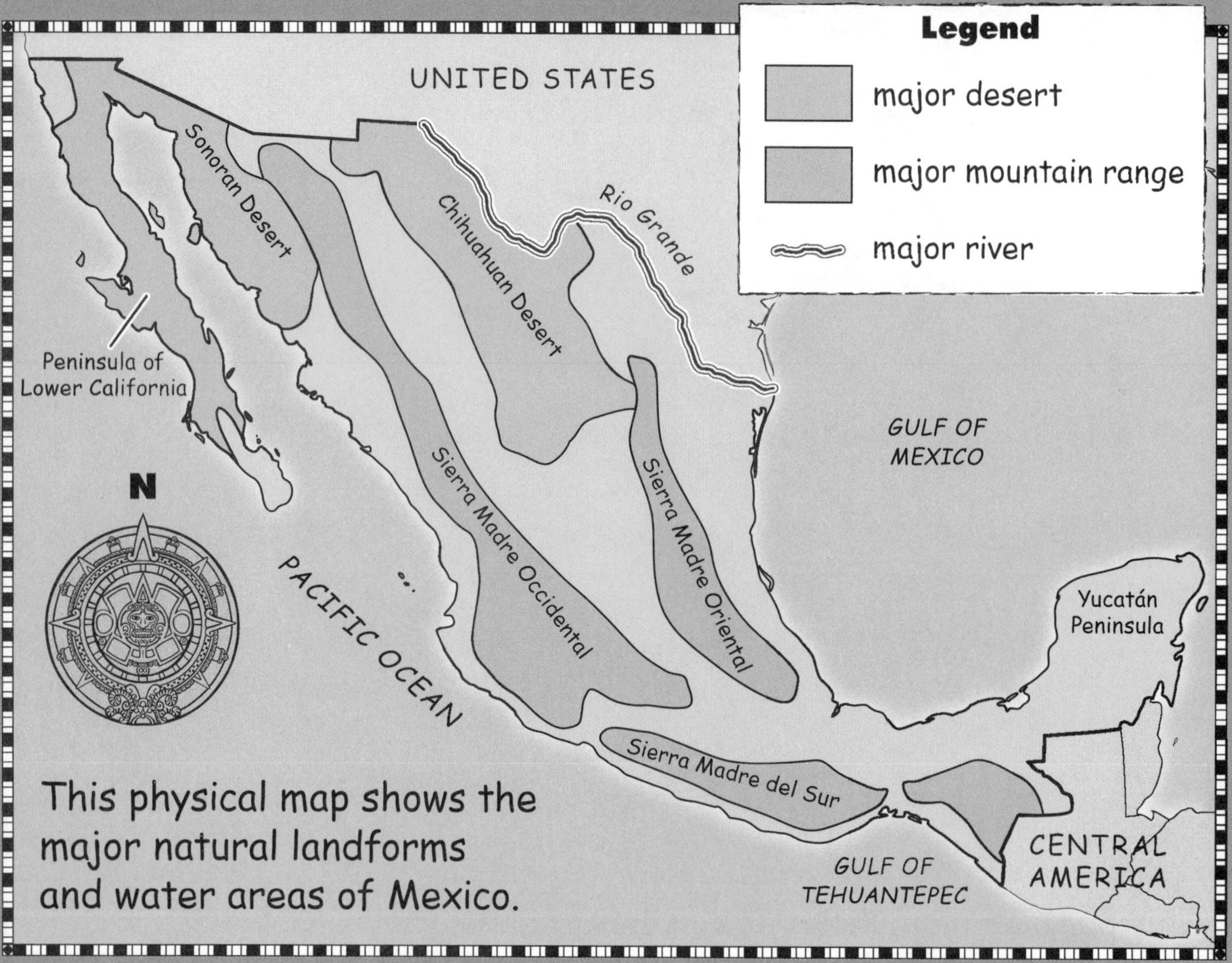
Legend
major desert
major mountain range
major river
UNITED STATES
Sonoran Desert
Chihuahuan Desert
Rio Grande
Peninsula of
Lower California
GULF OF
MEXICO
N
PACIFIC OCEAN
Sierra Madre Occidental
Sierra Madre Oriental
Yucatán
Peninsula
Sierra Madre del Sur
GULF OF
TEHUANTEPEC
CENTRAL
AMERICA

This physical map shows the major natural landforms and water areas of Mexico.

1. What does this map show?
   - A. cities and states in Mexico
   - B. landforms and waterways of Mexico
2. Which one is a desert?
   - A. Chihuahuan
   - B. Sierra Madre Occidental
3. Which one is a mountain range?
   - A. Rio Grande
   - B. Sierra Madre del Sur
4. Which waterway is east of Mexico?
   - A. Gulf of Mexico
   - B. Gulf of Tehuantepec

Types of Maps

A Product Map: Nebraska

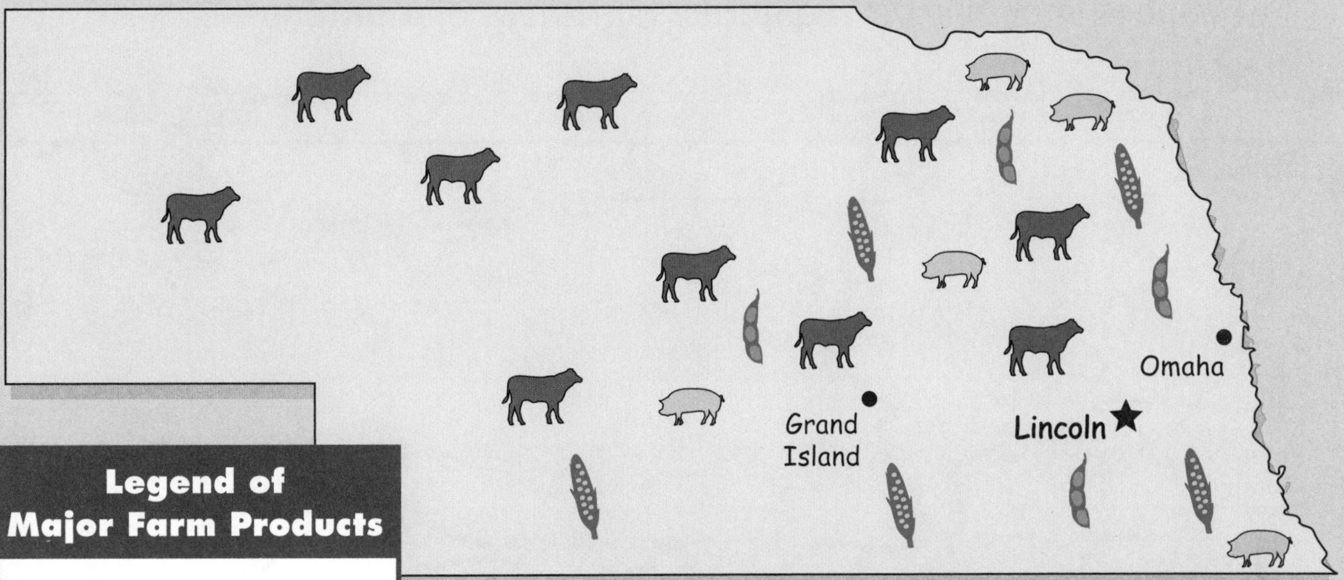
Grand Island
Lincoln
Omaha

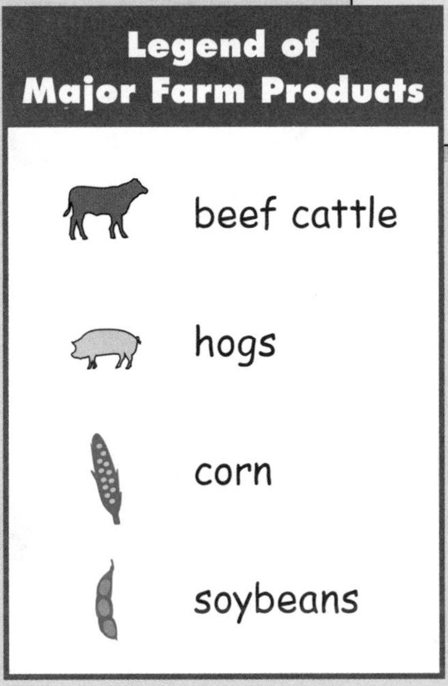
Legend of Major Farm Products
beef cattle
hogs
corn
soybeans

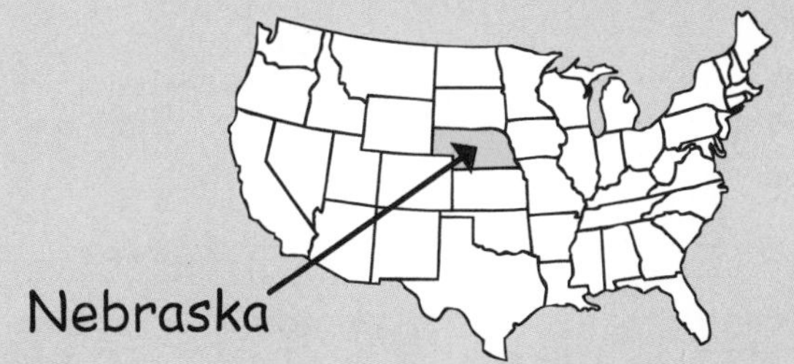
Nebraska

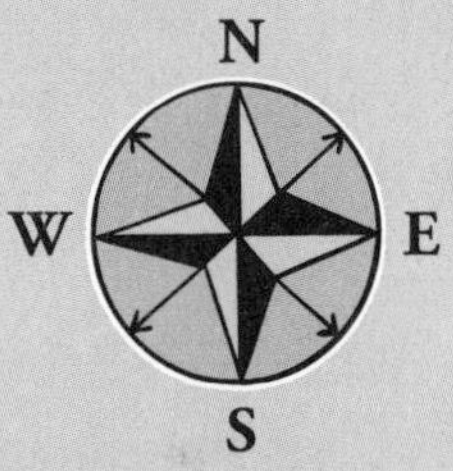
N
W
E
S

This product map shows the natural products that are grown or raised in Nebraska.

1. What does this map show?
   - A. all farm products of Nebraska
   - B. major farm products of Nebraska
2. How many areas raise hogs?
   - A. 5
   - B. 10
3. Where are beef cattle raised?
   - A. only in eastern Nebraska
   - B. throughout most of Nebraska
4. What are the major crops of Nebraska?
   - A. corn and soybeans
   - B. hogs and beef cattle

Types of Maps

A Road Map: Montana

This road map shows the major highways in Montana.

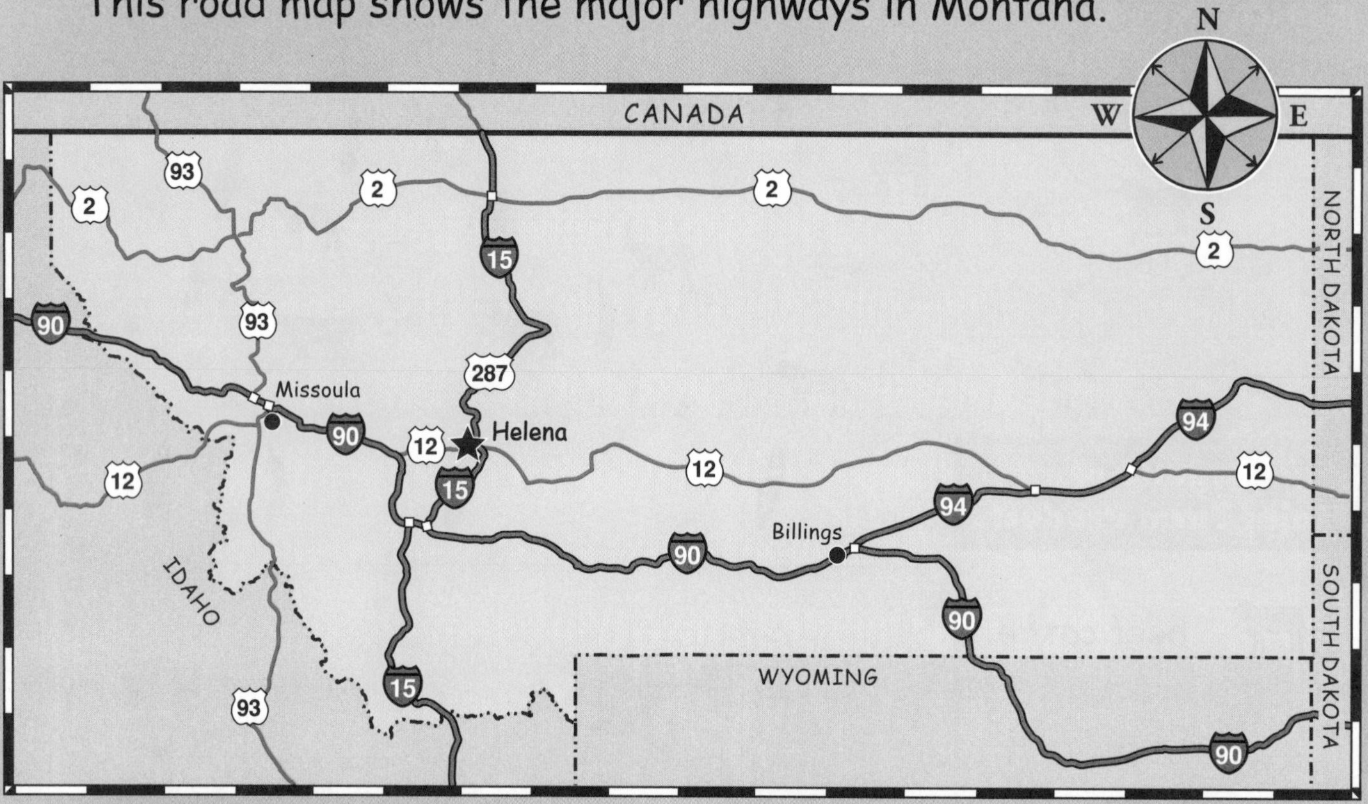
N
S
E
W
CANADA
NORTH DAKOTA
SOUTH DAKOTA
WYOMING
IDAHO
Missoula
Helena
Billings
2
93
90
15
287
12
94

Legend

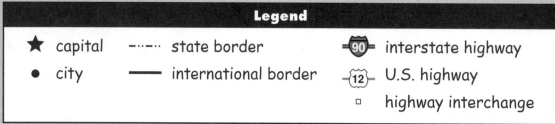

- ★ capital
- ● city
- -··-·· state border
- —— international border
- 90 interstate highway
- 12 U.S. highway
- ▫ highway interchange

1. What does the map show?
   - A. highways and streets in Montana
   - B. major highways in Montana

2. Which one is an interstate highway?
   - A. Highway 12
   - B. Highway 90

3. Which U.S. highway runs east and west?
   - A. U.S. Highway 2
   - B. U.S. Highway 93

4. The capital is at the interchange of which three highways?
   - A. 12, 15, and 287
   - B. 12, 90, and 93

Answer Key

Types of Maps

90

Lift the flap to check your answers.

Types of Maps

Part 1

A Political Map: Canada

1. A
2. A
3. B
4. B

A Physical Map: Mexico

1. B
2. A
3. B
4. A

A Product Map: Nebraska

1. B
2. A
3. B
4. A

A Road Map: Montana

1. B
2. B
3. A
4. A

Part 2

1. product map
2. road map
3. physical map
4. political map

Types of a Maps

Types of a Maps

©2005 by Evan-Moor Corp. • EMC 3718

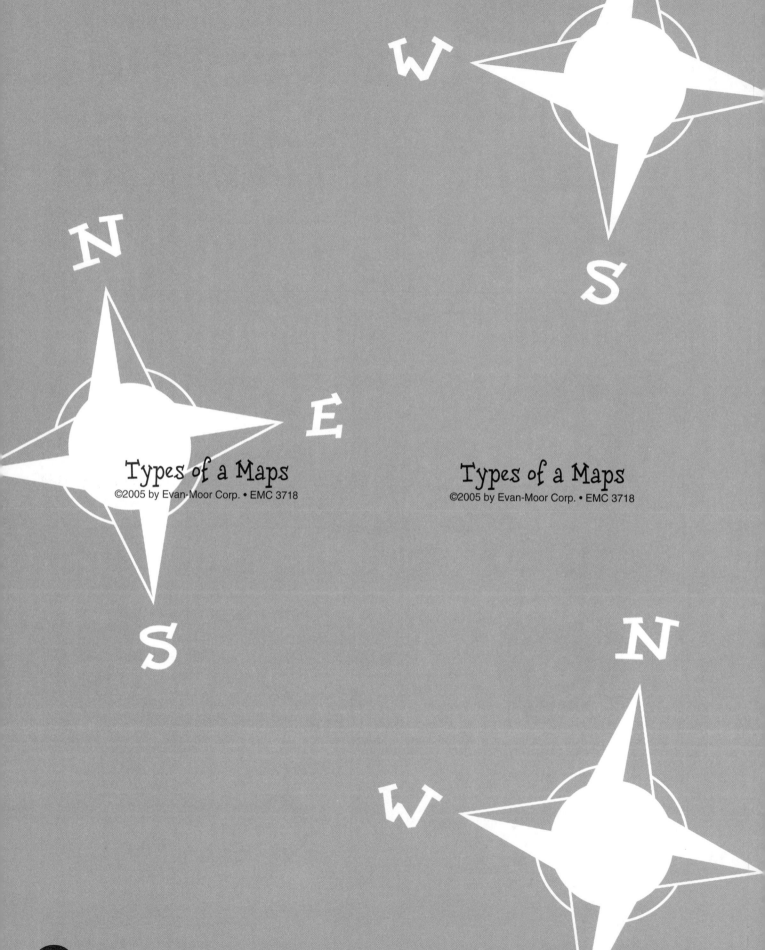

Earth's Landforms

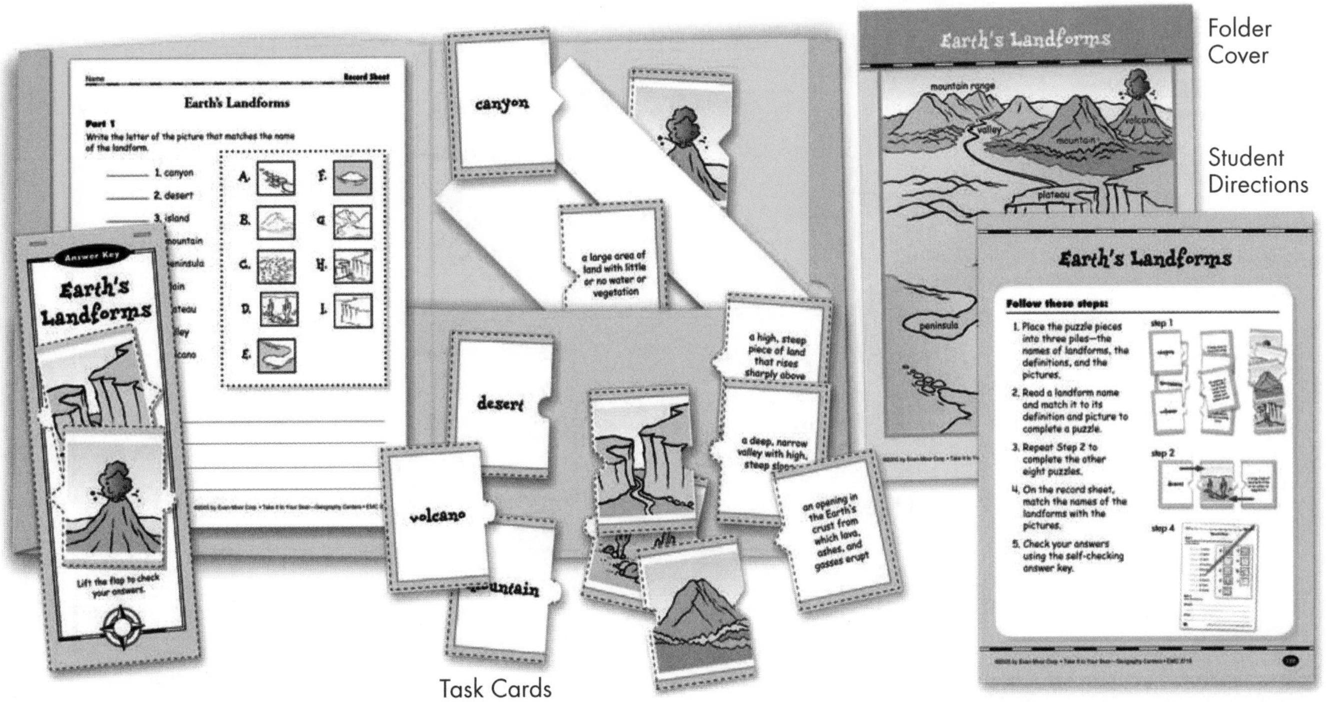
Earth's Landforms
Earth's Landforms
canyon
desert
volcano
Earth's Landforms
Earth's Landforms
Follow these steps:

Folder Cover

Student Directions

Task Cards

Preparing the Center

1. Prepare a folder following the directions on page 3.

   Cover—page 137

   Student Directions—page 139

   Puzzle Task Cards—pages 141–145
   - Landform Names
   - Definitions
   - Pictures

   Self-Checking Key—page 147

2. Reproduce a supply of the record sheet on page 136. Place copies in the left-hand pocket of the folder.

Using the Center

1. The student sorts the puzzle pieces into three piles—the names of landforms, the definitions, and the pictures.
2. Next, the student reads and matches three cards at a time to complete a puzzle. The puzzle is self-checking.
3. The student repeats the steps to complete the other eight puzzles.
4. On the record sheet, the student matches each term with its picture and writes two definitions.
5. Finally, the student uses the self-checking key to check answers.

Earth's Landforms

Part 1

Write the letter of the picture that matches the name of the landform.

_______ 1. canyon

_______ 2. desert

_______ 3. island

_______ 4. mountain

_______ 5. peninsula

_______ 6. plain

_______ 7. plateau

_______ 8. valley

_______ 9. volcano

A.

F.

B.

G.

C.

H.

D.

I.

E.

Part 2

Write the definitions.

peninsula: ____

____

plateau: ____

____

Earth's Landforms

mountain range
volcano
valley
mountain
plateau
canyon
plain
peninsula
isthmus
island
desert

W
S

N
E
S

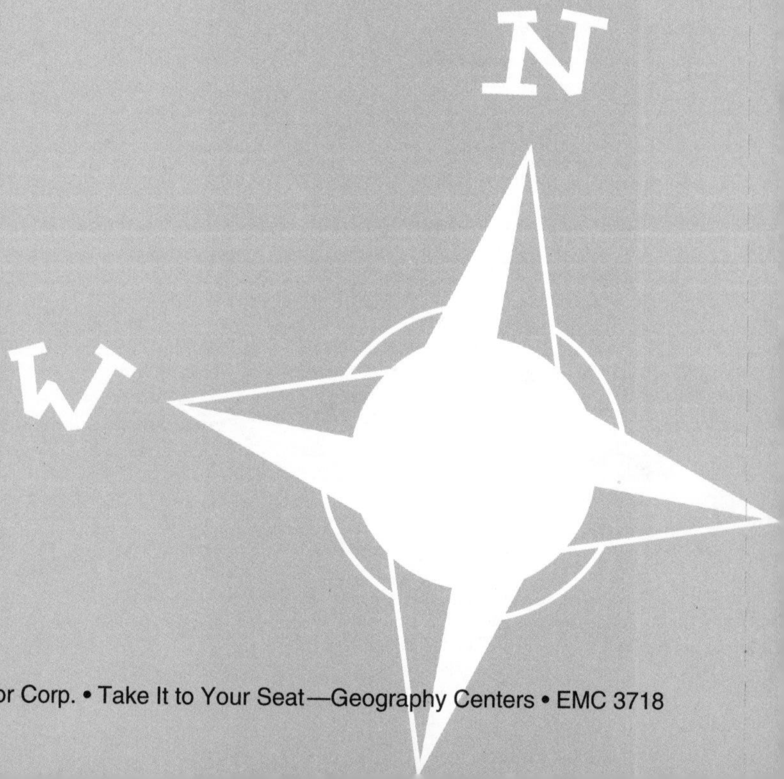
N
W

Earth's Landforms

Follow these steps:

1. Sort the puzzle pieces into three piles—the names of landforms, the definitions, and the pictures.

2. Read a landform name and match it to its definition and picture to complete a puzzle.

3. Repeat Step 2 to complete the other eight puzzles.

4. On the record sheet, match the names of the landforms with their pictures. Then do Part 2.

5. Check your answers using the self-checking answer key.

step 1

canyon
mountain
volcano
a large area of land with little
an opening in the Earth's crust from which lava, ashes, and gasses erupt
the surrounding area

step 2

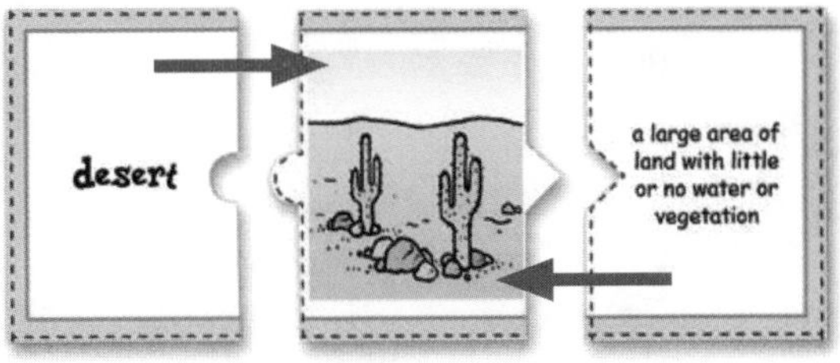
desert
a large area of land with little or no water or vegetation

step 4

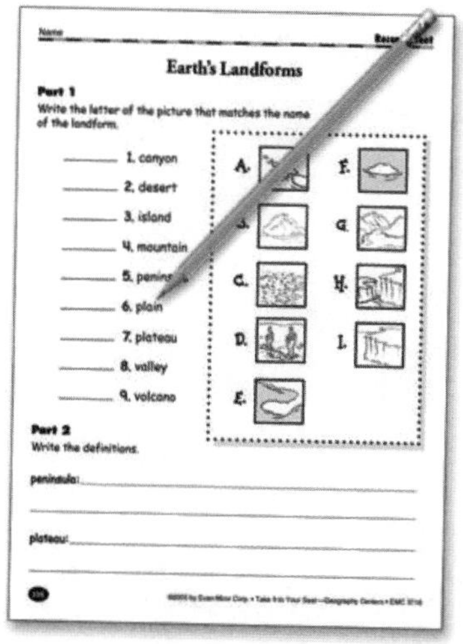
Earth's Landforms
Part 1
1. canyon
2. desert
3. island
4. mountain
6. plain
7. plateau
8. valley
9. volcano
Part 2
Write the definitions.
peninsula:
plateau:

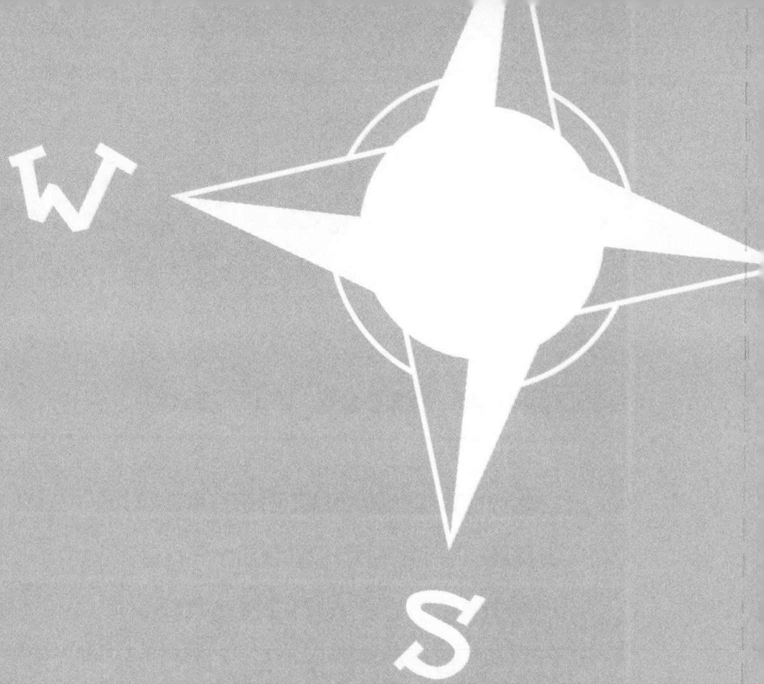
W
S

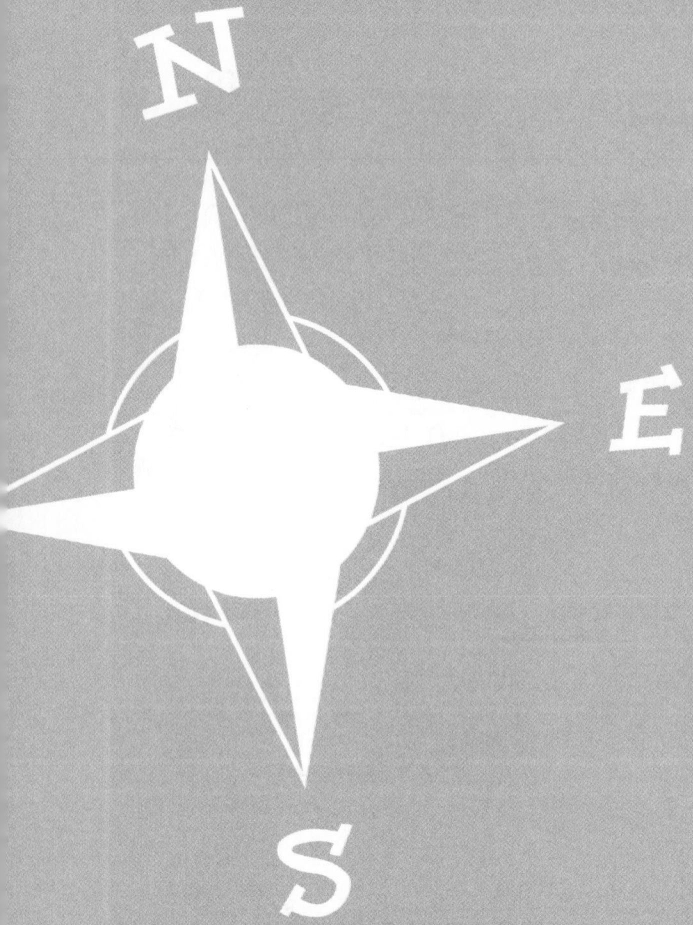
N
E
S

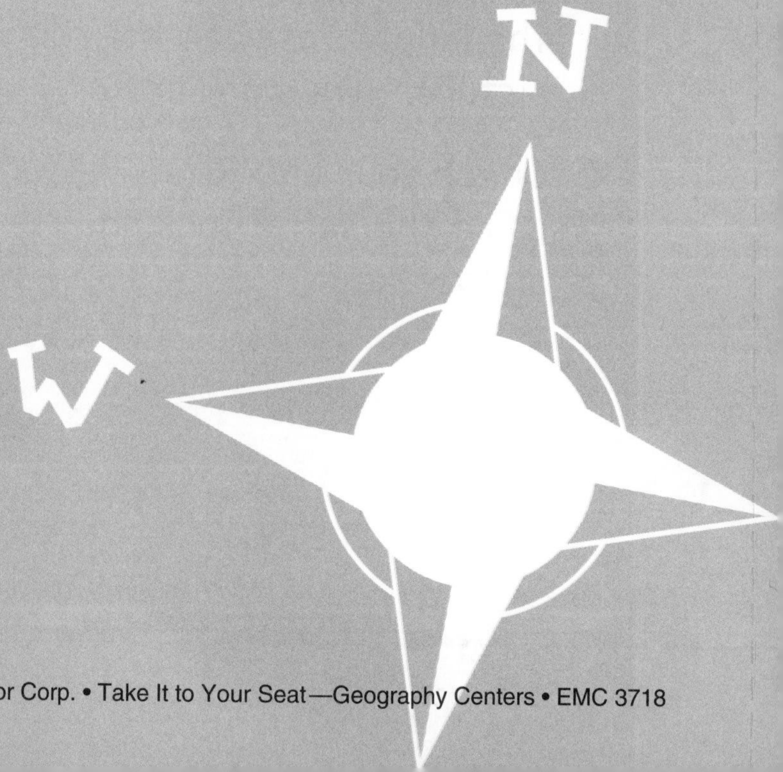
N
W

canyon

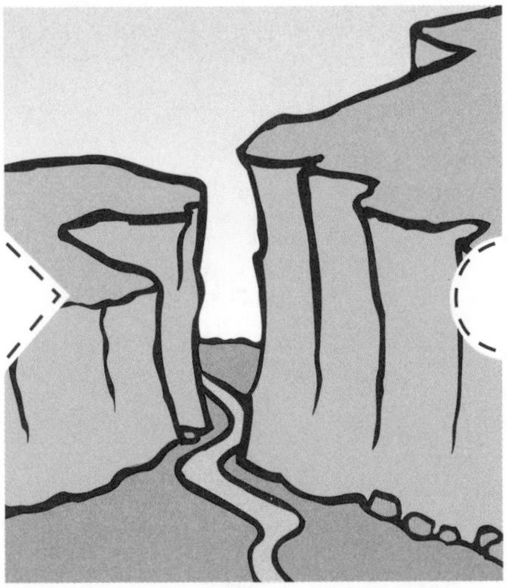

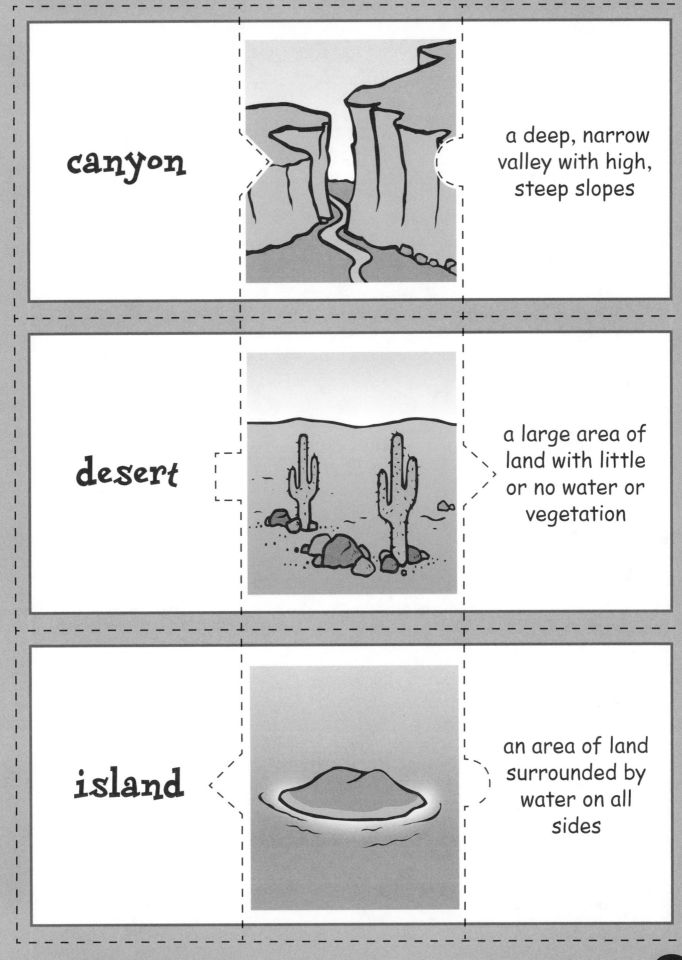

a deep, narrow valley with high, steep slopes

desert

a large area of land with little or no water or vegetation

island

an area of land surrounded by water on all sides

Landforms on Earth

Landforms on Earth

©2005 by Evan-Moor Corp.
EMC 3718

Landforms on Earth

©2005 by Evan-Moor Corp.
EMC 3718

Landforms on Earth

©2005 by Evan-Moor Corp.
EMC 3718

Landforms on Earth

©2005 by Evan-Moor Corp.
EMC 3718

Landforms on Earth

©2005 by Evan-Moor Corp.
EMC 3718

Landforms on Earth

©2005 by Evan-Moor Corp.
EMC 3718

Landforms on Earth

©2005 by Evan-Moor Corp.
EMC 3718

Landforms on Earth

©2005 by Evan-Moor Corp.
EMC 3718

mountain

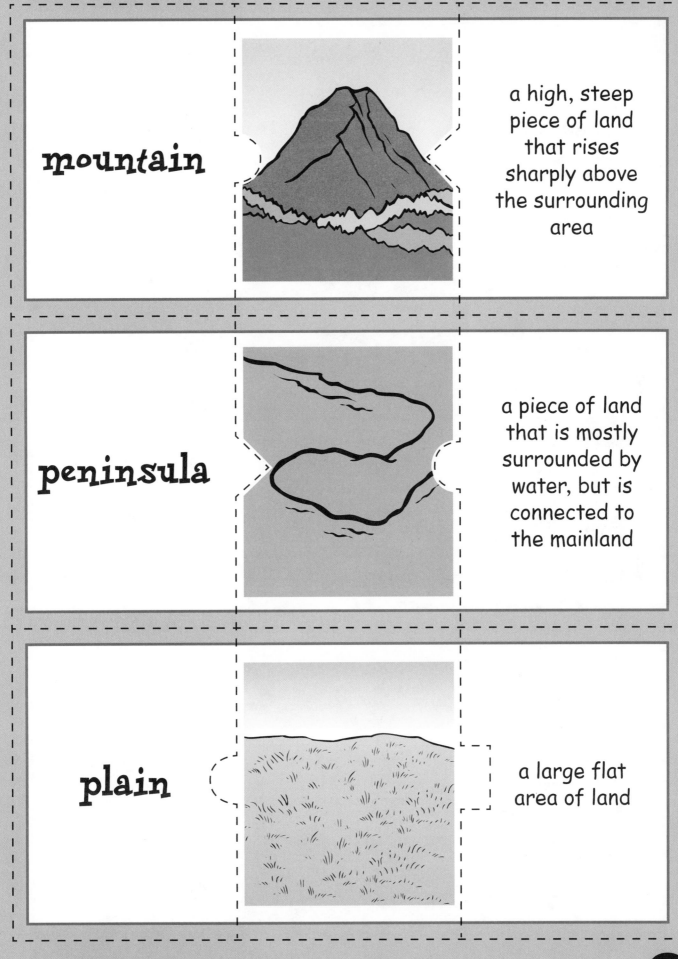

a high, steep piece of land that rises sharply above the surrounding area

peninsula

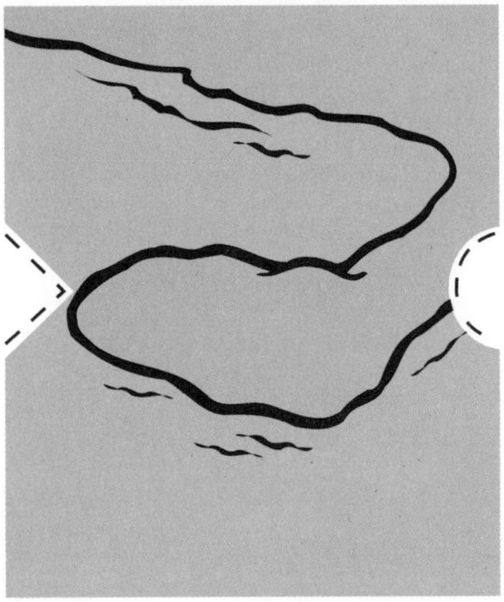

a piece of land that is mostly surrounded by water, but is connected to the mainland

plain

a large flat area of land

Landforms on Earth

Landforms on Earth
©2005 by Evan-Moor Corp.
EMC 3718

Landforms on Earth
©2005 by Evan-Moor Corp.
EMC 3718

Landforms on Earth
©2005 by Evan-Moor Corp.
EMC 3718

Landforms on Earth
©2005 by Evan-Moor Corp.
EMC 3718

Landforms on Earth
©2005 by Evan-Moor Corp.
EMC 3718

Landforms on Earth
©2005 by Evan-Moor Corp.
EMC 3718

Landforms on Earth
©2005 by Evan-Moor Corp.
EMC 3718

Landforms on Earth
©2005 by Evan-Moor Corp.
EMC 3718

plateau

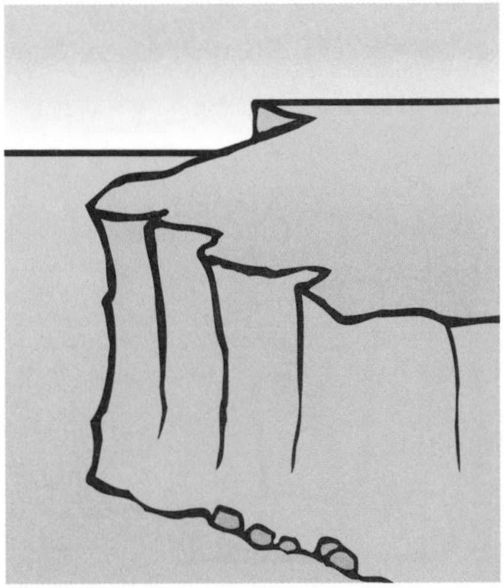

a large area of high, flat land

valley

land that lies between mountains or hills

volcano

an opening in the Earth's crust from which lava, ashes, and gasses erupt

Landforms on Earth

©2005 by Evan-Moor Corp.
EMC 3718

Landforms on Earth

©2005 by Evan-Moor Corp.
EMC 3718

Landforms on Earth

©2005 by Evan-Moor Corp.
EMC 3718

Landforms on Earth

©2005 by Evan-Moor Corp.
EMC 3718

Landforms on Earth

©2005 by Evan-Moor Corp.
EMC 3718

Landforms on Earth

©2005 by Evan-Moor Corp.
EMC 3718

Landforms on Earth

©2005 by Evan-Moor Corp.
EMC 3718

Landforms on Earth

©2005 by Evan-Moor Corp.
EMC 3718

Landforms on Earth

©2005 by Evan-Moor Corp.
EMC 3718

Answer Key

Earth's Landforms

Lift the flap to check your answers.

Earth's Landforms

Part 1

1. H
2. D
3. F
4. B
5. E
6. C
7. I
8. G
9. A

Part 2

peninsula: a piece of land that is mostly surrounded by water, but connected to the mainland

plateau: a large area of high, flat land

Landforms on Earth

Landforms on Earth

©2005 by Evan-Moor Corp. • EMC 3718

Bodies of Water

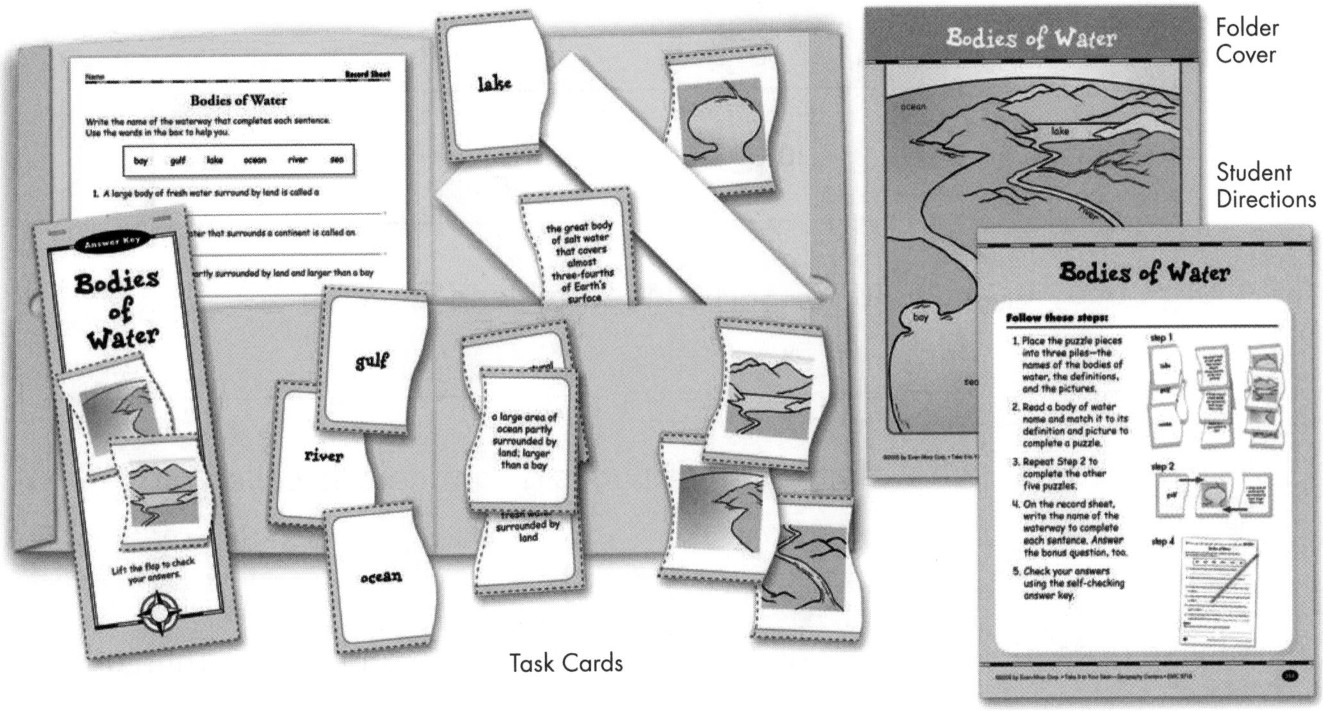
Folder Cover
Student Directions
Task Cards
Bodies of Water
Bodies of Water
lake
gulf
river
ocean
the great body of salt water that covers almost three-fourths of Earth's surface
a large area of ocean partly surrounded by land; larger than a bay
Answer Key
Lift the flap to check your answers.
Follow these steps:

Preparing the Center

1. Prepare a folder following the directions on page 3.

   Cover—page 151

   Student Directions—page 153

   Puzzle Task Cards—pages 155 and 157
   - Names
   - Definitions
   - Pictures

   Self-Checking Key—page 159

2. Reproduce a supply of the record sheet on page 150. Place copies in the left-hand pocket of the folder.

Using the Center

1. The student sorts the puzzle pieces into three piles—names, definitions, and pictures.
2. The student reads and matches three cards at a time to complete a puzzle.
3. The student repeats the steps to complete the other five puzzles.
4. On the record sheet, the student writes the name of the waterway to complete each sentence and answers the bonus question.
5. Finally, the student uses the self-checking key to check answers.

Bodies of Water

Write the name of the waterway that completes each sentence.
Use the words in the box to help you.

bay	gulf	lake	ocean	river	sea

1. A large body of fresh water surrounded by land is called a

   ______________________________.

2. A large body of salt water that surrounds a continent is called an

   ______________________________.

3. A large area of ocean partially surrounded by land and larger than a bay is called a ______________________.

4. A large natural stream of fresh water that flows into a lake or an ocean is called a ______________________.

5. An area of the ocean that is partially enclosed by land and smaller than a gulf is called a ______________________.

6. A body of water that is usually part of an ocean, and is partially or completely enclosed by land is called a ______________________.

Bonus:

What are the names of the four oceans of the world?

______________________ ______________________

______________________ ______________________

Bodies of Water

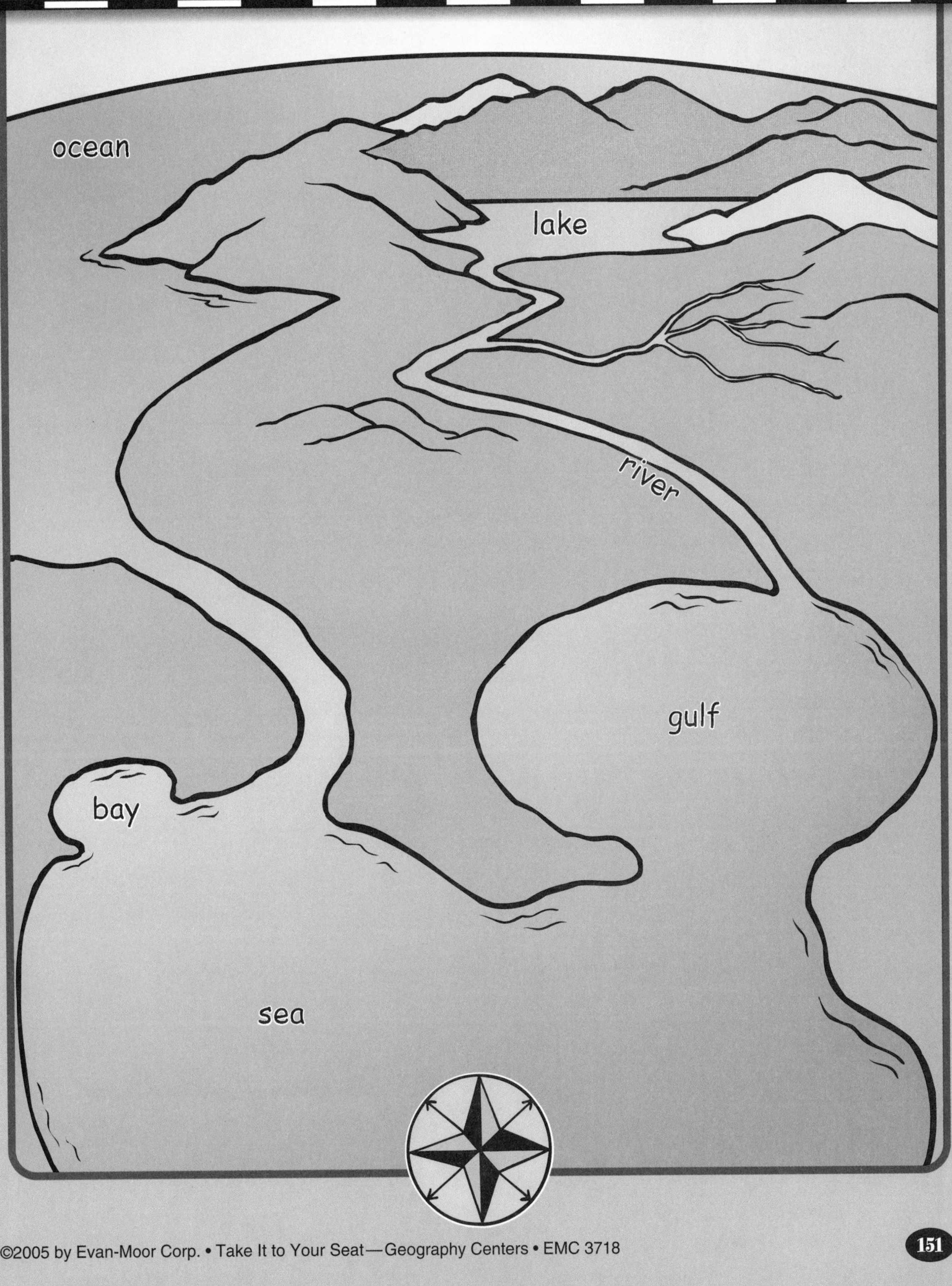
ocean
lake
river
gulf
bay
sea

W
S

N
E
S

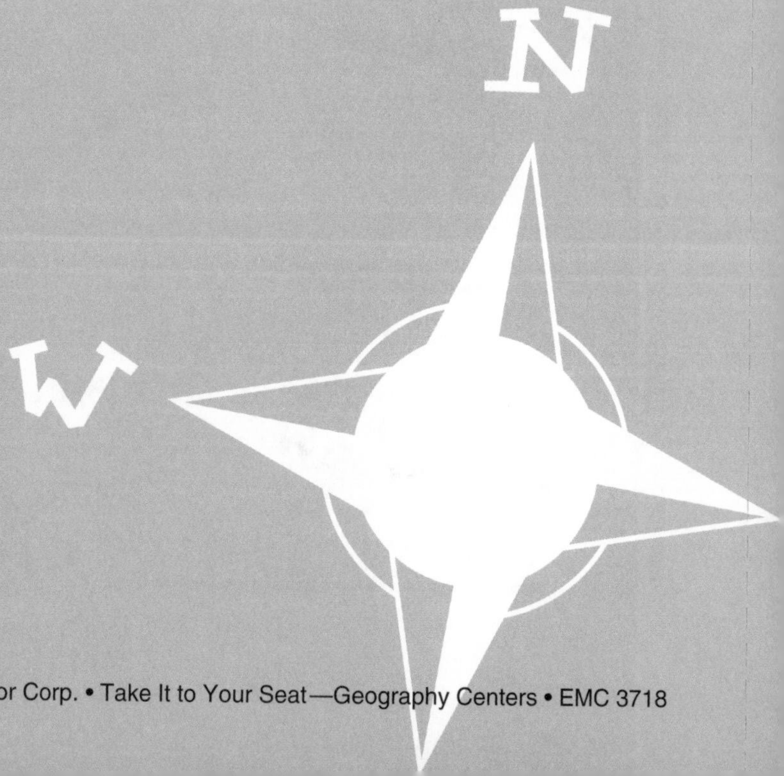
N
W

Bodies of Water

Follow these steps:

1. Sort the puzzle pieces into three piles—the names of the bodies of water, the definitions, and the pictures.
2. Read a body of water name and match it to its definition and picture to complete a puzzle.
3. Repeat Step 2 to complete the other five puzzles.
4. On the record sheet, write the name of the waterway to complete each sentence. Answer the bonus question, too.
5. Check your answers using the self-checking answer key.

step 1

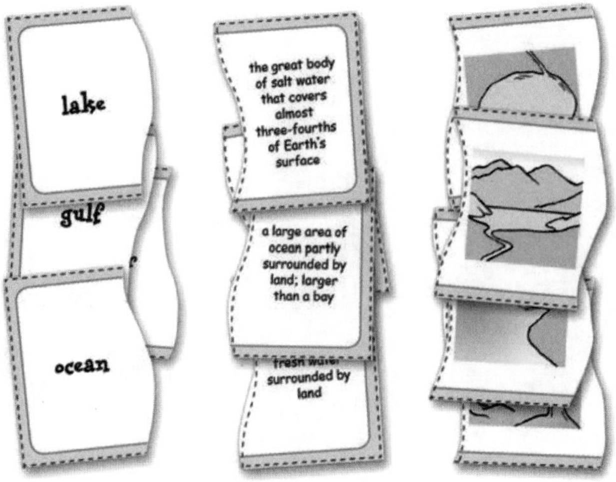
lake
gulf
ocean
the great body of salt water that covers almost three-fourths of Earth's surface
a large area of ocean partly surrounded by land; larger than a bay
surrounded by land

step 2

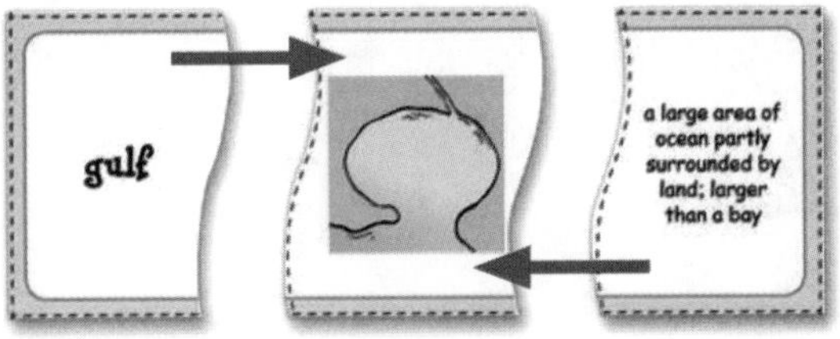
gulf
a large area of ocean partly surrounded by land; larger than a bay

step 4

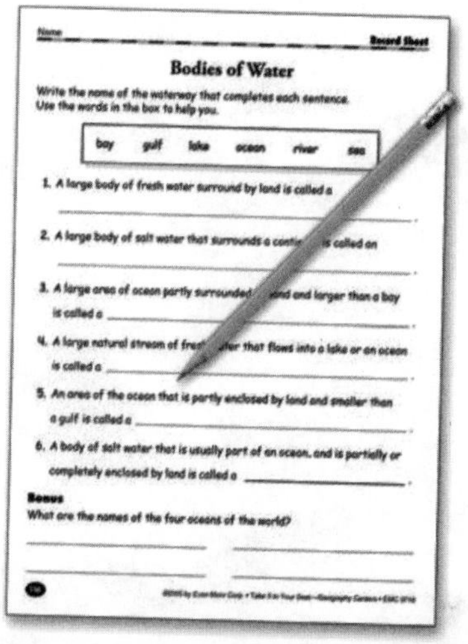
Bodies of Water
bay gulf lake ocean river sea

W
S

N
E
S

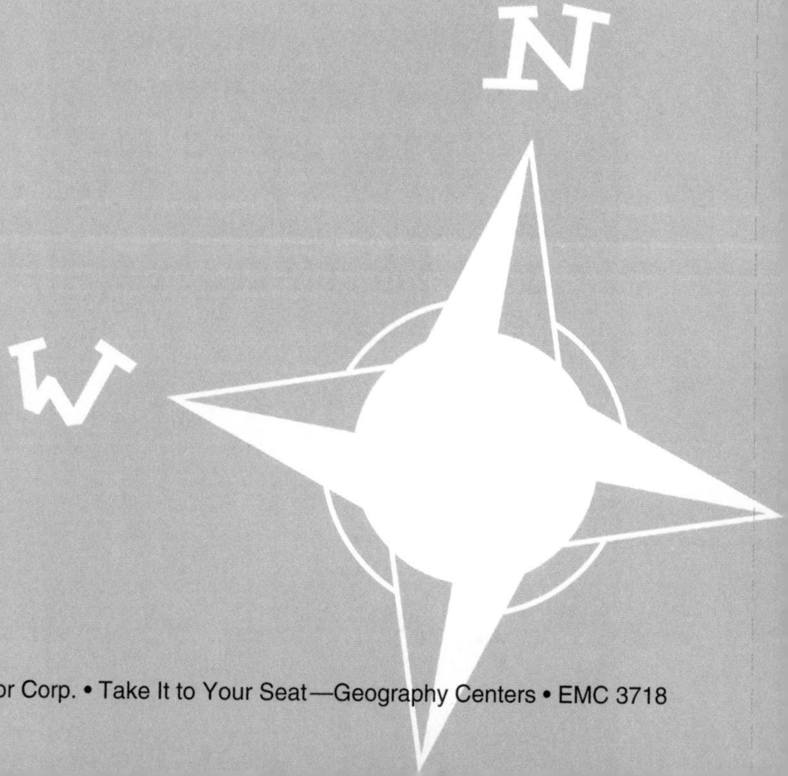
N
W

bay

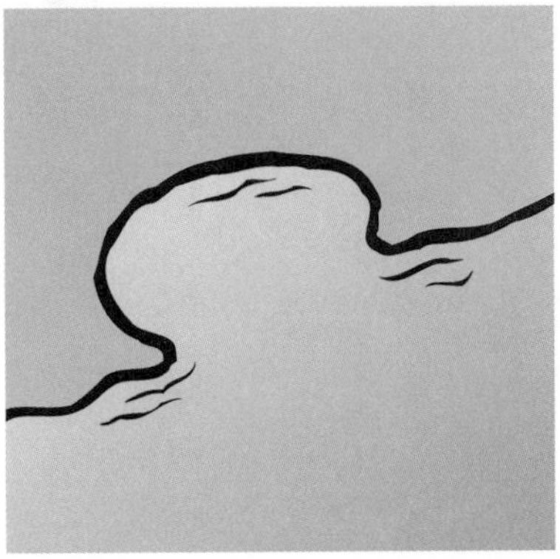

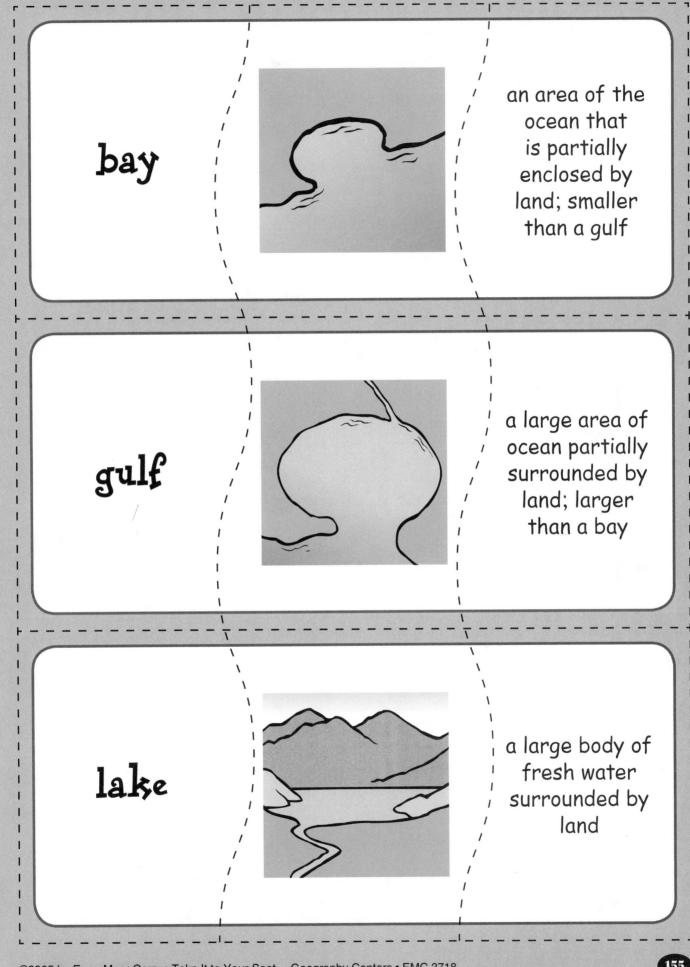

an area of the ocean that is partially enclosed by land; smaller than a gulf

gulf

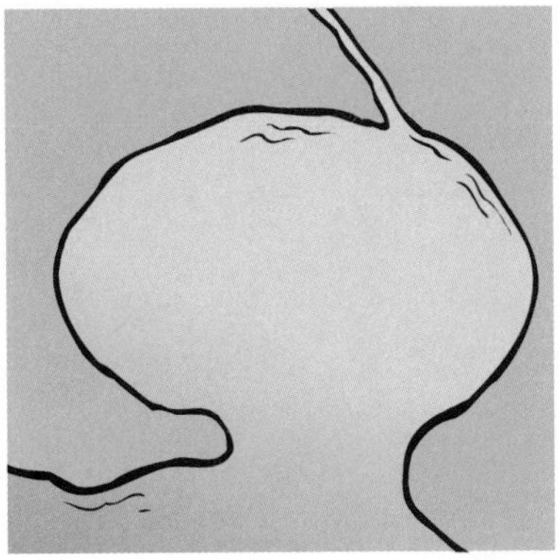

a large area of ocean partially surrounded by land; larger than a bay

lake

a large body of fresh water surrounded by land

Bodies of Water
©2005 by Evan-Moor Corp.
EMC 3718

Bodies of Water
©2005 by Evan-Moor Corp.
EMC 3718

Bodies of Water
©2005 by Evan-Moor Corp.
EMC 3718

Bodies of Water
©2005 by Evan-Moor Corp.
EMC 3718

Bodies of Water
©2005 by Evan-Moor Corp.
EMC 3718

Bodies of Water
©2005 by Evan-Moor Corp.
EMC 3718

Bodies of Water
©2005 by Evan-Moor Corp.
EMC 3718

Bodies of Water
©2005 by Evan-Moor Corp.
EMC 3718

Bodies of Water
©2005 by Evan-Moor Corp.
EMC 3718

ocean

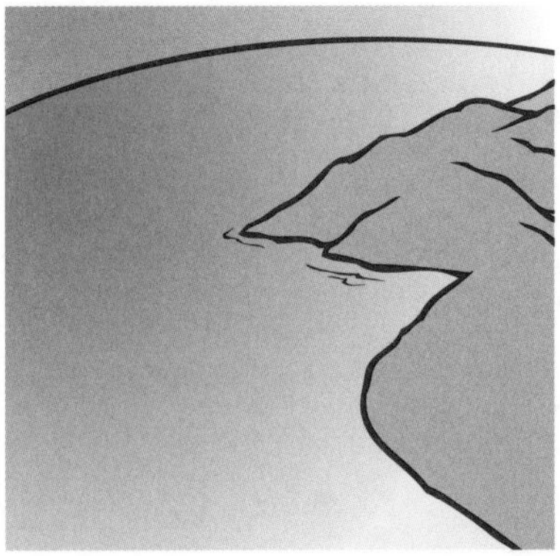

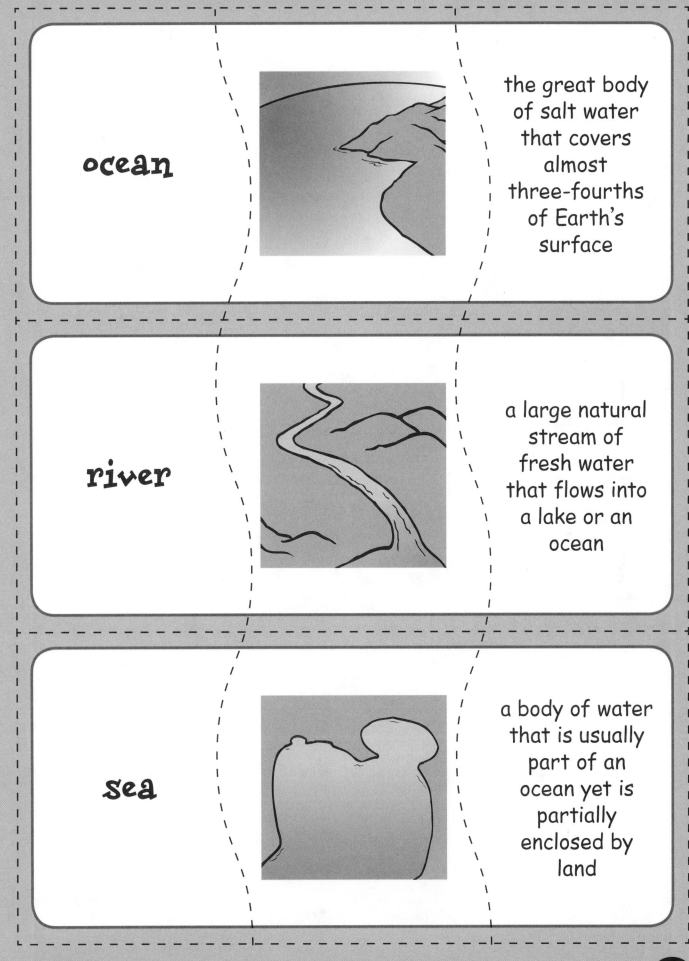

the great body of salt water that covers almost three-fourths of Earth's surface

river

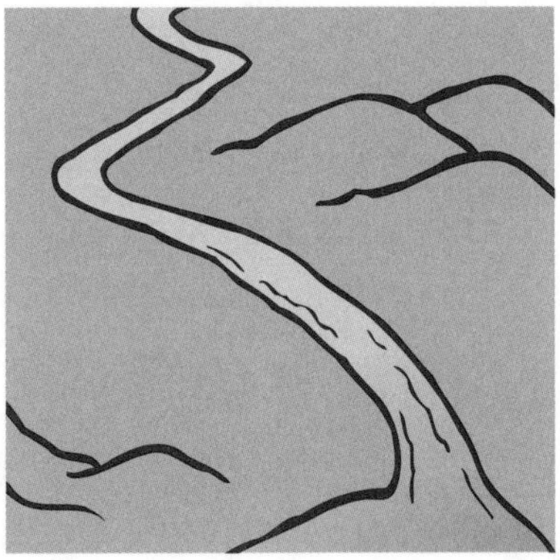

a large natural stream of fresh water that flows into a lake or an ocean

sea

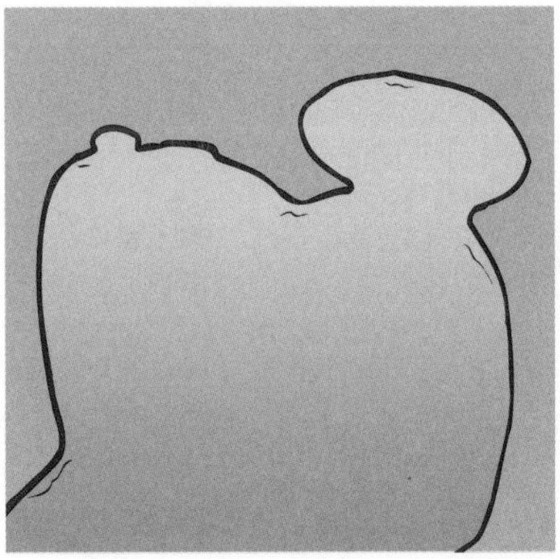

a body of water that is usually part of an ocean yet is partially enclosed by land

Bodies of Water

©2005 by Evan-Moor Corp.
EMC 3718

Bodies of Water

©2005 by Evan-Moor Corp.
EMC 3718

Bodies of Water

©2005 by Evan-Moor Corp.
EMC 3718

Bodies of Water

©2005 by Evan-Moor Corp.
EMC 3718

Bodies of Water

©2005 by Evan-Moor Corp.
EMC 3718

Bodies of Water

©2005 by Evan-Moor Corp.
EMC 3718

Bodies of Water

©2005 by Evan-Moor Corp.
EMC 3718

Bodies of Water

©2005 by Evan-Moor Corp.
EMC 3718

Bodies of Water

©2005 by Evan-Moor Corp.
EMC 3718

Answer Key

Bodies of Water

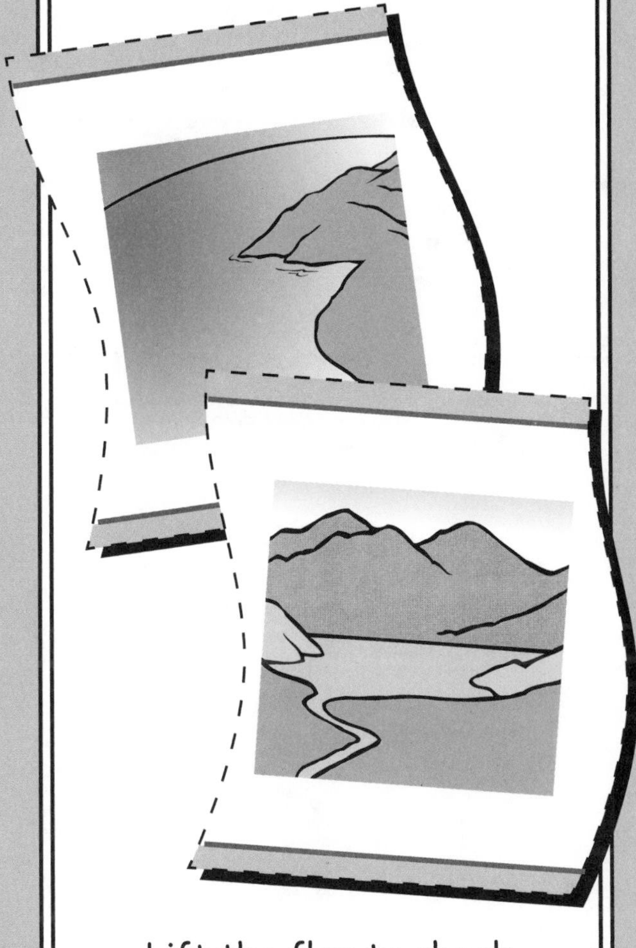

Lift the flap to check your answers.

Bodies of Water

1. lake
2. ocean
3. gulf
4. river
5. bay
6. sea

Bonus:

Arctic Ocean
Atlantic Ocean
Indian Ocean
Pacific Ocean

Bodies of Water

Bodies of Water

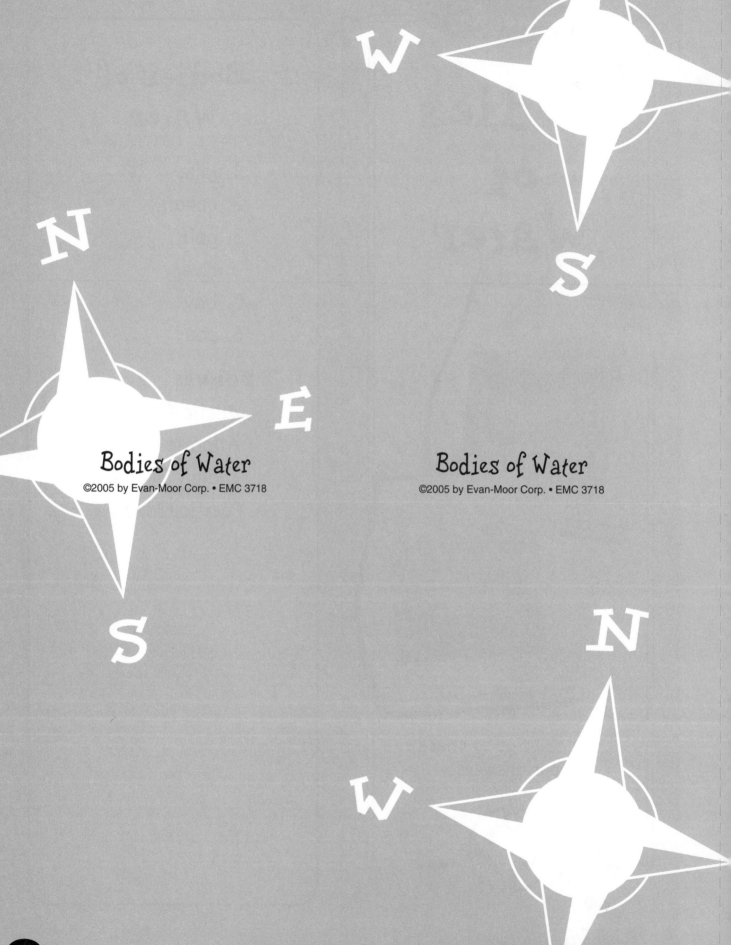

©2005 by Evan-Moor Corp. • EMC 3718

Name That Landmark!

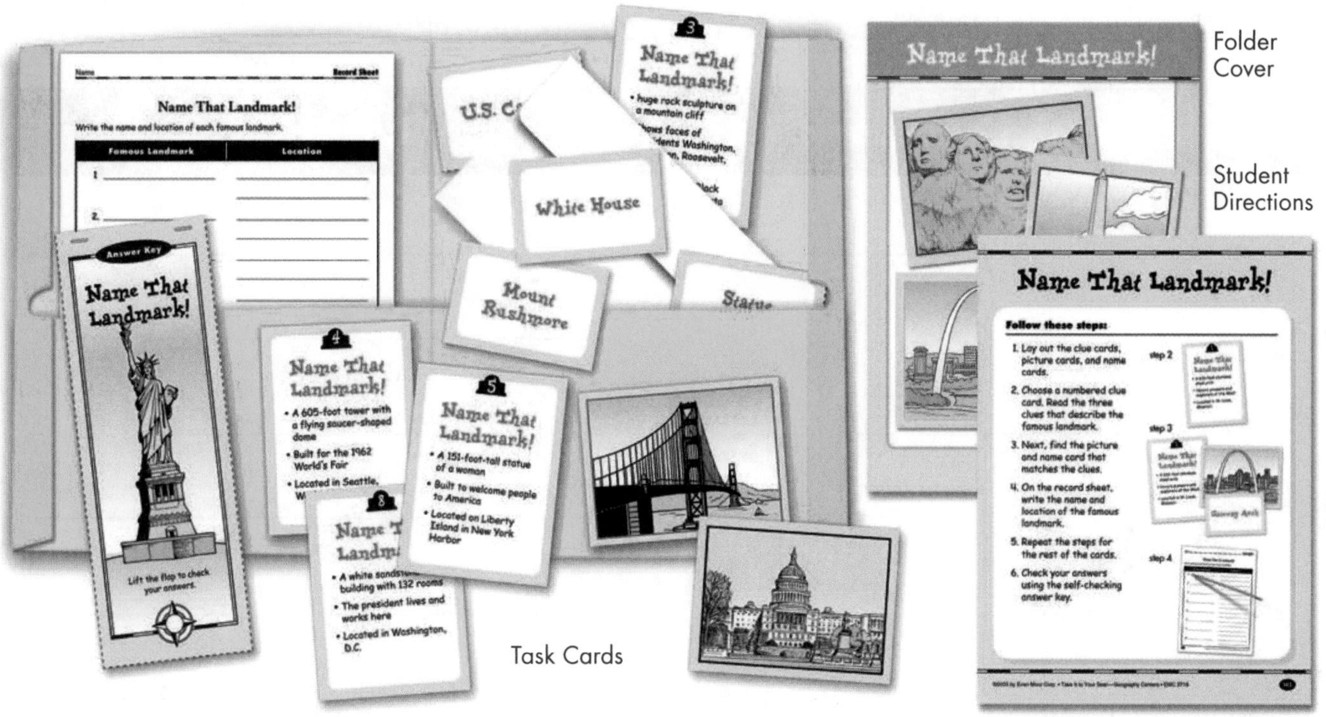
Folder Cover
Student Directions
Task Cards
Name That Landmark!
White House
Mount Rushmore
Name That Landmark!

Preparing the Center

1. Prepare a folder following the directions on page 3.

   Cover—page 163

   Student Directions—page 165

   Task Cards—pages 167–175
   - Clues
   - Names
   - Pictures

   Self-Checking Key—page 177

2. Reproduce a supply of the record sheet on page 162. Place copies in the left-hand pocket of the folder.

Using the Center

1. The student selects a numbered clue card and reads the three clues about a famous landmark.
2. Next, the student finds the picture and name card that is described on the clue card. The cards are self-checking.
3. Then the student records the name and location of the famous landmark on the record sheet.
4. The student repeats the above steps for the remaining cards.
5. Finally, the student uses the self-checking key to check answers.

Name That Landmark!

Write the name and location of each famous landmark.

Famous Landmark	Location
1. ______	______ ______
2. ______	______ ______
3. ______	______ ______
4. ______	______ ______
5. ______	______ ______
6. ______	______ ______
7. ______	______ ______
8. ______	______ ______

Name That Landmark!

W
S
N
E
S
N
W

Name That Landmark!

Follow these steps:

1. Lay out the clue cards, picture cards, and name cards.
2. Choose a numbered clue card. Read the three clues that describe the famous landmark.
3. Next, find the picture and name card that matches the clues.
4. On the record sheet, write the name and location of the famous landmark.
5. Repeat the steps for the rest of the cards.
6. Check your answers using the self-checking answer key.

step 2

1
Name That Landmark!
• A 630-foot stainless steel arch
• Honors pioneers and explorers of the West
• Located in St. Louis, Missouri

step 3

1
Name That Landmark!
• A 630-foot stainless steel arch
• Honors pioneers and explorers of the West
• Located in St. Louis, Missouri
Gateway Arch

step 4

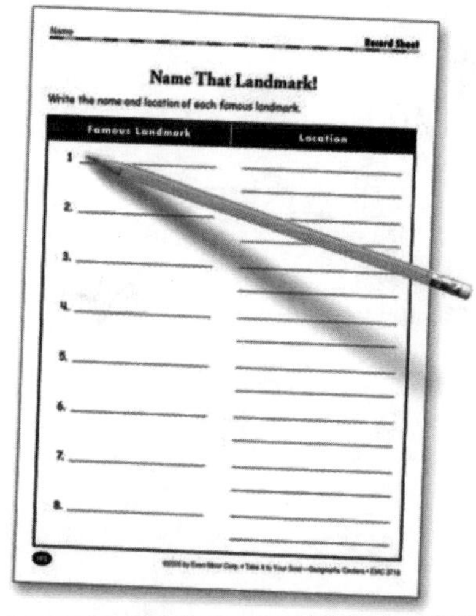
Name That Landmark!
Famous Landmark
Location

W
S

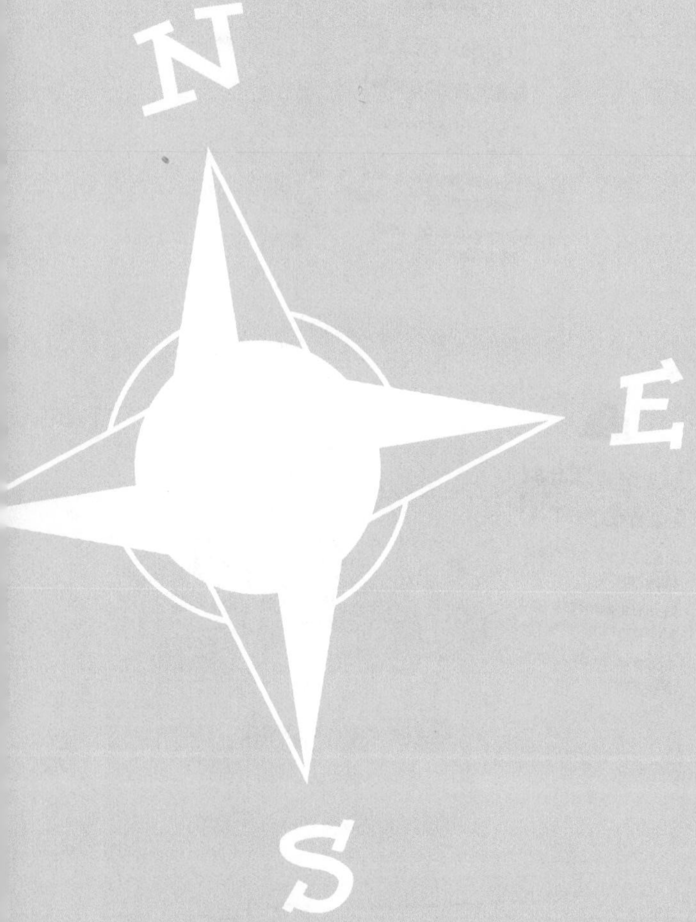
N
E
S

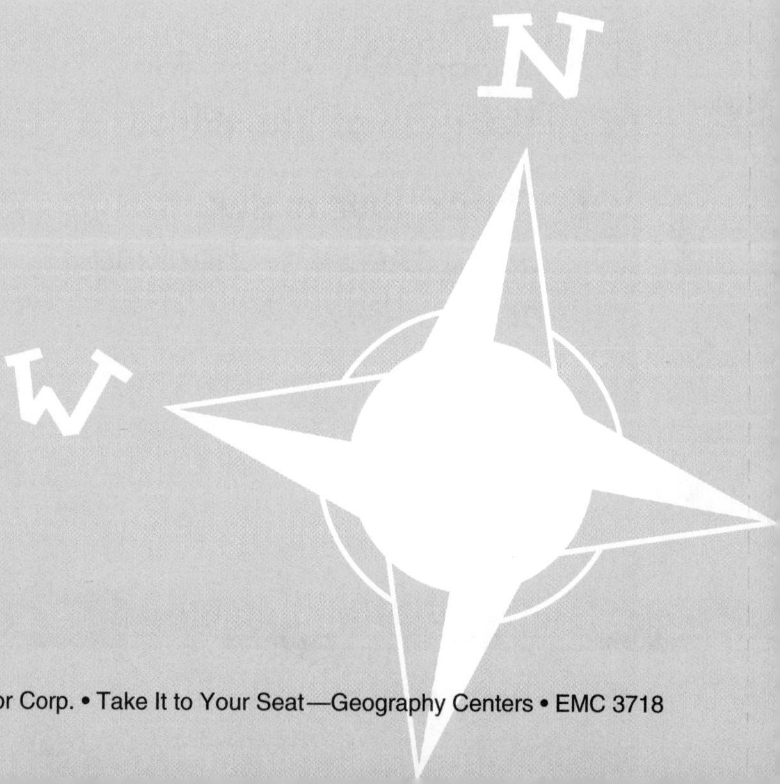
N
W

JULY
IV

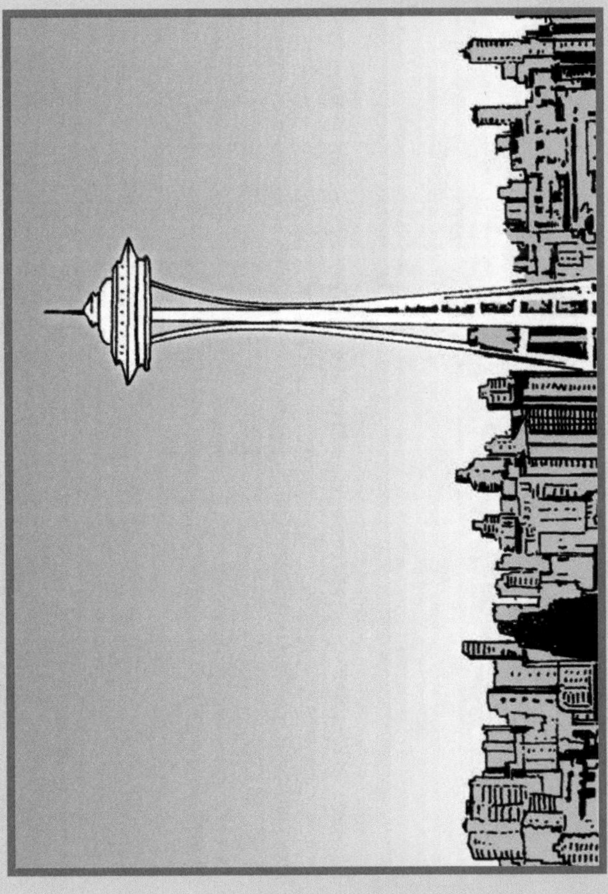

Name That Landmark!

Name That Landmark!

Name That Landmark!

Name That Landmark!

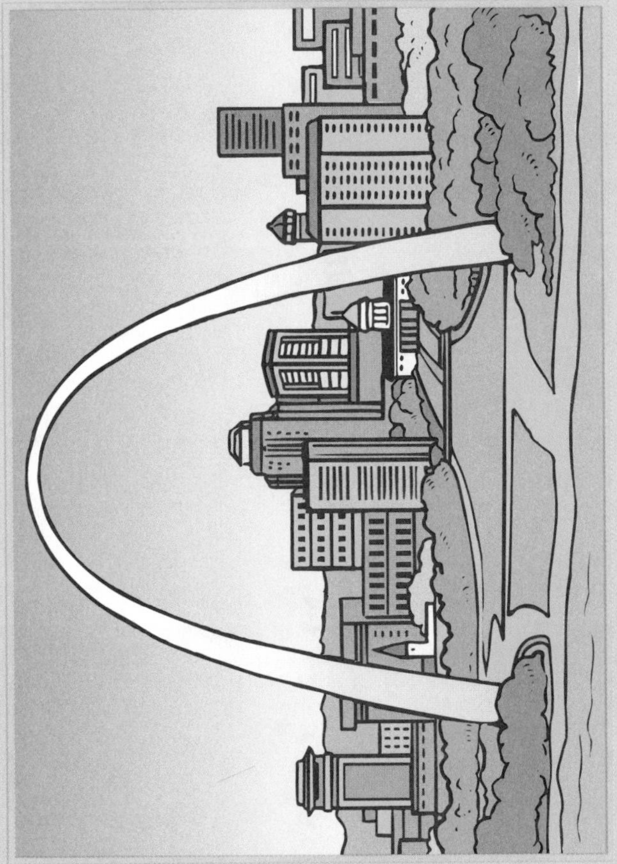

Name That Landmark!

Name That Landmark!

Name That Landmark!

Name That Landmark!

1

Name That Landmark!

- A 630-foot stainless steel arch
- Honors pioneers and explorers of the West
- Located in St. Louis, Missouri

3

Name That Landmark!

- Huge rock sculpture on a mountain cliff
- Shows faces of Presidents Washington, Jefferson, Roosevelt, and Lincoln
- Located in the Black Hills of South Dakota

2

Name That Landmark!

- Seventh-longest suspension bridge in the world
- Over 45 million vehicles cross it every year.
- Located in San Francisco, California

4

Name That Landmark!

- A 605-foot tower with a flying saucer-shaped dome
- Built for the 1962 World's Fair
- Located in Seattle, Washington

Name That Landmark!

Name That Landmark!

Name That Landmark!

Name That Landmark!

5

Name That Landmark!

- A 151-foot-tall statue of a woman
- Built to welcome people to America
- Located on Liberty Island in New York Harbor

7

Name That Landmark!

- A tall four-sided stone pillar with a pyramid on top
- Named after a president
- Located in Washington, D.C.

6

Name That Landmark!

- A white marble building with 540 rooms
- Congress makes laws here.
- Located in Washington, D.C.

8

Name That Landmark!

- A white sandstone building with 132 rooms
- The president lives and works here.
- Located in Washington, D.C.

Name That Landmark!

Name That Landmark!

Name That Landmark!

Name That Landmark!

Gateway Arch	Statue of Liberty
Golden Gate Bridge	U.S. Capitol
Mount Rushmore	Washington Monument
Space Needle	White House

Name That Landmark!

Name That Landmark!

Name That Landmark!

Name That Landmark!

Name That Landmark!

Name That Landmark!

Name That Landmark!

Name That Landmark!

Answer Key

Name That Landmark!

JULY IV

Lift the flap to check your answers.

Name That Landmark!

Famous Landmark	Location
1. Gateway Arch	St. Louis, Missouri
2. Golden Gate Bridge	San Francisco, California
3. Mount Rushmore	Black Hills of South Dakota
4. Space Needle	Seattle, Washington
5. Statue of Liberty	Liberty Island in New York Harbor
6. U.S. Capitol	Washington, D.C.
7. Washington Monument	Washington, D.C.
8. White House	Washington, D.C.

Name That Landmark!

Name That Landmark!

©2005 by Evan-Moor Corp. • EMC 3718

A Trip to Arizona

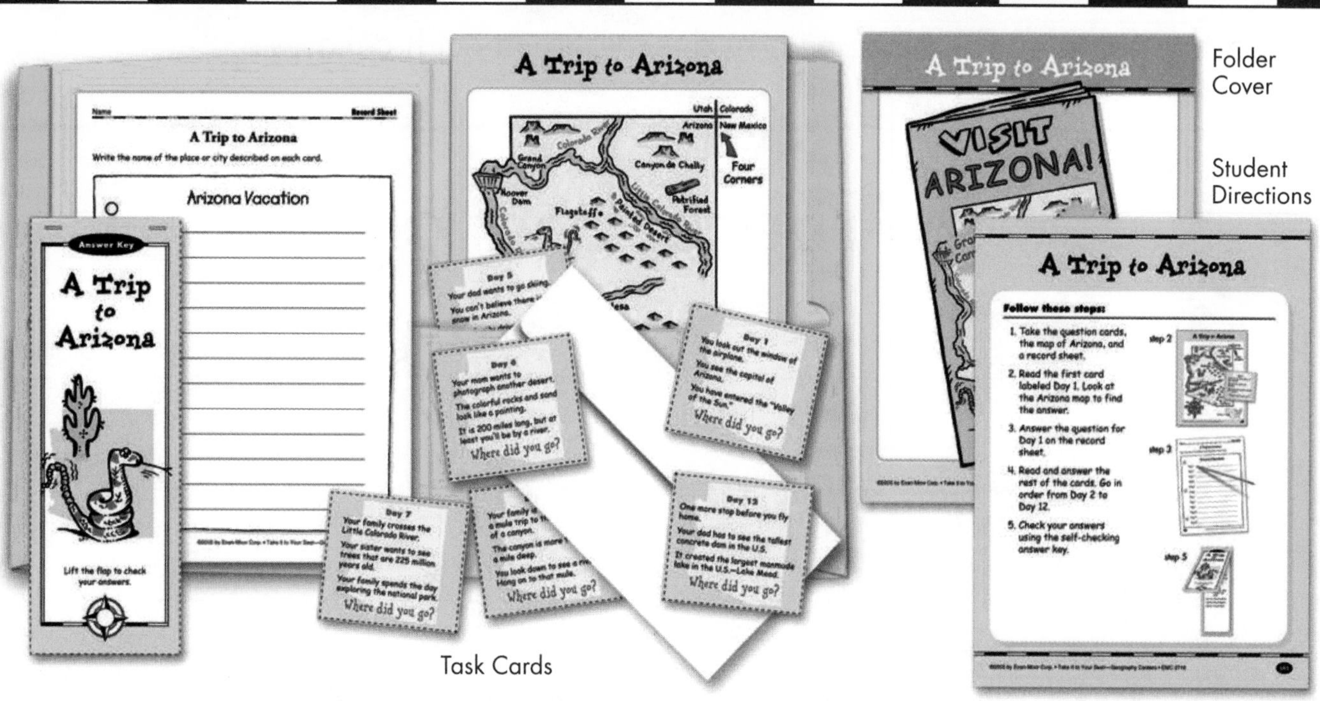
A Trip to Arizona
Folder Cover
Student Directions
Task Cards
Arizona Vacation
VISIT ARIZONA!
Answer Key
Where did you go?

Preparing the Center

1. Prepare a folder following the directions on page 3.

   Cover—page 181

   Student Directions—page 183

   Question Task Cards—pages 187 and 189

   Self-Checking Key—page 191

2. Laminate the tourist map of Arizona on page 185. Place the map card in the pocket for the student to use with the question cards.

3. Reproduce a supply of the record sheet on page 180. Place copies in the left-hand pocket of the folder.

Using the Center

1. The student takes the question cards, the map of Arizona, and a record sheet.

2. The student begins with Day 1 of the trip. The student reads the card and uses the map of Arizona to help answer the question.

3. On the record sheet, the student records the name of the tourist attraction described on the Day 1 card.

4. The student continues the same process in chronological order—from Day 2 to Day 12.

5. Finally, the student uses the self-checking key to check answers.

Name

A Trip to Arizona

Write the name of the place or city described on each card.

Arizona Vacation

Day 1 ____________________

Day 2 ____________________

Day 3 ____________________

Day 4 ____________________

Day 5 ____________________

Day 6 ____________________

Day 7 ____________________

Day 8 ____________________

Day 9 ____________________

Day 10 ____________________

Day 11 ____________________

Day 12 ____________________

A Trip to Arizona

VISIT ARIZONA!
Colorado River
Nature!
Grand Canyon!
Little Colorado River
Flagstaff
Colorado River
Phoenix
Mesa
Sun!
Gila River
Tucson
Tombstone

W
S

N
E
S

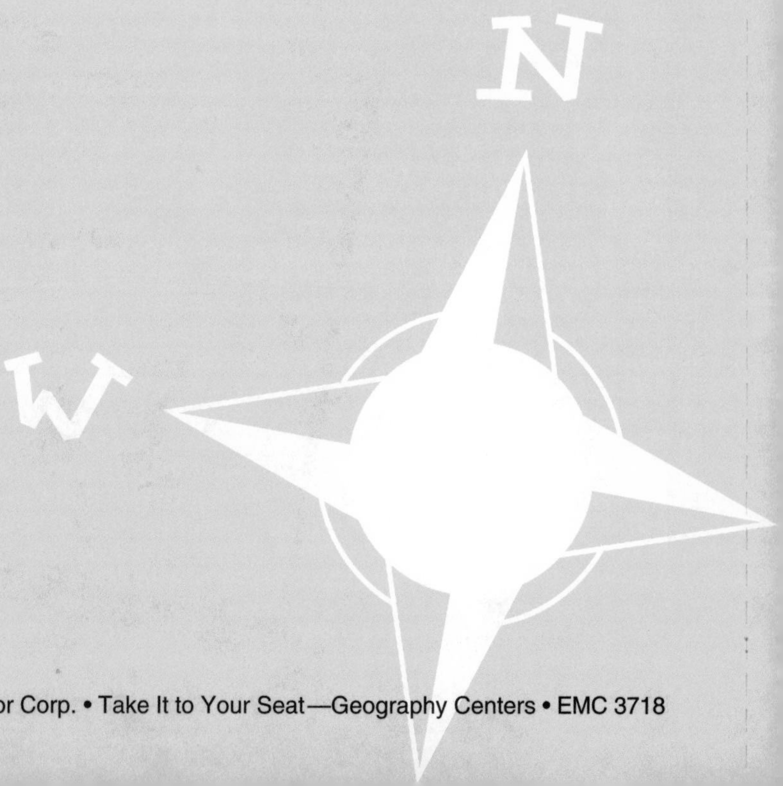
N
W

A Trip to Arizona

Follow these steps:

1. Take the question cards, the map of Arizona, and a record sheet.
2. Read the first card labeled Day 1. Look at the Arizona map to find the answer.
3. Answer the question for Day 1 on the record sheet.
4. Read and answer the rest of the cards. Go in order from Day 2 to Day 12.
5. Check your answers using the self-checking answer key.

step 2

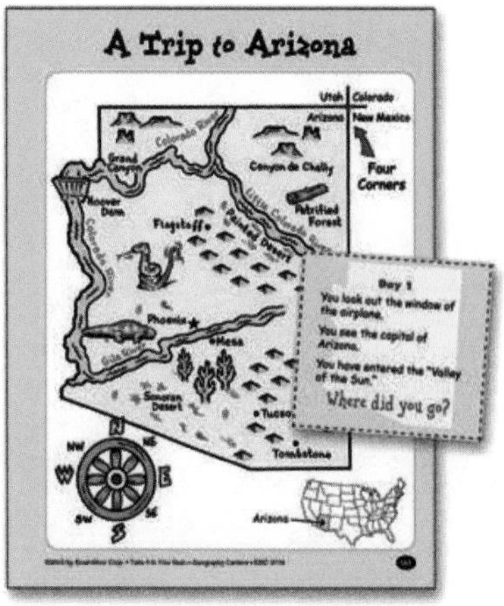
A Trip to Arizona
Where did you go?

step 3

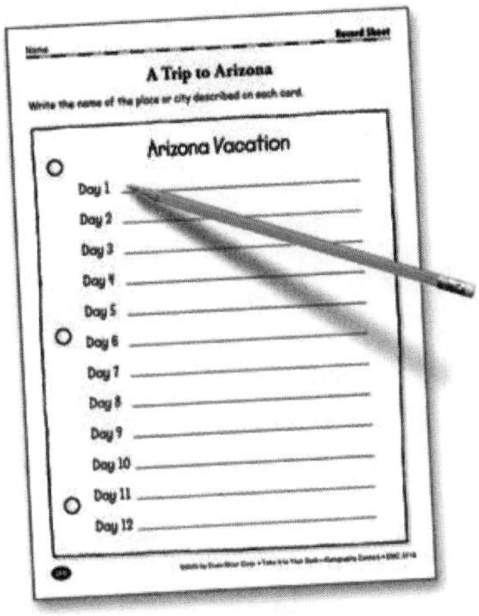
A Trip to Arizona
Arizona Vacation
Day 1
Day 2
Day 3
Day 4
Day 5
Day 6
Day 7
Day 8
Day 9
Day 10
Day 11
Day 12

step 5

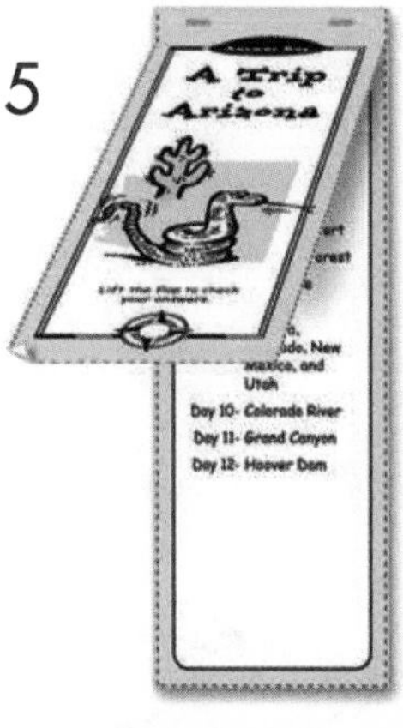
A Trip to Arizona
Day 10- Colorado River
Day 11- Grand Canyon
Day 12- Hoover Dam

W
S

N
E
S

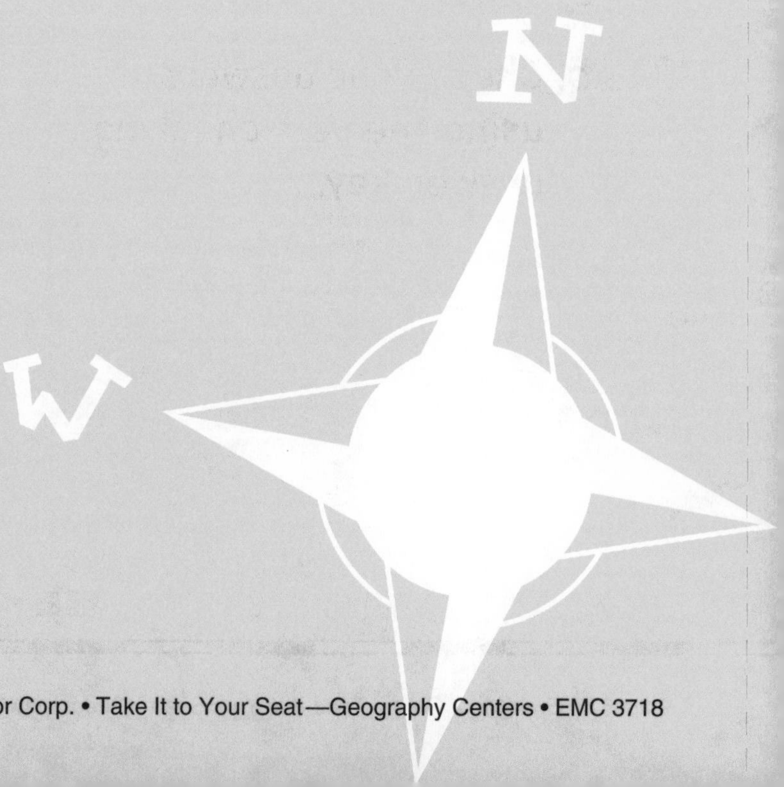
N
W

A Trip to Arizona

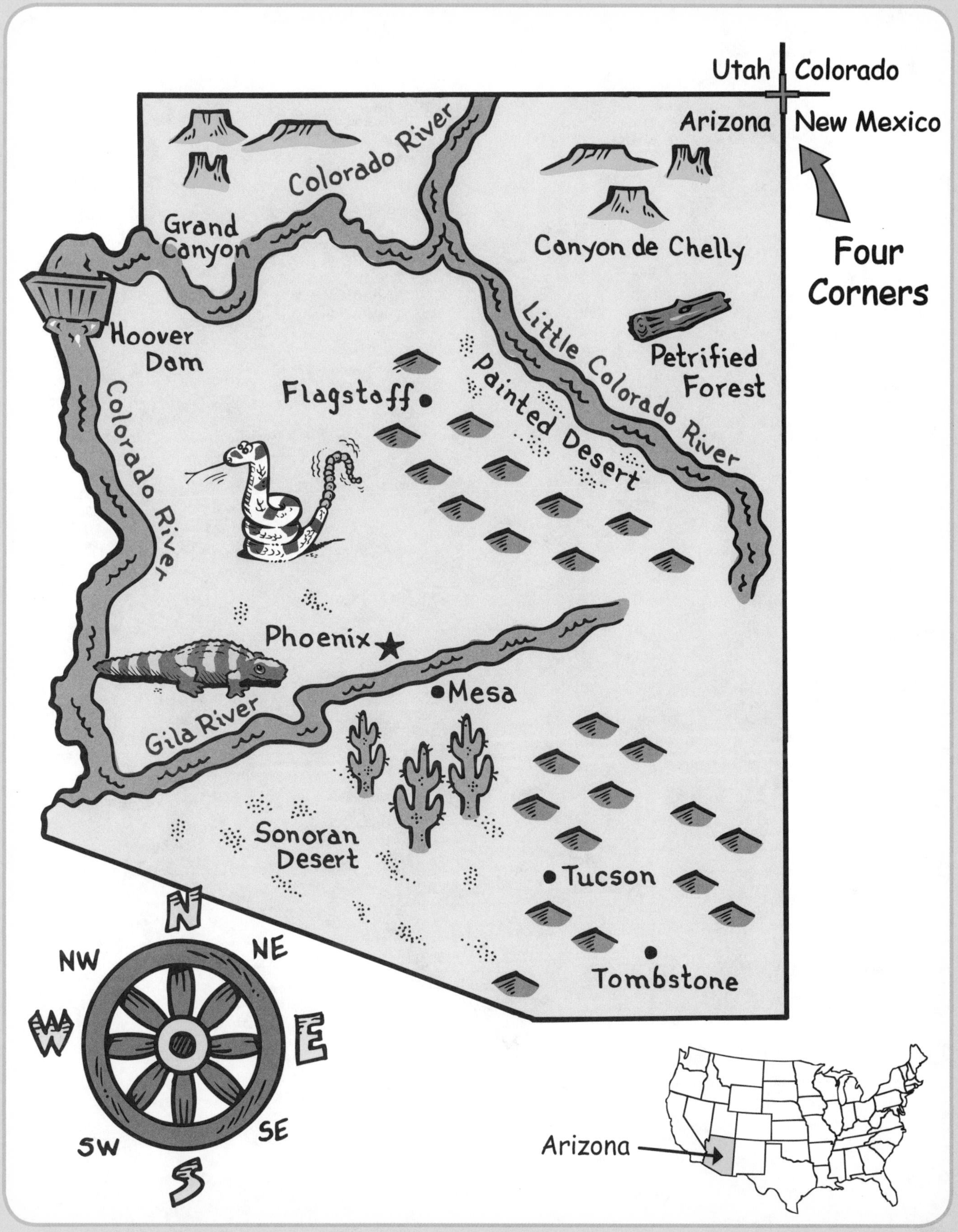
Utah
Colorado
Arizona
New Mexico
Four Corners
Colorado River
Grand Canyon
Canyon de Chelly
Hoover Dam
Little Colorado River
Petrified Forest
Painted Desert
Flagstaff
Colorado River
Phoenix
Mesa
Gila River
Sonoran Desert
Tucson
Tombstone
N
NE
NW
W
E
SW
SE
S
Arizona

W
S

N
E
S

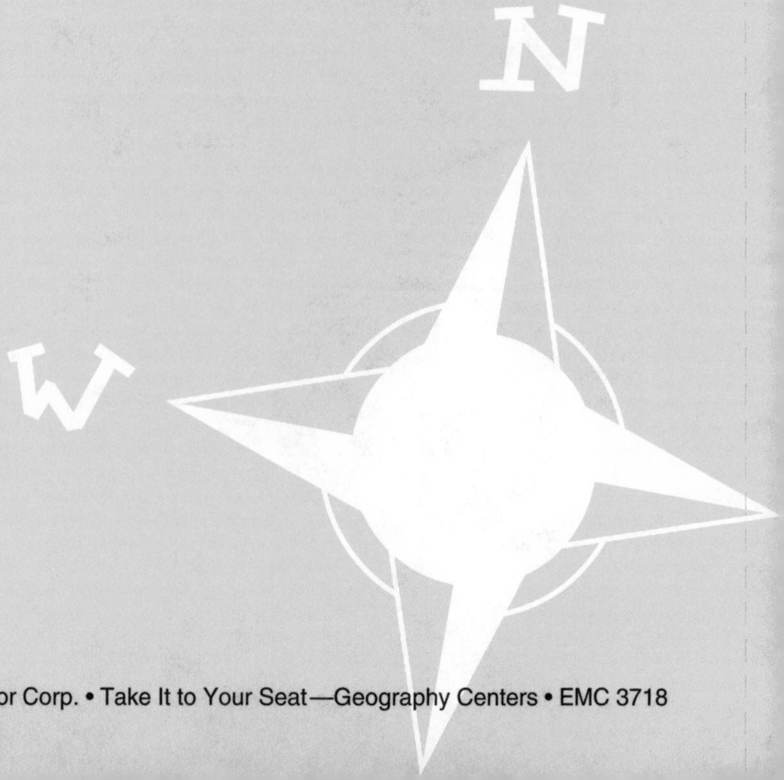
N
W

Day 1

You look out the window of the airplane.

You see the capital of Arizona.

You have entered the "Valley of the Sun."

Where did you go?

Day 4

Your big brother watched the old movie *Gunfight at the OK Corral.*

He really wants to visit "The Town Too Tough to Die."

Your family heads southeast to this old western town.

Where did you go?

Day 2

Your big sister wants to feel the heat of a desert.

You want to see a giant saguaro cactus.

You head south. Wear plenty of sunscreen.

Where did you go?

Day 5

Your dad wants to go skiing.

You can't believe there is snow in Arizona.

Your family drives northwest to stay at a ski resort near this city.

Where did you go?

Day 3

Your little brother loves planets and stars.

Your family heads to the city southeast of Mesa.

It is called the "Astronomy Capital of the World."

Where did you go?

Day 6

Your mom wants to photograph another desert.

The colorful rocks and sand look like a painting.

It is 200 miles long, but at least you'll be by a river.

Where did you go?

A Trip to Arizona

A Trip to Arizona

A Trip to Arizona

A Trip to Arizona

A Trip to Arizona

A Trip to Arizona

Day 7

Your family crosses the Little Colorado River.

Your sister wants to see trees that are 225 million years old.

Your family spends the day exploring the national park.

Where did you go?

Day 8

You know Arizona has many Native Americans.

You want to learn about Navajo history.

Your family heads north to a famous monument in a canyon.

Where did you go?

Day 9

Your big brother wants to stand on the spot where four states meet.

Your family drives north to Four Corners.

You name the four states for everybody.

Where did you go?

Day 10

Your family wants to have a wet and wild time.

You decide it is time for a river-raft trip.

You choose a trip on the longest river in Arizona.

Where did you go?

Day 11

Your family is ready for a mule trip to the bottom of a canyon.

The canyon is more than a mile deep.

You look down to see a river. Hang on to that mule.

Where did you go?

Day 12

One more stop before you fly home.

Your dad has to see the tallest concrete dam in the U.S.

It created the largest human-made lake in the U.S.—Lake Mead.

Where did you go?

A Trip to Arizona

A Trip to Arizona

A Trip to Arizona

A Trip to Arizona

A Trip to Arizona

A Trip to Arizona

Answer Key

A Trip to Arizona

Lift the flap to check your answers.

Day 1—Phoenix

Day 2—Sonoran Desert

Day 3—Tucson

Day 4—Tombstone

Day 5—Flagstaff

Day 6—Painted Desert

Day 7—Petrified Forest

Day 8—Canyon de Chelly

Day 9—Arizona, Colorado, New Mexico, and Utah

Day 10—Colorado River

Day 11—Grand Canyon

Day 12—Hoover Dam

A Trip to Arizona

A Trip to Arizona

©2005 by Evan-Moor Corp. • EMC 3718